Earth Habitat

Earth Habitat

Eco-Injustice and the Church's Response

EDITED BY

DIETER HESSEL
AND
LARRY RASMUSSEN

Fortress Press
Minneapolis

EARTH HABITAT
Eco-Injustice and the Church's Response

Cover image: Nick Daly. © 2001 Tony Stone. Used by permission.
Cover design: David Meyer
Book design: Ann Delgehausen
Chapter 1: From *Risks of Faith* by James H. Cone, copyright © 1999 by
    James H. Cone. Used by permission of Beacon Press, Boston.
"The Weaver's Shuttle Swiftly Flies": Text copyright © 1990 James Gert-
    menian. Used by permission.

Library of Congress Cataloging-in-Publication Data
Earth habitat : eco-injustice and the church's response / edited by Dieter Hessel and Larry Rasmussen.
    p. cm.
    Includes bibliographical references and index.
    ISBN 0-8006-3295-8 (alk. paper)
    1. Human ecology—Religious aspects—Christianity. 2. Environmental justice—Religious aspects—Christianity. I. Hessel, Dieter T. II. Rasmussen, Larry L.

BT695.5 .E265 2001
261.8'362—dc21   00-054353

Manufactured in the U.S.A.   AF 1-3295
05   04   03   02   01   1   2   3   4   5   6   7   8   9   10

Contents

Part 3. Environmentally Engaged Church and Community

Contributors

Ibrahim M. Abu-Rabi is Professor of Islamic studies and Muslim-Christian relations at Hartford Seminary, Connecticut, and coeditor with Jane Smith of *The Muslim World*.

Sarah Anderson-Rajarigam was born in Bangalore, India, and is a Ph.D. candidate at Union Theological Seminary, New York. She has taught at Indian Theological Seminary, Madras, where she was active in environmental concerns and initiated a rural women's action team.

Jim Cochrane is Director of the Research Institute on Christianity in South Africa and Professor in the Department of Religious Studies, University of Cape Town, Rondebosch.

James H. Cone is Charles Briggs Distinguished Professor of Systematic Theology at Union Theological Seminary, New York City. He is the author of *Black Theology and Black Power* and *Martin and Malcolm and America*.

Ernst Conradie teaches Christian studies at the University of the Western Cape, South Africa. He is author of *Rus vir die hele aarde* ("Rest for the Whole Earth"), *Hope for the Earth: Vistas on a New Century*, and an indexed bibliography on *Christian Theology and Ecology*. He is coauthor of *A Rainbow over the Land: A South African Guide on the Church and Environmental Justice*.

David Field is Senior Lecturer in Christian Ethics and Systematic Theology at Africa University, Mutare, Zimbabwe, and coordinates the Research Institute on Christianity in South Africa's Ecological Justice Project. "Reformed Theology, Modernity and the Environmental Crisis" was the title of his Ph.D. dissertation at the University of Cape Town. He is coauthor of *A Rainbow over the Land: A South African Guide on the Church and Environmental Justice.*

David G. Hallman has worked for more than two decades on the national staff of the United Church of Canada and in recent years has also served as climate-change program coordinator for the World Council of Churches. He is author of *Spiritual Values for Earth Community, A Place in Creation: Ecological Vision in Science, Religion and Economics,* and *Ecotheology: Voices from South and North.*

Dieter Hessel is founding director of the ecumenical Program on Ecology, Justice and Faith and codirector of TEMEC (Theological Education to Meet the Environmental Challenge). From 1965 to 1990, he was the social education and social policy director of the Presbyterian Church (U.S.A.). He authored *Social Ministry* and edited *After Nature's Revolt: Eco-Justice and Theology* and *Theology for Earth Community: A Field Guide.* He also coedited with Rosemary Radford Ruether the Harvard University Center for Study of World Religions' volume *Christianity and Ecology.*

Brigitte Kahl is Professor of New Testament at Union Theological Seminary, New York. An ordained minister of the Protestant Church of Berlin-Brandenburg, she previously studied and taught at Humboldt University, Berlin.

Charity Majiza is General Secretary of the South African Council of Churches, Johannesburg.

Deenabandhu Manchala taught at Gurukul Lutheran Theological College in Madras, India, before joining the staff of World Council of Churches as Executive Secretary for Peace Concerns, in 1999.

Troy Messenger is the Director of Worship at Union Theological Seminary, New York, and author of *Holy Leisure: Recreation and Religion in God's Square Mile.*

Victor Molobi is a member of the Faith and Earthkeeping Project, Research Institute for Theology and Religion, University of South Africa.

Kusumita Pedersen is chair of the Department of Religious Studies of St. Francis College, Brooklyn, and former director of the Project on Religion and Human Rights at Emory University, Atlanta, Georgia. She is specializing in research on religion and environmental ethics, and was an NGO leader at the 1992 Earth Summit. She is also on the board of the Council for a Parliament of the World's Religions.

Larry Rasmussen is Reinhold Niebuhr Professor of Social Ethics at Union Theological Seminary, New York, and he recently co-moderated Unit III (Justice, Peace, Creation) of the World Council of Churches. He is author of *Moral Fragments and Moral Community* and *Earth Community, Earth Ethics* (which won the 1997 Grawemeyer Award for Religion).

Martin Robra is the Executive Secretary of the World Council of Churches issues cluster, Justice, Peace, Creation. He is a minister of the Evangelical Church of Westfalia (Germany), with a Ph.D. in theology from Bochum University and is author of *Ökumenische Sozialethik*.

Steven C. Rockefeller is Professor Emeritus of Religion at Middlebury College in Vermont, and he chaired the Earth Charter drafting committee. He is the author of *John Dewey: Religious Faith and Democratic Humanism* and editor of *Spirit and Nature: Why the Environment Is a Religious Issue*.

Peggy M. Shepard is Executive Director and cofounder of West Harlem Environmental Action, Inc. (WE ACT).

Welile T. Sigabi is Director of the Moiplaas Methodist Training Centre in South Africa. He has held pastorates in Natal and Eastern Cape, and he formerly worked with the Department of Agriculture and Forestry.

Preface

THREE AREAS OF NEEDED WORK DISTINGUISH THIS VOLUME. One is the nature and mission of the church itself. Oddly, ecclesiology has been a missing locus in the busy circles of ecotheology and ethics, a hole as big as the church itself. We face this fact squarely, and these pages explore a church socioecologically reformed. They investigate new dimensions of church and community in creation, from the opening section on "Theology for Habitat Earth" to the closing one on "Environmentally Engaged Church and Community."

A second area of constructive work is the search for Earth-honoring expressions of Christianity and the quest for normative common ground. While the heart of this is justice-centered Christianity, it is a particular notion of justice, one that expands moral horizons and adds moral substance to the notions of justice that presently reign. We seek inclusive socioecological justice aimed at shedding the remnants of complex domination systems that, in a humanly dominated biosphere, continue to oppress both peoples and the land. The moral boundary is creation itself—the societal, biophysical, even geoplanetary, together.

Along the way another area of joint endeavor surfaces. We document the local impact of global forces, from economic globalization to accelerated climate change and pervasive violence, and the way these forces are experienced by local churches and communities. Also documented are creative responses from disparate quarters, responses that range from liturgical renewal to community organizing.

Perhaps such work as this developed naturally, given the cosponsors of the October 1998 conference that generated this volume and the agenda of its participants: EATWOT (Ecumenical Association of Third World Theologians); TEMEC (Theological Education to Meet the Environmental Challenge); the World Council of Churches Unit III–Justice, Peace, Creation; the U.S. Ecumenical Women's Network: Beijing and Beyond; and Auburn and Union theological seminaries. We gratefully acknowledge the in-kind support contributed by all of the cosponsors and TEMEC's grant to Union Seminary, which seeded conference planning.

This was an international conference on social justice and ecology that focused on the churches and their communities, and it enjoyed a lively international representation ranging from New York City neighborhoods to communities in India, South Africa, South America, Europe, Korea, and Canada. An inclusive analysis, coupled with reconstructive work in ecclesiology, ethics, and community, was fostered by the range of participants themselves: theologians and community organizers, farmers and liturgists, church staff, seminary students, and journalists from hither and yon. Both practical and theoretical efforts to grasp the realities that bear down on "ecumenical Earth"[1] permeated the conference. The editors thank those participants, the cosponsors, those who wrote the papers from which this volume was born, the planning committee of Auburn and Union seminaries chaired by Dean Robert Reber (Auburn) and Larry Rasmussen (Union), and Nancie Erhard for help both with the administration of the conference and the editing of this volume.

Dieter Hessel, TEMEC, Princeton, New Jersey
Larry Rasmussen, Union Theological Seminary, New York City

Introduction

ECO-JUSTICE: CHURCH AND COMMUNITY TOGETHER

Larry Rasmussen

PRESENT THREATS TO THE WHOLE COMMUNITY OF LIFE, human and more-than-human, require different boundaries for our spiritual-moral universes. Moral exclusion of other persons is sometimes the culprit. Despite Jesus' example and command, we don't habitually place the well-being of others in the same framework as our own. Moral privilege thus treats insiders at the expense of outsiders. The result is society's perennial plague of "us" versus "them."

At other times, moral exclusion of other-than-human life is the culprit. Homo sapiens lives as though we constituted an ecologically segregated species. The result is "species apartheid." One "race"—the human race—subjugates the rest of the biosphere for human benefit alone. Moral privilege here can be severe, so severe that moral standing and rights are denied to other-than-human life except when its welfare aligns with human welfare. (It is always the welfare of some humans more than others, we must add. Apartheid comes in many interlinking forms.)

But now threats to the whole community of life—global inequalities; climate change; loss of species and biodiversity as well as topsoil, safe water, and wetlands; urban growth and pollution; resource depletion; and

1

numerous internecine wars—mean the ascendancy of ethics and a review of the moral systems we live and die by. Threats to planetary life systems in fact compel community spiritual-moral formation of a different sort than is written in the hearts and heads of most of us as "moderns." The key questions themselves may well be the old ones of justice, even when the answers take new twists and turns. The lead essay, by James H. Cone, puts it this way: "Whose Earth Is It, Anyway?"[1] Kusumita Pedersen's follow-up is similar: "The question of who belongs to 'us,' with whom are we willing to share, and for whom are we ready to sacrifice,"[2] is the pertinent one. Such are the questions for this volume as a whole, itself the outgrowth of an international conference on social justice and ecology.[3]

Addressing Social and Ecological Reality

How do we answer these questions now? Consider two vignettes. Each highlights dimensions—the "social" and the "ecological"—that must now be addressed *together* in a crowded and humanly dominated biosphere.

The first vignette is from the movie *A Time to Kill*. It is about the Canton, Mississippi, trial of Carl Lee Haley, an African American, for the murder of two young white men who raped and brutally beat his ten-year-old daughter Tanya, then tossed her in a river to die. The scene I am about to describe finds Carl Lee in prison on the eve of the trial summation. The Mississippi jury is all white. The year, judging from the car models, falls somewhere in the late '60s, early '70s. The dialogue in Carl Lee's cell is between the defendant and the young white lawyer representing him, Jake Breganz. Jake has taken his own knocks by accepting Carl Lee's case. His house has been burned by the Klan, his wife and their ten-year-old daughter have left town for safety at his in-laws'. Here is the prison dialogue:

JAKE BREGANZ: "We're gonna lose this case, Carl Lee; I wanna cop a plea, maybe second degree murder, with life in prison."

CARL LEE HALEY: "I can't do no life in prison."

JAKE: "The jury has to identify with the defendant. And I'm a lawyer and you're a gardener; I live in the valley, you're on Thomas Hill . . . "

CARL LEE: "Yeah, and you're white and I'm black. See, Jake, you think just like them, that's why I picked you. You one of them. Oh, you think you ain't 'cause you on TV, trying to get me off, talking 'bout black and white. But when you look at me, you don't see a man, you see a black man."

JAKE: "Carl Lee, I'm your friend."

CARL LEE: "We ain't no friends, Jake. We're on different sides of the line. You live in a different part of town. I don't think you even know where I live. Our daughters ain't never gonna play together."

JAKE: "What are you talkin' about?"

CARL LEE: "America. America is a war and you is on the other side. How a black man ever gonna get a fair trial with the enemy on the bench, and in the jury box, and my life in white hands? You, Jake, that's how. You my secret weapon 'cause you one of the bad guys. You don't mean to be, but that's how you raised: nigger, Negro, black, African American; no matter how you sees me, you sees me as different. If you was on that jury, what would it take to convince you to set me free? That's how you save my ass, *that's how you save us both.*"[4]

The relationship of Carl Lee and Jake is a "structured" enemy relationship. The two men have to find a way to be allies—"that's how you save my ass, that's how you save us both." But their relationship is race-riddled, mired in a history reaching back to the Middle Passage and to slaves and slave owners in Mississippi. That relationship is essentially antagonistic, and it will be as long as America's most deep-seated social problem—white racism—persists. Jake pushes that relationship away because he thinks he's crossed over, as Carl Lee's friend. But his ten-year-old Hannah and Carl Lee's ten-year-old Tanya won't likely share a common future, perhaps won't even play together. Their own innocent relationship was already a structured enemy relationship the day their mothers—privileged white and poor black—pushed them with pain and joy from the womb.

Structured enemy relationships and varieties of moral privilege and exclusion define our time, whatever the personal attitudes of individuals may be and whatever working alliances might be cobbled together. Carl Lee and Jake reflect racial "enemyhood" in the United States. But we might also have named other inimical connections reflected in this volume and elsewhere: colonized and colonizer, poor and rich, female and male, South African black and South African white, *dalit* ("backward") and "casted," Muslim and Christian, Jew and Gentile, gay and straight, worker and manager, Native American and Euro-American, tenant and landlord, debtor and creditor, nation here and nation there. Do individual bonds matter here? Of course. But far less than the systemic power relationships that govern conflicting collective interests. Far less than the contours of social justice and injustice.

Structured enemy relationships and moral privilege and exclusion are not all of life. But *in* all of life there are socially constructed hostilities and historically clashing interests. No soul is immune from harm, no life is without some violation, no community remains at peace indefinitely, no paradise is unspoiled. Indeed, "to be human is to be in conflict, to offend and to be offended."[5] So the question for viable, sustainable community, finally, is whether there is a gospel and ethic for enemies.[6] Or, to sharpen it in the way Jesus of Nazareth, Mohandas Gandhi, and Martin Luther King Jr. all did, whether love of enemy is not a life imperative itself and the reconciliation of enemies the only way to new creation.

"New creation" necessarily passes by way of "old creation." New creation is creation as we know it, redeemed. So consider a second vignette and a second dimension of creation.

The American Museum of Natural History, New York City, is on Central Park West at 79th Street. Get off the C train and walk underground into the museum itself. Ascend one floor to the new Hall of Biodiversity. The centerpiece is a detailed cross section of the Dzanga-Sangha rain forest, an extension of the Congo Basin rain forest in the Central African Republic. The purpose is clearly educational, though the effect is esthetic as well. The nature and indispensability of biodiversity is explained, as are the efforts needed to sustain the forest and its peoples. Of course, biodiversity isn't only a matter of rain forests. It's the sum of all species living on earth and their habitats, and we rely on it for most everything. Not only for "food, fuel, fiber, medicine, and countless natural products," just to start the list, but also for the functions that all life requires to sustain itself—cleansing, recycling, renewing. Biodiversity, the exhibit goes on to explain, makes and keeps the earth habitable through "purification of air and water, control of floods and droughts, protection from ultraviolet light, generation and renewal of soil fertility, detoxification and decomposition of wastes, pollination of crops and natural vegetation, maintenance of diverse habitats and ecosystems, control of agricultural pests, cycling of crucial nutrients, moderation of temperature extremes and the forces of wind and waves."[7] Moreover, biodiversity isn't only essential to our physical survival. It is "a force in our cultural lives. It is the medium through which our aesthetic and spiritual values are expressed." "Around the world," a panel reads, "traditions of faith have drawn upon biodiversity for both insight and imagery."[8]

Still, the attention getter on this visit is not the re-created slice of rain forest. It's the panoramic displays of habitats nearby: eighteen waist-high, tilted panels. Across the panels move slow-motion, full-color video displays of Earth's diverse habitats: coral reefs, tropical forests, freshwater wetlands, rivers, and lakes, deserts, oceans, temperate and boreal forests, tundra, grasslands and savannas, islands. The scenes change, then change again. Sometimes a single habitat unfolds across all eighteen panels—a sixty-foot panorama of fish on their reefs, an ocean shoreline, a mountainside in autumn, a high desert in spring bloom or caught in the austerity of winter, a swamp of much more color than you ever expect of swamps. Now and again scenes of humanly induced degradation move into the panels and interrupt the more pristine presentations. Then sentences emerge, enlarge a little, and move left and right to the same slow rhythm as the display of life. No argument is made and nothing is really explained. There is just a drumbeat of data.

An area of rainforest the size of Switzerland is lost each year in Southeast Asia. Only 6% of the world's forests are protected. Acid rain can fall as far as 200 miles from a pollution source. 80% of the mangrove swamps in the Philippines were destroyed by 1985. Humans have developed 1/2 to 2/3 of Earth's land surface. Only about 1/10% of pesticides actually reach their target. Habitat loss has resulted in the loss of 90 Native Amazonian cultures since 1900. Humans erode 71 tons of topsoil on a typical day. 1/3 of the population of developing countries lacks access to safe drinking water. Three million tons of oil pour into the sea annually. Since 1970 the world's fishing fleet has expanded twice as much as the catch. Over 2/3 of the world's fisheries have collapsed or are threatened. Since 1950 1/5 of the world's topsoil has been lost. Human population has grown more since 1950 than in all previous history. Global water usage has tripled since 1950.[9]

All this time, the kids scurry about, apparently enamored with the colorful motion of the displays. Some try to catch the virtual fish. The adults are quieter and pensive. It's sinking in: A beautiful world is being lost, and the drumbeat is really about ourselves. We are enemies, structured enemies, massively structured enemies of much of the rest of life.

Biodiversity is the name science gives a fierce "ontology of communion"[10] and an intimacy of all life. But human and other-than-human life, invariably together, is at enmity, an enmity at the hands of those who, without wincing, still dare to name themselves creation's stewards.

Focus and Assumptions

The mission of the churches beyond 2000 is to help create community among structured enemies in a shared but humanly dominated biosphere. The task is creating reconciling and reconciled socioenvironmental community. And the obstacle is not diversity, biological or otherwise. It is injustice, moral privilege, and exclusion.

Such reconciling and reconciled local "Earth" community is in fact the only community that genuinely saves, whether the dividing lines of hostility be racial, ethnic, gendered, sexual, class-born, species-born, national, or cultural. Such community is the only truly redeemed community, the only expression of genuinely "new creation." Community is not reformed or redeemed if, to recall Jesus's word, we love only redundantly, if we love only those who like us and who are like us. But such a redeemed community is a work of art far more difficult than present language lets on. Exuberant declarations "celebrating" differences and "embracing" community cover harsher realities. Ask Carl Lee Haley. Or, if you could, ask those species now extinct at human hands.

Eco-justice is one way to name the moral norm and goal. "The community of life" is another way to name it, "ecumenical Earth" or "habitat Earth" yet another. And church and community together in creation is a way to designate the kind of partnership required for the pursuit of Earth community by Christian believers.

What would such community spiritual-moral formation for eco-justice mean for churches working together with other institutions and movements? It would mean a different "social" Christianity as well as a different "ecological" one. Most simply put, it would require shedding the remnants of complex domination systems that have oppressed both peoples and the land. This volume is about practical and theoretical efforts to do that.

There are assumptions necessary to this task. While they cannot be discussed here, many are explored in the pages that follow. In any case, displaying these assumptions at the outset can help introduce the volume as a whole and prepare the reader for what follows.

• Until matters of eco-justice are seen to rest somewhere near the heart of Christian faith, the environment will be relegated to the long list of important "issues" clamoring for people's attention. The proper subject of justice is not *the environment*. It is inclusive *creation* as Earth—the other-than-human and human, together. (All the essays assume this.)

• Differently said, all creation has standing before God and is the object of redemption. Creation's well-being rests at the center, not the edge, of Christian moral responsibility and practices, liturgical and contemplative practices included. (On the latter, see Troy Messenger's chapter, "These Stones Shall be God's House: Tools for Earth Liturgy.")

• A significant work for Christian communities for the foreseeable future is adapting their major teachings and practices—the "deep traditions" of Christianity, together with its reading of Scripture—to the task of revaluing nature/culture together so as to prevent their destruction and contribute to their sustainability. (See Brigitte Kahl's rereading of Earth and Eve in Genesis, Kusumita Pedersen's reflections on salvation and moral exclusion, and Dieter Hessel's concluding chapter, "The Church Ecologically Reformed.")

• There are no pristine Christian traditions for this task. This means that conversions to Earth on the part of Christianity are crucial to Christianity's role in the interreligious, panhuman vocation of Earthkeeping. "Conversion" here means what it has commonly meant in religious experience; namely, both a break with the past and yet a preservation of essential trajectories; both a rupture and a new direction, yet with a sense that the new place is also "home" or truly "home"; both a rejection of elements of tradition yet the making of new tradition in fulfillment of the old; both difference from what has gone before and solidarity with it. Substantively, *conversion to Earth* means measuring all Christian impulses by one stringent criterion: their contribution to Earth's well-being. (All the essays assume conversion of this kind as well as this criterion.)

• A valorizing of Christian pluralism is necessary and desirable. It is necessary for the sake of the integrity of diverse Christian traditions themselves. They are many, they are wildly different from one another, even in the same family, and they ought to be treated in ways that honor their genealogy and merit the respect and recognition of their devotees. "Catholicity" is the name for the nature of the church as the community of churches, present and past, that manifest the ecumenical range of historically incarnate faiths lived across two millennia on most of Earth's continents. Such catholicity is inherently plural; it can only exist as internally diverse. A faithful remembering of the Christian past thus means respecting and retrieving this variety. This is not—to point up the contrast—"faithfulness" in the manner of imperial Christianities large and small, which consists in the selective forgetting or repression of this variety, usually in the name of theological heresy or moral or cultural deviance. [11] (Many of the chapters that follow speak from this enhanced notion of catholicity. See Robra, Deenabandhu and Anderson-Rajarigam for one account, based in the Theology of Life Program of the World Council of Churches, and Conradie et al., for an account from South Africa.)

• Valorizing Christian pluralism is desirable for another reason. The "eco-crisis" is comprehensive of nature and culture together. No one tradition, religious or secular, can satisfactorily address the full range of matters that require planetary attention. It is therefore necessary to think ecologically about ecumenism and ecumenically about ecological well-being. ecumenical Earth, or habitat Earth, is one way to capture this comprehensive ecological/ecumenical orientation.[12] (David G. Hallman's "Climate Change and Ecumenical Engagement Toward Sustainable Community" nicely illustrates this on a new and compelling issue.)

• The revelation of God and God's ways are not, it is assumed here, limited to those known in the Christian churches. This can be and has been argued on Christian grounds: Just as the God Israel worships is not the God of the Jews alone, by their own confession, so the God of Christians is not the God of Christians alone, by their own confession. In this volume, this means that any reading of tradition has more to do "with a Christian reading of the past than it does with an exclusive reading of the Christian past."[13] The Spirit blows where it will. (The Ecumenical Earth Conference that generated this volume carried an interreligious, crosscultural, and international tone.)

• The investigation of plural Christian traditions in search of a common Earth ethic should center in community practices and discrete ways of life. This assumes two things relevant to spiritual-moral formation: (1) that the way a community "*does* the truth"—its practices—reflects its operative understandings and its hopes or aspirations, and (2) that the community's moral values and beliefs cannot be separated from other beliefs and prizings. How community members understand their lives comprehensively and enact them in their practices already entails norms for their conduct and exhibits their sense of moral responsibility as a whole. Morality isn't a sector in life; it is a dimension of life intimately related to other dimensions. (All the essays assume this.)

• Against the reigning assumption that Christianity is a text-based and not a place-based religion, the assumption here is that there are always meaningful connections of spirituality and practice to place, to environs, often to the natural landscape itself. The investigation of communities should therefore include a description of flora, fauna, and geology as well as the details of the built environment, precisely as spiritually and morally significant. The connection of locale and the spiritual-moral universe is not made in the manner of the tourist or the scientist, however. It is Earth as alive in a particular locale and alive among those who live their lives in this place. It is local Earth as seen in reigning metaphors and symbols; in diet and dress, art and architecture; in liturgy, hymnody, prayer, and preaching; in the designation of "special" or "sacred" places; in the tasks and meaning of everyday work; and in the issues local communities address. Part of a genuine conversion to Earth of multiple Christianities is simply to recognize Earth's presence and influence already there, as numerous chapters in this book do. (See the discussion of Theology of Life and South African cases mentioned above, as well as Peggy Shepard's treatment of community environmental action in Harlem in her essay, "Issues of Community Empowerment.")

• The descriptive account of each community's place and the presence of that in the community's life—its "eco-location"—is only part of good analysis, however. Good analysis includes other elements, most of them reflected in these pages:

- interstructured moral analysis (social/eco-location seen in factors of race, gender, class, culture);
- reflection and theory as emergent from the practices and ways of life described;
- use of interdisciplinary methods;
- analysis that is theologically as well as morally explicit;
- analysis that can be ably communicated to the churches and communities it serves;
- proposals that aim at community spiritual-moral formation and public policy;
- a working style that is itself collaborative from onset to conclusion; and

- work that reconstructs Christian moral theory and clarifies the nature and contributions of plural expressions of Christianity as an Earth-honoring faith.

All this said, these pages also assume that community and social justice is the strongest and most enduring vocational emphasis of the "peoples of the Book"—Judaism, Islam, Christianity. Divine power in these traditions is experienced as the power to create a people whose way of life is to exemplify righteousness and moral responsibility. Dorothee Soelle has it right, and she echoes a major theme of the conference: "The tradition that joins us together is justice. 'God is the universe,' 'God is the maker of the cosmos,' 'God is energy,' 'God is the light'—I can say all that, too. But, coming from the Judeo-Christian tradition, I must first say, God is justice. To know God means to do justice."[14] In fact, the whole purpose of eco-justice formation is precisely to extend this tradition, not diminish it.

- The specific theological-moral point of departure here draws largely, although not exclusively, from liberation theologies. It therefore seeks out Christian traditions of opposition to experienced and perceived injustice as crucial sources of knowledge and participation for Christian revaluing of nature/culture and for the construction of just and sustainable communities.

- Engaging Christian communities who have suffered more than benefited from the forces of modernity is the path this liberative work takes. This is the case in part because the forces of modernity have largely created the present threats to life. Those who have known firsthand the destructive side of modernity offer critical knowledge largely neglected or hidden by/to those who have benefited. (This and the foregoing assumption are prominent in all sections of this volume.)

- The forces of modernity can be described in many ways. Determining how to describe them rightly is essential. The crucial nexus suggested here is the interaction of the global economy and global life systems. One fruitful means of treating this is an analysis of three successive waves of "globalization": (a) conquest and colonization, Christianity and commerce moving outward from Europe beginning in the fifteenth century and understood as the spread of "civilization"; (b) post–World War II "development" and its economic criterion for social well-being: namely, that the well-being of all peoples is to be judged on the basis of rising production and consumption enabled by unending economic growth; and

(c) pre- and post-1989 free-trade capitalism and its use of market logic and relationships as the model for society itself. The old Western "*mission civilisatrice*" is reaffirmed by each wave, sometimes in religious and sometimes in secular form but always to the transformation of local nature/culture and often to their destruction. There are profound race, class, gender, cultural, and "natural" dimensions across all three waves. Any one of them—white supremacy, for example, or the modern turns of patriarchy—could be as effective an entry point and organizing venue as "globalization." And in fact all are represented in these pages, beginning with James H. Cone's "Whose Earth Is It, Anyway?" and continuing with Ibrahim M. Abu-Rabi's response to the Western *mission civilisatrice* and globalization in "The Muslim World: Globalization and Ecology."

• It is assumed, at least as a starting point, that the deep traditions and practices of Christian communities may harbor local knowledge important for building just and sustainable local communities among structured enemies. This includes the ways of "traditional ecologists," persons whose knowledge of local and regional life systems can undergird potentially sustainable practices. Generally speaking, premodern religions are comprehensive healing systems that include important local arts. Often these are arts for healing the land, arts that have, together with their practitioners, been largely disdained and shunted aside by modernity's scientific and industrialized ways, industrialized agriculture and mining included. (See, for example, the discussion of *dalit* communities in chapter 5 as well as current programmatic efforts in South Africa.)

• This kind of work also assumes that a scheme of inquiry and interpretation which begins in suspicion of current arrangements can, through the uncovering of subjugated pasts, move beyond retrieval of neglected memories and practices to positive construction of an Earth ethic, provided the table is set for a dialogue of equals. It assumes as well that setting the table in this way requires great labor and is far more difficult than the talk of "embracing diversity" in the interests of "community" lets on. Granting subjugated knowledges equal voice means granting subjugated peoples equal voice. And granting peoples equal voice means sharing power. (See Steven C. Rockefeller's chapter on the important process used in formulating and revising the proposed Earth Charter. See also, in keeping with earlier assumptions, Rockefeller's call for plural expressions of Christianity.)

For this writer's own tradition—one of the Western Christian strands present in the "neo-Europeanizing" of nature/culture that accompanied globalization—these assumptions carry a radical reorientation. To illustrate this and further introduce the volume as a whole, we will take the time and space to discuss one element. Namely, affirming Christian pluralism by way of challenging the notion that Christianity is a European religion.

CHRISTIANITIES BEYOND THE EUROPEAN NORM

The varieties of Christianity that accompanied white supremacy and globalization, especially in its initial phase of conquest, colonization, and commerce, were largely the imperial Christianities of expanding and competing European tribes. They sought and taught both religious and moral orthodoxy in the manner largely favored since Constantine's vision and Theodosius's decree: that is, "one Lord, one faith, one baptism" translated as "one king, one church, one creed, one people, one morality." This is the ethics of empire and master narrative and it accords poorly, in religious or secular form, with any truly common good across multicultural reality on varied terrain. Alfred Crosby Jr.'s commentary in *The Columbian Exchange* is chilling and true. He, an environmental historian, speaks of a dominant Christian morality that saw itself as part and parcel of European civilizational superiority: "Again and again, during the centuries of European imperialism, the Christian view that all men are brothers was to lead to persecution of non-Europeans—he who is my brother sins to the extent that he is unlike me."[15] This is not Cain's moral world; Cain does not really consider himself his brother's keeper.[16] This is the moral world of those who *do* profess the unity of the human family in God, but who norm it with a deadly conformity—"*he who is my brother sins to the extent that he is unlike me.*"

Powerful dissent from imperial ecclesial ethics and spiritual-moral formation of this sort arose on European turf itself, in the work of the Enlightenment. Among other things, the Enlightenment eventually yielded liberalism's answer to the problem Martin Luther King Jr. identified. A widely separated family has in effect, King said, inherited a house in which they have to live together, a great "world house" of "black and white, Easterner and Westerner, Gentile and Jew, Catholic and Protestant, Moslem and Hindu." These peoples comprise "a family unduly separated in ideas, culture and interest who, because we can never again live apart, must learn somehow to live with each other in peace."[17] Liberalism's answer to the problem of "world house" pluralism was civic moral formation promoting the virtue and value of tolerance. But this does not suffice, either. Yes, it takes fewer lives than the ethics of empire and offers welcome breathing space. Both are genuine moral treasures in a world of endless internecine conflict. But tolerance does not, as such, reconcile structured enemies, either people-to-people enemies or people-and-life-systems enemies. In fact—this is its Achilles' heel—tolerance tends to leave in place the power arrangements and social stratifications that generate and sustain enemyhood. Tolerance calls for inclusiveness; but inclusiveness without substance in a concrete set of community-creating, enemy-reconciling practices adds up to little more than "letting be" (we tolerate and perhaps "appreciate" the other, then go our separate ways).

So has Christianity as a European religion been deconstructed by its own dissenters, secular or religious? Not if the collective socioenvironmental power arrangements remain largely in place, as they do (white supremacy and male control, for example, together with an economy that threatens environments). The task for many churches is still to recover from the notion that Christianity is normatively, though not geographically, a European religion.

As a starting point, it is vital to see that Christianity as a European and neo-European religion is erroneous from a historical-geographical point of view. Churches arose on three continents simultaneously and Christianity, like the Judaism from which it emerged, was multiethnic, multiracial, multicultural, multilingual, and heterodox, from the outset. The Pentecost account of Parthian, Medes, Elamites, and other residents of Mesopotamia turns out to be a rather accurate index of a contested faith that radiated from Jerusalem and the Mediterranean basin. Early accounts place Christians in Edessa, beyond the borders of the Roman Empire to the east—that is, at the edge of that which called itself the *oikumene* (inhabited Earth). Legend already has Thomas founding the church in India; and if a first-century date is unlikely, there are clear records of a flourishing Mar Thoma church in the far south of the Asian subcontinent by the fourth century. Armenians, to cite a West Asian case, were a self-declared Christian nation already in the third century. Moreover Persian or Assyrian Christianity, now completely lost in the

"Christianity is European" narrative, not only arose very early on, but at one point extended from the Euphrates to the border of Korea—a full 5,000 miles—and included 250 dioceses. There were fifteen metropolitan provinces among Persians and Mongolians and five missionary provinces in China and India. One estimate numbers 12 million or so Persian Christians by the year 1000. This Christianity flourished under Islam for several hundred years. (It was also decimated by Islam after the conversion to Islam of Mongolian and Turkish emperors.)[18]

Not only was this three-continent Christianity culturally and ethnically pluralist from the start, its faith was heterodox in all three locales— Europe, Asia, and Africa. It continued so, both before *and after* a series of ecumenical councils convened by emperors and in which bishops declared an official creed that pushed large numbers of chiefly Asian and African Christians, such as Nestorians and Monophysites, outside the pale of a now established orthodoxy. Emperors and bishops did what they did, east, west, north, and south, not least because an imperial religion in a shaky empire makes its contribution to social and political order by socializing around common beliefs and a common morality. Baptism under Charlemagne, the reader may recall, was an offer (at sword point) that one couldn't refuse. But even as late as Charlemagne (800 C.E.) Christianity isn't "European." "Europe" doesn't yet exist as either a consciousness or a civilization. It exists only as a continent. Franks, Celts and Germanic sorts, Anglo-Saxon peoples of differing kinds, Goths and Visigoths, Greeks and Romans and Iberians exist. The "Europe" of "Western Christianity" is actually rather late-breaking news. The call-up to the crusades generates a certain cross-tribal European consciousness, to be sure. And Charlemagne's empire should not be forgotten. But the real boost is the first wave of globalization initiated in the late fifteenth century; that is, conquest, colonization, commerce, and Christianity under the sponsorship of rival European tribes and deemed a common "civilizing" mission to heathen peoples in distant lands, a mission, we must remind ourselves, that changed nature on a mass scale together with peoples. Yet as late as the Reformation itself, Christianity is portrayed as a three-petaled flower where one petal is Europe, one Asia, and one Africa. And the center that joins them is not Rome, much less Geneva, Wittenberg, Constantinople, or Canterbury. It is Jerusalem.

Here we return to the Enlightenment. It plays an ironic role. As mentioned, the notion that the Christian West is the bearer of a Christianity normative for all is a notion the Enlightenment, which sought to foster trans-tribal European consciousness and a genuinely cosmopolitan morality, strongly challenged. The Enlightenment challenged hegemonic religious claims, often in starkly anticlerical, antichurch tones and helped set in motion the process of Western secularization. It did this at the very same time the colonizing process and the settlement of neo-Europes around the world reproduced "Christian civilization" in a Western mode as normative for morality and society everywhere else! And here the Enlightenment quest for a genuinely cosmopolitan global ethic usually merged, despite some real fights, with the civilizational mission of European Christianities. So the Enlightenment, to which we owe so much in the way of critical consciousness, ends up as an uneasy but real ally of a normative Christian ethic that is imperial on a global scale. It really did not undo the double assumptions that were so fatal to so many peoples, their cultures, and the land itself. Namely, that Christianity could supply the religious and moral unity of civilization, and that this civilization was superior to the ways of non-European peoples.

Take one instance of a tribal neo-European Christianity as civilizationally normative. This is a case on U.S. soil. The example is "Orthodox Alaska." The Orthodox Church in Alaska has been in the hands of Native Alaskans essentially since the Russians sold "the Great Land" to the United States. In fact the Orthodox Church was, because of the assimilationist policies of the U.S. government, about the only institution left in native hands after the Russians sailed back across the Bering Strait. In any case, there were never more than nine hundred Russians in Alaska even when it was a Russian colony. The U.S. government, in a remarkable violation of church and state separation, assigned various Indian reservations to specific Protestant Christian bodies and paid the salaries of missionaries to carry out the civilizing task. Two of the key players in assimilationist policy were Presbyterian ministers—Reverend S. Hall Young and Reverend Dr. Sheldon Jackson. Young wrote in his autobiography about the need to counter Orthodoxy's habit of using indigenous languages and customs:

> One strong stand, so far as I know I was the first to take, was the determination to do no translating into . . . any of the native dialects. I realized . . . that the task of making an English-speaking race of these Natives was much easier than the task of making a civilized and Christian language out

of the Native languages. We should let the old tongues with their superstitions and sin die—the sooner the better—and replace these languages with that of Christian civilization, and compel the Natives in our schools to speak English and English only.[19]

In 1912 the United States government closed St. Paul's, the Orthodox Church school in the Pribilof Islands, for the crime of teaching Aleut. There will be, the government said, no Natives teaching Natives native ways, or teaching anything else in Native languages.[20] And when an Orthodox bishop protested the policies Dr. Jackson was carrying out, and lodged his complaints with President McKinley, the *New York Tribune* attacked the bishop for his "blind and unwarranted prejudice against this Protestant country and its excellent schools."[21]

The words of the commissioner of education made the point even plainer: "We have no higher calling in the world than to be missionaries to these people who have not yet achieved the Anglo-Saxon frame of mind."[22]

Or plainer yet, in a citation that is raw in its exposure of the connections of commerce, [Protestant] Christianity, and assimilationist policies. This is from official school philosophy as promulgated by the U.S. government in 1900:

> If the Native population of Alaska can be brought under the influence of Christianity and be given a rudimentary English-language education, it follows that the white population [comprised of immigrants from other states] could employ them in mining, transportation, and the production of food.[23]

The phrase *brought under the influence of Christianity* is especially telling in that many of the "Native population" were Orthodox Christians! But this is just another trait of the controlling narrative—it filters out, or declares as illegitimate, dissenting Christianities. So the second task for Earth-honoring and eco-justice-oriented churches, after decentering Christianity as normatively white and European, is to recover and amplify dissenting perspectives and practices, whether minority or majority. That is happening now and is a great gift of recent decades. With it comes a different sense of ecumenism and Christian unity. This is ecumenism and unity cognizant that all vibrant religion is local and incarnational and that churches are always particular. Fabian Eboussi Boulaga speaks of African churches, but his remarks have ecumenical sweep.

> Because [the churches] are frankly given as particular and plural, each church posits the need for the others, by which and thanks to which each is passé, [and] by which each transcends itself. The deficiency of all the churches is that they are so far from being the origin and principle. None can claim to possess the fullness of truth. Thus it is in reciprocal recognition and acknowledgment, in exchange and confrontation, that they will discover the principle of unity and an active universality. . . . [T]he human being journeys in partiality, and each church should be speaking the divine transforming action that is under way in the historical and social space in which it finds itself immediately inserted. Nowhere and at no moment does totalizing practice, or the absolute, synoptic viewpoint, simply emerge. Unity and universality are in the process of communication of the particular, different churches.[24]

BENEFITS FOR ECUMENICAL EARTH

Boulaga's effort to voice an ecclesiology joining solidarity and difference, pluralism and re-creating tradition together, without assuming the normative narrative of European Christianity, yields three benefits for Earth-positive spiritual-moral formation among structured enemies. We cite Dale Irvin here, as we have earlier. The reader will see evidence of exactly these three benefits throughout this volume.

A "*self-corrective* capacity for criticism and renewal" would issue from the awareness of multiple communities and practices within the plural Christian traditions themselves and the exchanges, both public and muted, of dominant and oppositional voices. "*New options opening for the churches' future(s)*" would emerge from the expression of diversity and multiplicity in and across the churches. And "*new modes of Christian community*" itself would be encouraged and explored when the table of community is set in this way. A pluralist ecclesiology that discovers the unity and universality of the church in the vibrancy of its diversity would be intrinsically restless and creative and make common cause in working alliances with other institutions and movements.[25] The church catholic, then, is a community of communities that share and honor a common Earth with others. It is "church and community in creation," to recall the subtitle of the originating conference.

Of course, the bump and grind and clash of fashioning open communities among structural enemies in the churches has its own requirement, something Irvin calls "costly flexibility"—that is, a disposition to experience the holy in new and diverse ways offered by the stranger and enemy as well as soul mate and friend.[26] Costly flexibility is more than the "letting be" of liberal tolerance, since it is more likely to face the systemic power issues that generate conflict and hostility. So perhaps it is most fitting to conclude this introduction by highlighting a few appropriate reminders, given what has been said thus far.

Churches *are*, not only *have*, a social ethic. They form—or malform—those whose lives are shaped by liturgy, instruction, moral witness, church order, or any other expression of church life. This includes churches' roles in working alliances with nonchurch organizations and movements. The churches' own structures and the ways in which their members relate to one another and the wider society thus comprise a way of being in the world, a social ethic. Moral formation (and malformation) are the inevitable outcome of what is done (and not done) and the way in which it takes place (or fails to take place).

An inescapable pluralism will and should reign here. Churches create, modify, and draw deeply from differing traditions. They face different moral challenges or meet the same global challenges in different ways. Understandings and expressions of formation thus differ accordingly. The sense of identity, the ordering of community, and the place and meaning given specific rites and practices will, even amid strong continuity, vary from locale to locale as compelling needs and issues arise and evolve.

This means that spiritual-moral formation is irreducibly concrete and local, even when it is formation of a shared Earth ethic. It happens person by person, congregation by congregation, institution by institution, system by system. And it happens by way of multiple points of entry and multiple means as expressed by the whole people of God—young and old, lettered and unlettered, male and female, of whatever race, clan, nationality, or ecclesial tradition. Yet the point of all this is *the effort to fashion and share normative common ground.* It is normative common ground for eco-justice as near the center of varied expressions of Christian faith. Dieter Hessel's concluding chapter names four interactive norms that help build this common ground: (a) solidarity with other people and creatures in Earth community; (b) ecological sustainability, that is, environmentally fitting habits that enable life to flourish; (c) sufficiency as a standard of organized sharing; and (d) socially just participation in decisions about how to obtain sustenance and manage the common good.[27] These norms have already shaped the landscape of some church-and-community thought and work, around the notion of "sustainable community."[28]

Differently said, and on the terms where we began, this normative common ground presents new boundaries and substance for the spiritual-moral universe of an Earth-honoring faith, boundaries and substance that encompass the whole community of life—the societal, the biophysical, and the geoplanetary—and that recognize structured enemies across it.[29] The questions are the same, "Whose Earth is it, anyway?" or "Who belongs to 'us,' with whom are we willing to share, and for whom are we willing to sacrifice?"[30] But the answers, inherently socioecological, carry new twists. There are new dimensions of church and community in creation to confront and to fashion for the sake of habitat Earth. The call is for "the church ecologically reformed."

PART I

THEOLOGY FOR HABITAT EARTH

1

Whose Earth Is It, Anyway?

James H. Cone

The earth is the LORD's and all that is in it,
   the world, and those who live in it.
      —Psalm 24:1

We say the earth is our mother—we cannot own her; she owns us.[1]
      —Pacific peoples

THE LOGIC THAT LED TO SLAVERY AND SEGREGATION IN THE AMERICAS, colonization and apartheid in Africa, and the rule of white supremacy throughout the world is the same one that leads to the exploitation of animals and the ravaging of nature. It is a mechanistic and instrumental logic that defines everything and everybody in terms of contribution to the development and defense of white world supremacy. People who fight against white racism but fail to connect it to the degradation of the earth are anti-ecological—whether they know it or not. People who struggle against environmental degradation but do not incorporate in it a disciplined and sustained fight against white supremacy are racists—whether they acknowledge it or not. The fight for justice cannot be segregated but must be integrated with the fight for life in all its forms.

Until recently, the ecological crisis has not been a major theme in the liberation movements in the African American community. "Blacks don't care about the environment" is a typical comment by white ecologists. Racial and economic justice has been at best only a marginal concern in the mainstream environmental movement. "White people care more about the endangered whale and the spotted owl than they do about the survival of young blacks in our nation's cities" is a well-founded belief in the African American community. Justice fighters for blacks and the defenders of the earth have tended to ignore each other in their public discourse and practice. Their separation from each other is unfortunate because they are fighting the same enemy—human beings' domination of each other and nature.

The leaders in the mainstream environmental movement are mostly middle- and upper-class whites who are unprepared culturally and intellectually to dialogue with angry blacks. The leaders in the African American community are leery of talking about anything with whites that will distract from the menacing reality of racism. What both groups fail to realize is how much they need each other in the struggle for "justice, peace and the integrity of creation."[2]

In this essay, I want to challenge the black freedom movement to take a critical look at itself through the lens of the ecological movement and also challenge the ecological movement to critique itself through a radical and ongoing engagement of racism in American history and culture. Hopefully, we can break the silence and promote genuine solidarity between the two groups and thereby enhance the quality of life for the whole inhabited earth—humankind and otherkind.

EXPANDING THE RACE CRITIQUE

No threat has been more deadly and persistent for black and indigenous peoples than the rule of white supremacy in the modern world. For more than five hundred years, through the wedding of science and technology, white people have been exploiting nature and killing people of color in every nook and cranny of the planet in the name of God and democracy. According to the English historian Basil Davidson, the Atlantic slave trade "cost Africa fifty million souls."[3] Author Eduardo Galeano claims that 150 years of Spanish and Portuguese colonization in Central and South America reduced the indigenous population from 90 million to 3.5 million.[4]

During the twenty-three-year reign of terror of King Leopold II of Belgium in the Congo (1885–1908), scholarly estimates suggest that approximately ten million Congolese met unnatural deaths—"fully half the territory's population."[5] The tentacles of white supremacy have stretched around the globe. No people of color have been able to escape its cultural, political, and economic domination.

Blacks in the United States have been the most visible and articulate opponents of white racism. From Frederick Douglass and Sojourner Truth to Martin Luther King Jr., Malcolm X, and Fannie Lou Hamer, African Americans have waged a persistent fight against white racism in all its overt and covert manifestations. White racism denied the humanity of black people, with even theologians debating whether blacks had souls. Some said blacks were subhuman "beasts."[6] Other more progressive theologians, like Union Seminary's Reinhold Niebuhr, hoped that the inferiority of the Negro was not "biological" but was due instead to "cultural backwardness," which could gradually be overcome with education.[7]

Enslaved for 244 years, lynched and segregated another one hundred, blacks, with militant words and action, fought back in every way they could—defending their humanity against all who had the nerve to question it. Malcolm X, perhaps the most fierce and uncompromising public defender of black humanity, expressed the raw feelings of most blacks: "We declare our right on this earth . . . to be a human being, to be respected as a human being, to be given the rights of a human being in this society, on this earth, in this day, which we intend to bring into existence by any means necessary."[8]

Whites bristled when they heard Malcolm talk like that. They not only knew Malcolm meant what he said but feared that most blacks agreed with him—though they seldom said so publicly. Whites also knew that if they were black, they too would say a resounding, "Amen!" to Malcolm's blunt truth. "If you want to know what I'll do," Malcolm told whites, "figure out what you'll do."[9]

White theologians thanked God for being "truly longsuffering, 'slow to anger and plenteous in mercy' (Ps. 103:8)," as Reinhold Niebuhr put it, quoting the Hebrew scriptures. Niebuhr knew that white people did not have a leg to stand on before the bar of God's justice regarding their treatment of people of color. "If," Niebuhr wrote, "the white man were to expiate his sins committed against the darker races, few would have the right to live."[10]

Black liberation theology is a product of a fighting spirituality derived from nearly four hundred years of black resistance. As one who encountered racism first as a child in Bearden, Arkansas, no day in my life has passed in which I did not have to deal with the open and hidden violence of white supremacy. Whether in the society or the churches, at Adrian College or Union Seminary, racism was always there—often smiling and sometimes angry. Since writing my first essay on racism in the white church and its theology thirty years ago, I decided that I would never be silent about white supremacy and would oppose it with my whole being.

While white racism must be opposed at all cost, our opposition will not be effective unless we expand our vision. Racism is profoundly interrelated with other evils, including the degradation of the earth. It is important for black people, therefore, to make the connection between the struggle against racism and other struggles for life. A few black leaders recognized this need and joined the nineteenth-century abolitionist movement with the suffragist movement and the 1960s civil rights movement with the second wave of the women's movement. Similar links were made with the justice struggles of other U.S. minorities, gay rights struggles, and poor peoples' fight for freedom around the world. Martin Luther King Jr.'s idea of the "beloved community" is a potent symbol for people struggling to build one world community where life in all its forms is respected. "All life is interrelated," King said. "Whatever affects one directly affects all indirectly. . . . There is an interrelated structure of reality."[11]

RACE, ECOLOGY, AND AFRICAN AMERICAN CHURCHES

Connecting racism with the degradation of the earth is a much-needed work in the African American community, especially in black liberation theology and the black churches. Womanist theologians have already begun this important intellectual work. Delores Williams explores a "parallel between defilement of black women's bodies" and the exploitation of nature. Emilie Townes views "toxic waste landfills in African American communities" as "contemporary versions of lynching a whole people." Karen Baker-Fletcher, using prose and poetry, appropriates the biblical and literary metaphors of dust and spirit to speak about the embodiment of God in creation. "Our task," she writes, "is to grow large hearts, large minds, reconnecting with earth, Spirit, and one another. Black religion must grow ever deeper in the heart."[12]

The leadership of African American churches turned its much-needed attention toward ecological issues in the early 1990s. The catalyst, as usual in the African American community, was a group of black churchwomen in Warren County, North Carolina, who in 1982 lay their bodies down on a road before dump trucks carrying soil contaminated with highly toxic PCBs (polychlorinated biphenyl) to block their progress. In two weeks, more than four hundred protesters were arrested, "the first time anyone in the United States had been jailed trying to halt a toxic waste landfill."[13] Although local residents were not successful in stopping the landfill construction, that incident sparked the attention of civil rights and black church leaders and initiated the national environmental justice movement. In 1987 the United Church of Christ Commission of Racial Justice issued its groundbreaking "Report on Race and Toxic Wastes in the United States." This study found that "among a variety of indicators race was the best predictor of the location of hazardous waste facilities in the U.S."[14] Forty percent of the nation's commercial hazardous-waste landfill capacity was in three predominantly African American and Hispanic communities. The largest landfill in the nation is found in Sumter County, Alabama, where nearly 70 percent of the 17,000 residents are black and 96 percent are poor.

In October 1991 the First National People of Color Environmental Leadership Summit was convened in Washington, D.C. More than 650 grassroots and national leaders from fifty states, the District of Columbia, Mexico, Puerto Rico, and the Marshall Islands participated. They represented more than three hundred environmental groups of color. They all agreed that "If this nation is to achieve environmental justice, the environment in urban ghettoes, barrios, reservations, and rural poverty pockets must be given the same protection as that provided to the suburbs."[15]

The knowledge that people of color are disproportionately affected by environmental pollution angered the black church community and fired up its leadership to take a more active role in fighting against *environmental racism,* a phrase that was coined by Benjamin Chavis, who was then the director of the United Council of Churches (UCC) Commission on Racial Justice.[16] Bunyan Bryant, a professor in the School of Natural Resources and Environment at the University of Michigan and a participant in the environmental justice movement, defines environmental racism as "an extension of racism."

It refers to those institutional rules, regulations, and policies or government or corporate decisions that deliberately target certain communities for least desirable land uses, resulting in the disproportionate exposure of toxic and hazardous waste on communities based upon certain prescribed biological characteristics. Environmental racism is the unequal protection against toxic- and hazardous-waste exposure and the systematic exclusion of people of color from environmental decisions affecting their communities.[17]

The more blacks found out about the racist policies of the government and corporations the more determined they became in their opposition to environmental injustice. In December 1993, under the sponsorship of the National Council of Churches, leaders of mainline black churches held a historic two-day summit meeting on the environment in Washington, D.C. They linked environmental issues with civil rights and economic justice. They did not talk much about the ozone layer, global warming, the endangered whale, or the spotted owl. They focused primarily on the urgent concerns of their communities: toxic and hazardous wastes, lead poisoning, landfills, and incinerators. "We have been living next to the train tracks, trash dumps, coal plants, and insect-infested swamps for many decades," Bishop Frederick C. James of the African Methodist Episcopal Church said. "We in the Black community have been disproportionately affected by toxic dumping, disproportionately affected by lead paint at home, disproportionately affected by dangerous chemicals in the workplace." Black clergy also linked local problems with global issues. "If toxic waste is not safe enough to be dumped in the United States, it is not safe enough to be dumped in Ghana, Liberia, Somalia, nor anywhere else in the world," proclaimed Charles G. Adams, pastor of Hartford Memorial Baptist Church in Detroit. "If hazardous materials are not fit to be disposed of in the suburbs, they are certainly not fit to be disposed of in the cities."[18]

Like black church leaders, African American politicians also are connecting social justice issues with ecology. According to the League of Conservation Voters, the Congressional Black Caucus has "the best environmental record of any voting bloc in Congress."[19] "Working for clean air, clean water, and a clean planet," declared Rep. John Lewis of Georgia, "is just as important, if not more important, than anything I have ever worked on, including civil rights."[20]

Black and other poor people in all racial groups receive much less than their fair share of everything good in the world and a disproportionate amount of the bad. Middle-class and elite white environmentalists have been very effective in implementing the slogan "Not In My Backyard" (NIMBY). As a result, corporations and the government merely turned to the backyards of the poor to deposit their toxic waste. The poor live in the least desirable areas of our cities and rural communities. They work in the most polluted and physically dangerous workplaces. Decent health care hardly exists. With fewer resources to cope with the dire consequences of pollution, the poor bear an unequal burden for technological development while the rich reap most of the benefits. This makes racism and poverty ecological issues. If blacks and other hard-hit communities do not raise these ethical and political problems, they will continue to die a slow and silent death on the planet.

Ecology touches every sphere of human existence. It is not just an elitist or a white middle-class issue. A clean, safe environment is a human- and civil-rights issue that affects the lives of poor blacks and other marginalized groups. We therefore must not let the fear of being distracted from racism blind us to the urgency of the ecological crisis. What good is it to eliminate racism if we are not around to enjoy a racist-free environment?

The survival of the earth, therefore, is a moral issue for everybody. If we do not save the earth from destructive human behavior, no one will survive. That fact alone ought to be enough to inspire people of all colors to join hands in the fight for a just and sustainable planet.

EXPANDING THE ECOLOGICAL CRITIQUE

We are indebted to ecologists in all fields and areas of human endeavor for sounding the alarm about the earth's distress. They have been so effective in raising ecological awareness that few people deny that our planet is in deep trouble. For the first time in history, humankind has the knowledge and power to destroy all life—either with a nuclear bang or a gradual poisoning of the land, air, and sea.

Scientists have warned us of the dire consequences of what human beings are doing to the environment. Theologians and ethicists have raised the moral and religious issues. Grassroots activists in many communities are organizing to stop the killing of nature and its creatures. Politicians are paying attention to people's concern for a clean, safe environment. "It is not so much a question of whether the lion will one day lie down with the lamb," writes Alice Walker, "but whether human beings will ever be able to lie down with any creature or being at all."[21]

What is absent from much of the talk about the environment in First World countries is a truly radical critique of the culture most responsible for the ecological crisis. This is especially true among white ethicists and theologians in the United States. In most of the essays and books I have read, there is hardly a hint that perhaps whites could learn something of how we got into this ecological mess from those who have been the victims of white world supremacy. White ethicists and theologians sometimes refer to the disproportionate impact of hazardous waste on blacks and other people of color in the United States and Third World and even cite an author or two, here and there throughout the development of their discourse on ecology. They often include a token black or Indian in anthologies on ecotheology, eco-justice, and eco-feminism. It is "politically correct" to demonstrate a knowledge of and concern for people of color in progressive theological circles. But people of color are not treated *seriously*, that is, as if they have something *essential* to contribute to the conversation. Environmental-justice concerns of poor people of color hardly ever receive serious attention, not to mention organized resistance. How can we create a genuinely mutual ecological dialogue between whites and people of color if one party acts as if they have all the power and knowledge?

Since Earth Day in 1970, the environmental movement has grown into a formidable force in American society and ecological reflections on the earth have become a dominant voice in religion, influencing all disciplines. It is important to ask, however, Whose problems define the priorities of the environmental movement? Whose suffering claims its attention? "Do environmentalists care about poor people?"[22] Environmentalists usually respond thus, as Rafe Pomerance puts it: "A substantial element of our agenda has related to improving the environment for everybody." Others tell a different story. Former Assistant Secretary of Interior James Joseph says, "Environmentalists tend to focus on those issues that provide recreative outlets instead of issues that focus on equity." Black activist Cliff Boxley speaks even more bluntly, labeling the priorities of environmentalists as "green bigotry." "Conservationists are more interested in saving the habitats of birds than in the construction of low-income housing."[23]

Do we have any reason to believe that the culture most responsible for the ecological crisis will also provide the moral and intellectual resources for the earth's liberation? White ethicists and theologians apparently think so, since so much of their discourse about theology and the earth is just talk among themselves. But I have a deep suspicion about the theological and ethical values of white culture and religion. For five hundred years whites have acted as if they own the world's resources and have forced people of color to accept their scientific and ethical values. People of color have studied dominant theologies and ethics because our physical and spiritual survival partly depended on it. Now that humanity has realized the possibility of its extinction, one would think that a critical assessment of how we got to where we are would be the next step for sensitive and caring theologians of the earth. While there is some radical questioning along these lines, it has not been persistent or challenging enough to compel whites to look outside of their dominating culture for ethical and cultural resources for the earth's salvation. One can still earn a doctorate degree in ethics and theology at American seminaries, even here at Union Seminary in New York, and not seriously engage racism in this society and the world. If we save the planet and have a society of inequality, we wouldn't have saved much.

According to Audre Lorde, "The master's tools will never dismantle the master's house."[24] They are too narrow and thus assume that people of color have nothing to say about race, gender, sexuality, and the earth—all of which are interconnected. We need theologians and ethicists who are interested in mutual dialogue, honest conversation about justice for the earth and all of its inhabitants. We need whites who are eager to know something about the communities of people of color—our values, hopes, and dreams. Whites know so little about our churches and communities that it is often too frustrating to even talk to them about anything that matters. Dialogue requires respect and knowledge of the other—their history, culture, and religion. No one racial or national group has all the answers, but all groups have something to contribute to the earth's healing.

Many ecologists speak often of the need for humility and mutual dialogue. They tell us that we are all interrelated and interdependent, including human and otherkind. The earth is not a machine. It is an organism in which all things are a part of each other. "Every entity in the universe," writes Catherine Keller, "can be described as a process of interconnection with every other being."[25] If white ecologists really believe that, why do most still live in segregated communities? Why are their essays and books about the endangered earth so monological—that is, a conversation of a dominant group talking to itself? Why is there so much talk of love, humility, interrelatedness, and interdependence, and yet so little of these values reflected in white people's dealings with people of color?

Blacks and other minorities are often asked why they are not involved in the mainstream ecological movement. To white theologians and ethicists I ask, Why are you not involved in the dialogue on race? I am not referring primarily to President Clinton's failed initiative, but to the initiative started by the civil rights and black power movements and black liberation theology more than forty years ago. How do we account for the conspicuous white silence on racism, not only in the society and world but especially in theology, ethics, and ecology? I have yet to read a white theologian or ethicist who has incorporated a sustained, radical critique of white supremacy in a theological discourse similar to an engagement of anti-Semitism, class contradictions, and patriarchy.

To be sure, a few concerned white theologians have written about their opposition to white racism but not because race critique was essential to their theological identity. It is usually just a gesture of support for people of color when solidarity across differences is in vogue. As soon as it is no longer socially and intellectually acceptable to talk about race, white theologians revert back to their silence. But as Elie Wiesel said in his Nobel Peace Prize acceptance speech, "We must always take sides. Neutrality helps the oppressor, never the victim. Silence encourages the tormentor, never the tormented."[26] Only when white theologians realize that a fight against racism is a fight for *their* humanity will we be able to create a coalition of whites, blacks, and other people of color in the struggle to save the earth.

Today ecology is in vogue and many people are talking about our endangered planet. I want to urge us to deepen our conversation by linking the earth's crisis with the crisis in the human family. If it is important to save the habitats of birds and other species, then it is at least equally important to save black lives in the ghettos and prisons of America. As Gandhi said, "The earth is sufficient for everyone's need but not for everyone's greed."[27]

2

Inclusion and Exclusion: Reflections on Moral Community and Salvation

Kusumita Pedersen

THE PHEASANT AND THE BLACKSNAKE

In a vast, eroded area somewhere in the American West, Loren Eiseley was crossing a barren valley. He came across a hen pheasant and a blacksnake with their bodies entwined in a mortal struggle. The snake was coiled around the wings of the pheasant. The bird was trying vainly to fly and kept leaping up, then falling back and pounding the snake against the ground. Neither animal would normally be food for the other. Their fight, Eiseley thought, must be over the eggs of the pheasant. "Here in this silent waste, like an emanation from nowhere, two bitter and desperate vapors, two little whirlwinds of contending energy, were beating each other to death because their plans—something, I suspected, about whether a clutch of eggs was to turn into a thing with wings or scales—this problem, I say, of the onrushing nonexistent future, had catapulted serpent against bird."[1] I could have waited to see what would happen, he later thought; perhaps that would have been the scientific thing to do. Instead, Loren Eiseley separated the blacksnake from the bird and continued across the valley with the snake around his arm.

After letting the snake go, he went on his way pondering what he had done, and why. "The bird had contended for birds against the oncoming future; the serpent writhing into the bunch grass had contended just as desperately for serpents. And I, the apparition in that valley—for what had I contended?" If the pheasant had fought for her species, and the blacksnake for its species, had the human being, in bringing their contest to an end, somehow fought for humans? But what advantage could be gained for the human species by this action? Could his behavior be explained by science? Eiseley grappled then, as he did on so many occasions, with the perception that nature cannot be explained by "the laws of nature," and that there is something perpetually appearing in nature which is hauntingly and profoundly "unnatural"—or is this "unnatural" thing itself the secret of nature, and also of the onrushing future?

"For what then had I contended, weighing the serpent with the bird in that wild valley? I had struggled, I am now convinced, for a greater, more comprehensive vision of myself."

Eiseley said later, "I contained, to put it simply, the serpent and the bird. I would always contain them. I was no longer one of the contending vapors; I had embraced them in my own substance and, in some insubstantial way, reconciled them. . . . I had not known what I sought, I was aware that something had found me. I no longer believed that nature was either natural or unnatural."[2]

"MAY ALL BEINGS BE HAPPY!"

What is the human, that it should "embrace other species within its own substance and reconcile them?" Any Buddhist would understand the necessity to separate the snake and the bird, based on a moral imperative to end or minimize the suffering of living beings wherever it might be found. The fact that "instinct" or, in Buddhist terms, the karmic impressions of past lives might drive two animals to fight would be no reason to refrain from helping. The snake's need to eat and the pheasant's passion to protect her eggs are each inherent in their natures, while kindness is a particularly human quality, aspiring to grow into a "boundless heart for all beings."

One of the best known of all Buddhist texts, the *Metta Sutta* or "Discourse on Lovingkindness" expresses this compassion.[3]

May all beings be at ease, secure;
may they be happy in heart.
whatever they may be,
wandering or stable,
all creatures long or great,
medium-sized or small,
all creatures seen or unseen,
living far or near,
born or awaiting birth,
may all be happy at heart!

One should cultivate an unlimited mind
toward all beings
the way a mother protects her only child
with her life.

One should cultivate an unlimited loving mind
without obstruction, anger or opposition,
to the whole world
above, below, across.[4]

This text is chanted formally three times a day by monks in the Theravada tradition and, though not obliged to do so, monks should also recite it silently whenever they are able to concentrate.[5] The more elaborate and systematic meditation practice directed to the same goal of boundless love is the four "boundless states" or "sublime attitudes" of lovingkindness, compassion, sympathetic joy, and equanimity. In this practice a natural affection for those near and dear is expanded outward to those toward whom one is neutral, then to one's enemies, and finally to all beings, with the intention of "unspecified pervasion" to measureless beings everywhere in the universe.[6] These wishes and attitudes are expressed in the often-repeated condensed formula, "May all beings be happy!"

Mahayana Buddhism centers on the ideal of the Bodhisattva, one who will be a Buddha, or fully enlightened being, in the future. The Bodhisattva's compassionate intention or vow has many different expressions in scripture and liturgy, the essence of which is the vow to attain the most complete enlightenment not for one's own sake, but for the benefit of "all beings." The phrase *all beings* occurs frequently in Mahayana writings from the earliest period.[7]

What is most important morally in the wish "May all beings be happy!" is its all-ness or total inclusiveness. The word *sattva* is often translated as "sentient being," but even this is augmented; the word simply means "a being," while *sarva* means "all." Buddhist commentary makes clear that *sarva* means all beings of all kinds, whether lovingkindness and compassion are manifested by an average practitioner, an adept, or a Buddha.[8]

Precisely analogous in the Hindu tradition is the teaching of the Bhagavad Gita that the person who attains spiritual knowledge "rejoices in the welfare of all beings" (*sarvabhutahite ratah* repeated twice: 5.25 and 12.4).[9] The same words used in Buddhism, lovingkindness (*maitri*) and compassion (*karuna*) are used in the Gita for the virtues of the illumined person (12.13). In the context of the Vedantic ontology of the self or soul (*atman*) which is in all existence, unqualified love arises from the perception of one's own identity with the other. The aspirant knows that his or her own self "has become the self of all beings" (*sarvabhutatmabhutatma,* 5.7) and "sees the Self present in all beings and all beings present in the Self" (6.29). God as the *atman* abides in all, thus: "By that knowledge, you shall see all beings in yourself, and also in Me" (4.35). "He who sees the Supreme Lord existing alike in all beings (*sarvesu bhutesu*), not perishing when they perish, truly sees" (13.27). On this verse Anant Rambachan comments,

> With regard to the presence of God, therefore, all beings must be equally regarded. No one is excluded and no qualifications can be introduced here. . . . The Sanskrit term *bhuta* is inclusive, incorporating all beings. The presence of God is not limited to the human species, so we must also discern God in other-than-human life forms. These forms must be within the reach of our concern and compassion. Our understanding of God grows as we learn to recognize God's presence in them.[10]

The verse following says, "Seeing the same Lord established everywhere, he does not injure the Self by the self" (13.28). The person who has understood that his or her own self is the same as the self "of all" and the divine "in all" refrains from any kind of harm and destructiveness, has no hatred or anger toward any being, develops inclusive love and "compassion for beings" (6.2), and intentions for the well-being of all. References to "all beings," as well as the word *sarvatra* (translated by such words as "everywhere," "in everything" or "in all cases") are frequent in the Bhagavad Gita. References to a loving relation to "all beings" can be found elsewhere in the Mahabharata epic, of which the Bhagavad Gita is a part, as well as in the Yajur Veda and other Hindu scriptures.

One of the most famous invocations in the Veda, the root scriptures of Hinduism, is the Shanti Mantra or mantra of peace:

> To the heavens be peace, to the sky and the earth,
> to the waters be peace, to plants and all trees,
> to the Gods be peace, to Brahman be peace,
> to all people be peace, again and again—
> peace also to me! (*Yajur Veda* 36.17)[11]

Here the sense of "all-ness" is not abstract but is constituted by the accumulation of particulars in the rehearsal of the parts of the cosmos. This comprehensive enumeration, also found in Hindu ritual, brings to mind the prayer and ceremony of Native Americans, from which many illustrations could be given.

The great opening prayer given at the beginning of any formal gathering of the Haudenosaunee, or Six Nations of the Iroquois Confederacy, addresses, in the sequence of their making by the Creator, thanks to all beings in the cosmos who have given and still are giving their shares of life to the world and to humankind.[12]

A similar structure is found in the Lakota dedication of the offering of the sacred pipe to different groups of beings in the universe, naming them each by name.[13] The Lakota not only name the parts of the cosmic community one by one, even up to 405 kinds of beings individually, but they also say, "*mitak' oyas'in*" or "all my relations" after a prayer or act of offering; this phrase may be repeated many times during a single ceremonial occasion by all or any of the participants. The story of the bringing of the sacred pipe to the people by the White Buffalo Calf Woman tells that she gave instructions to them to pray, "I want to live with all my relations, that is why I am doing this." Thus the Lakota may repeat this phrase precisely, or more extemporaneously, pray or sing in words such as the following: "I pray to Wakantaka, above whom nothing exists, and who should be regarded first in all sacred things. I pray that through this pipe I may gain knowledge, and that I may live with all my relations."[14]

Prayers and offerings may ask that oneself or others may receive life, knowledge, blessings, or well-being of any kind, and help in trouble. The concluding "all my relations" is integral to this cry or "voice" that is sent forth, which is a request for help from all life—seen as one's own family— for harmony with all life, and also the intention that "all my relations" will benefit from the prayer and ceremony. The closing words "That is why I am doing this" and "all my relations" state a dedication or purpose, much like the Buddhist "dedication of merit" of any good action, after it is done, to the welfare of all beings. Oren Lyons, a traditional leader of the Onondaga Nation of the Haudenosaunee, recently emphasized the inclusiveness of "all my relations." "I know what they mean when they say this," he said. "They mean everything."[15]

In these examples from Buddhism, Hinduism, and Native American traditions I have attempted to show that the vision of the community of all life is not a vague idea or a mere sentiment. It is a highly conscious and deliberate moral orientation, articulated carefully and liturgically impressed through repetition of the word *all*, formed in will and awareness by meditation practices, and a moral concept defined with philosophical precision. It is also reinforced and concretized through a detailed listing of the different kinds of beings to be included in the "all" whose welfare is the highest value.

MORAL EXCLUSION

In opposition to this sense of the all-inclusive community of living beings is the state of consciousness called "moral exclusion" by psychologists who have studied it empirically. There is a significant literature in psychology on moral exclusion and such related areas as genocide, violence, conflict resolution, the psychology of justice, prejudice, and moral development. Susan Opotow offers this definition: "Moral exclusion occurs when individuals or groups are perceived as outside the boundary in which moral values, rules and considerations of fairness apply. Those who are morally excluded are perceived as nonentities, expendable, or undeserving; consequently harming them appears acceptable, appropriate, or just."[16] She adds, "Moral exclusion is neither an isolated nor inexplicable event, but occurs with great frequency, depends on ordinary social and psychological processes to license previously unacceptable attitudes and behavior, and causes great harm, from personal suffering to widespread atrocities."[17] Studies of moral exclusion have looked at a variety of issues, including job loss, public schools, refugees and immigration policy, war, and genocide. Opotow notes that there are degrees in moral exclusion, but whether it involves horrendous active evil such as genocide, or passive unconcern for the suffering of others in more ordinary situations, it has similar characteristics and underlying patterns that can be outlined as follows.

For most people moral community has boundaries; for example, the moral community may be confined to humans while animals are excluded, or one may apply different rules of conduct for one's immediate family than for others. The boundaries of moral community, however, are variable and may change with changing conditions. People always recognize differences and categorizations of some kind; this is a cognitive function. Some of these categorizations may already have positive or negative value based on the prevailing social order, but when moral exclusion is under way, differences previously without salience can become highly charged. Differences that define moral boundaries receive special attention and may be dramatized, while new or more minutely distinguished "differences" may be defined.

Under conditions of social stress and when conflict escalates, the boundaries of groups are reinforced, groups cohere more strongly, outsiders are treated badly, and fairness between groups declines. Inside the group, moral rules apply. Outside, it is "no holds barred." The "scope of justice" becomes smaller as the moral community contracts.

Most people have internalized moral controls that prevent them from behaving in ways that are inconsistent with their moral norms, but in moral exclusion a process of "selective disengagement" of these moral controls takes place. In other words, the moral controls apply in a narrower range of situations than before, and behavior previously considered immoral or inhumane is accepted. Albert Bandura has described the characteristic patterns of this process as follows: The inhumane actions themselves may be euphemistically labeled, considered normal, or even glorified. There may be "palliative comparison," such as, "What we did was nothing compared to what the enemy did." Most important, the actions may be morally justified in various ways, which may require a new morality or "moral restructuring." Responsibility for the actions may be displaced ("I simply executed orders from above") or diffused, as when one performs only a small part of a large operation of war or genocide. Psychological "splitting" or "doubling" is an extreme form of displacement of responsibility, documented by Robert Jay Lifton in *The Nazi Doctors,* where the perpetrator develops a second "self" to carry out atrocities.[18] The consequences of the action may be minimized or denied, ignored or misconstrued. The perpetrator will seek literal or psychological distance from the victims. Finally, the victims of the inhuman actions may be delegitimized, dehumanized, or seen as guilty and deserving of what is done to them, or all of these.[19]

In blaming the victim, categorizations often define the victims as outside the moral community by describing them as "less than human." Dehumanization can be a deliberate strategy in removing inhibitions and disengaging moral controls. In moral justification, as just noted, the victims may be described not only as inferior or nonhuman, but as guilty or deviant, deserving of bad treatment (or undeserving of good treatment).[20] A Japanese soldier in World War II was recently quoted in the *New York Times* as saying that subjects of "experiments" (including vivisection) done during the war were "logs" or *maruta*. "They were logs to me," he said to explain why he believed nothing wrong had been done. "Logs were not considered to be human. They were either spies or conspirators," and as such, "They were already dead. So now they die a second time. We just executed a death sentence."[21] Here the attribution of guilt results in dehumanization, a conflation of two strategies in moral exclusion.

A common pattern in moral justification is "just-world" thinking, the belief that in the world things always happen in a fair and just manner. If something good happens to someone, he or she must be a good person; if something bad happens to someone, she or he must have done something wrong or is a bad person. "Just-world thinking leads observers to devalue innocent victims," says Ervin Staub. "The belief that the world is just helps people feel safe, since in a just world they themselves will not become the victims of random, unpredictable suffering. Just-world thinking provides perpetrators with a way to justify their actions. In a just world, where victims deserve to suffer, people can see their own victims as deserving to suffer, due to their character or past actions; the suffering they themselves inflict becomes a source of further devaluation of the victims."[22] Just-world thinking, psychologists report, is common and occurs from early childhood. It can easily be incorporated into ideologies used to justify moral exclusion, including religious worldviews.

In Ervin Staub's account, when a personal or collective goal that is nonmoral conflicts with moral norms, "moral equilibration" may occur and cause a shift to a lower level of moral reasoning. A nonmoral goal may be "bolstered" by adding moral claims or replacing moral goals altogether, as when the protection of the purity of the race replaced the value of human life in Nazi Germany. Inhibitions against ill-treatment of the outsider are then removed. Perpetrators of abuses learn to abuse more by participating. Both they and the "bystander" are changed by their actions. They are desensitized to violence so that a progression along a continuum of violence occurs and they devalue the victims further.[23] "Ultimately adverse social circumstances create the conditions necessary for ordinary people to dehumanize, harm, and act with incredible cruelty toward others."[24] At worst, moral exclusion results in "principled resort to destructiveness."[25]

To end atrocities, violence, and injustice, deterrence of moral exclusion and *expansion* of the moral community seems called for, and a vision of the "community of all life" resembling that which seems to be normative for Buddhism, Hinduism, and Native American traditions has now become a major theme in Christian theology engaging the environmental crisis. This raises the question, however, of how far we are ready to go, of the costliness of extending moral responsibility. Susan Opotow reminds us of how hard it may be in practice to draw the boundaries farther out. The members of one's own moral community, she says, are those whose well-being concerns us, for whom we will make sacrifices, and with whom we will share our resources, but "the more extended the moral community, the more numerous the claims on the resources of the community. And if the resources do not expand at the same rate as the claims, an inclusive moral community automatically entails greater scarcity of resources than does an exclusive or restricted one."[26] "How does the extended moral community deal with the resource scarcity that invariably results from moral inclusion?"[27] This dilemma is at the heart of the matter in environmental ethics: Who belongs to "us," with whom are we willing to share, and for whom are we ready to sacrifice?

THE SOTERIOLOGICAL DILEMMA

Expanded moral community has become central to ecotheology, yet Christianity has for most of its history carried a heavy baggage of exclusion. A serious moral inconsistency persists and must be resolved if, on the one hand, we speak of "the community of all life" and extending love of neighbor to nonhuman beings while, on the other, we still sidestep the question of who is excluded from the Christian community and the implications of this exclusion. This fact must be scrutinized if Christian environmental ethics is to be viable. Where exactly and how do we draw the boundary between who is "in" the community of the people of God and who is "out"—and what is at stake when we do this? If little or nothing is at stake, why have such a community?

Traditionally the question of inclusion and exclusion has revolved around the question of salvation. What is "church" or a particular church for, if not for salvation? To find the boundary line we must then ask, What does it actually mean to be "saved" and what difference does it make if we are saved or not? This is one of the very few critical interreligious questions, and theologians have grappled with it in various ways in the context of religious pluralism. I would like to consider soteriology here in light of "moral exclusion" and its opposite moral attitude, the wish "May all beings be happy!" Ecclesiology and ecotheology may be facing in different directions, but the question of the boundaries of the moral community must be looked at consistently across the board, or cognitive dissonance in moral consciousness results. To put it more bluntly, the traditional belief that being "saved" means that one goes to heaven after death (or to purgatory, then heaven) and not being "saved" means going to hell has exerted an enormous moral and psychic force on history. The impact of this force is still affecting lives and events globally, especially as many millions of Christians still hold to this belief, something of which non-Christians are keenly aware.[28]

Highly abstracted or demythologized ideas of salvation can gloss over these very same particularistic, concrete, and eschatological soteriological views that have great positive and negative moral valence, so that in attempting to solve an interreligious problem, a liberal theologian may risk neglecting the ecumenical task of bridging Christian positions, and at the same time inadvertently wish away the most recalcitrant aspects of the interreligious question. In his critique of theologian John Hick, S. Mark Heim says, "Because Hick insists that the one true religious end must not be proximately more consistent with the claims of one tradition than another, he removes that end to extremes of eschatological distance and philosophical generality"; in Hick's account, Heim says, the goal of salvific transformation is a "formal ultimate" and the transcendent Real becomes dispensable.[29] Wilfred Cantwell Smith, more down-to-earth than Hick, declares that he is certain that all who have faith, whatever be their religion, are indeed "saved." He believes this because, as a Christian, he himself has faith that the God revealed in Christ is a God who "reaches out to all men and women everywhere in compassion and

yearning, who delights in a sinner's repentance, who delights to save."[30]
As for what it means to be saved, Smith says that "mundane" salvation is
liberation from despair and meaninglessness, but avoids talking about
"extra-mundane" salvation. Smith says:

> I *am* sure that those of us who have been saved for all eternity by God's
> grace have been saved also here on earth from some appalling bathos of
> vacuity within and bleakness without. In fact, I am more sure of that than
> I am of how to speak about the extra-mundane dimension of salvation,
> which both Christians and Muslims for a time, and some others, ex-
> pressed through the metaphor of Heaven but for which just now the
> Church is having difficulty finding either prose or poetry.[31]

Hans Urs von Balthasar's account of the matter is therefore bracing,
as he meets this question head-on, apparently taking heaven and hell seriously while remarking that St. Augustine knew "too much" about
hell, and wryly noting his theological opponents' anger at the thought
that "hell is empty."[32] Von Balthasar is properly troubled by the power
that belief in damnation possesses to foster moral exclusion. Referring
to the belief that each person is destined for heaven or hell, he wonders:

> One really has to ask oneself how, given an eternally valid bifurcation of
> mankind like this, simple love of one's neighbor, or even love of one's
> enemy in the Christian sense, could still be possible. It should not remain
> unmentioned, however, that certain late Catholic Scholastics, for their
> part, had racked their brains about whether, assuming that God were to
> reveal to me privately that one of my fellow men was destined to hell, I
> should still love that person with Christian love or would, instead, have
> to treat him with politeness only.[33]

He reflects on the psychological fact that most people think of hell as
"hell for others," and finds odious any acceptance of joy in damnation or
even lack of pity.[34] He gives moving testimony from saints and mystics
who, having broadened their hearts through contemplation, found the
idea of hell even "for others" intolerable, desired to share the sufferings of
hell's inhabitants, and wished to offer themselves to save others—like
Catherine of Siena, who wanted to place herself in front of the entrance to
hell and block it off so that no one could enter hell any more.[35]

Theologians agree that Scripture offers an ambivalent testimony. There is abundant evidence that God's will is that "all" should be saved. Von Balthasar assembles New Testament relevant uses of the word *all.* Some are: "When I am lifted up from the earth, I will draw all men to myself" (John 12:31). God was pleased, through Christ "to reconcile to himself all things whether on earth or in heaven" (Col. 1:20) and God purposes "to unite all things in him, things in heaven and things on earth" (Eph. 1:10). Christ is "the savior of all men, especially of those who believe" (1 Tim. 4:10), and "God . . . desires all men to be saved and to come to a knowledge of the truth" (1 Tim. 2:4 ff). "God does not wish that any should reach perish but that all should reach repentance" (2 Peter 3:9). "All Israel will be saved" (Rom. 11:26).[36] Some of these passages, indeed, give intimations of the salvation which is not only universal for "all men" but cosmic for "all things," also spoken of in Romans 8, so often cited in theology of the environment. Still, God has commanded, "I have set before you this day life and good, death and evil, . . . blessing and curse, therefore choose life" (Deut. 30:15, 19). Human freedom is real. Jesus came into the world to save all, but how if some refuse this gift? Von Balthasar says: "The question, to which no final answer is given, or can be given, is this: 'Will he who refuses it now refuse it to the last?' To this there are two possible answers: the first says simply 'Yes.' It is the answer of the infernalists. The second says: 'I do not know, but I think it permissible to hope . . . that the light of divine love will ultimately be able to penetrate every human darkness and refusal.'"[37]

The dilemma of soteriology can be summed up thus: Can human freedom set a limit to God's universal grace, and if so, where is this limit? The doctrine of universal salvation or *apokatastasis* had an important history among the church fathers beginning with Origen, but in simple form does not provide a satisfactory solution to the dilemma for von Balthasar and some others. As Dermot Lane puts it, "Any doctrine of universal salvation calls into question the absolute importance of human freedom within the history of the world. Further, *apokatastasis* seriously ignores the realities of evil and sin in the course of human history. In addition the doctrine of universal salvation devalues the struggle to do good and create a more just society. Lastly *apokatastasis* clashes directly with the [traditional] Christian doctrine of the eternity of hell."[38] The soteriology accepted by von Balthasar, Karl Rahner, Lane, and others is one where hell, for reasons just given, must be accepted as "a real possibility" without our saying that we know anyone is in hell. We are obliged in our love for our neighbor and our faith in God's universal gift of grace to *hope* that all will be saved, as "Love hopes all things" (1 Cor.13:7).

In this there is a reverent agnosticism before God's ways, and also before the realities of life after death. Indeed, a good part of this soteriology of hope is to find it possible that death does not "freeze for eternity" the state of a soul,[39] but to believe that salvation as a process may continue in the next life in ways we cannot conceive; hence von Balthasar gives importance to the descent of Jesus into hell after the crucifixion, which is also treated in the new Catechism of the Roman Catholic Church.[40]

Such serious attempts not to demythologize but to re-understand traditional ideas of salvation are promising. They are not acceptable, however, to many Christians who hold fast to some version of what von Balthasar calls "infernalism." Evangelical theologian Clark H. Pinnock states that "the majority of evangelicals today are hard-line restrictivists in my estimation. The only possibility for encountering God and receiving salvation in this view is to exercise explicit faith in Jesus Christ in this earthly life. General revelation is not sufficient; all must receive God's revelation in Christ. Outside of this special revelation, there is near-total darkness. Other religions are error and falsehood and non-Christians with a few exceptions are on their way to hell."[41] Pinnock writes to qualify this view. Like Balthasar and others, he recognizes the soteriological dilemma and sees that the belief in damnation has consequences for moral consciousness and human relations:

> Dark thoughts have clouded our minds. For centuries, thanks largely to the Augustinian tradition that has so influenced evangelicals, we have been taught that God chooses a few who will be saved and has decided not to save the vast majority of humanity. God is planning (in his sovereign freedom) to send most of those outside the church to hell, and he is perfectly within his rights to do so. If as a result large numbers perish, theologians have assured us that God would feel no remorse and certainly deserve no blame. The result of such instruction is that many read the Bible with pessimistic control belief and find it hard to relate humanly to other people.[42]

Pinnock recognizes that this picture has "driven" some into theocentric pluralism, as they morally cannot accept a God or a religious belief that destines most humans to everlasting torment. As an uncompromisingly Christocentric evangelical, he rejects theocentric pluralism entirely but attempts to construct a more encouraging soteriological picture, in which first, God is seen as generous and God's universal love is affirmed, and second, many human souls will be saved rather than just a few. He outlines an evangelical global theology of "salvation optimism" in which access to salvation is broadened and proposes an eschatological resolution to the problem religious diversity presents to belief in the finality of Christ as Savior of the world. Pinnock's eschatological solution is that religions themselves are changing and will continue to change. God is working through religions, Christianity and others, in ways the outcome of which is only foreseeable by God, and in any case, souls will be saved not by the church or by Christianity but by Jesus Christ. He still speaks, however, in terms of the "victory" over other religions.

Pinnock also entertains the possibility of salvation after death through a "post-mortem encounter" with Christ, especially for the unevangelized. He believes, however, that for those who did not accept Jesus Christ in life on earth, there is every possibility that they will not change even if given another chance after they die. Those who have been evangelized but not "adequately" and those who in life have been sincere in their search for God may still be saved after death. But what of those of any religion who were given every opportunity to believe in Jesus but did not? They are, it seems, still destined for hell in Pinnock's view, be they Jews, Muslims, Hindus, Buddhists, Native Americans, or followers of any other religions. Pinnock rejects the Roman Catholic teaching in the papal encyclical *Redemptor Hominis* (1979) and elsewhere that Christ is salvifically united with every human person, even those who do not know Christ outwardly or know him incompletely, saying that this undercuts the need for conversion and for continuing missions as well as "truth-seeking dialogues" as an instrument of evangelization.[43]

The final point in Pinnock's only somewhat ameliorated account of the soteriological dilemma is that hell may not be, after all, the state of everlasting torment that is seen as morally intolerable by many. Hell may rather be a state moving towards nonexistence. Pinnock, referring to a number of evangelical theologians who support this view, says, "It is very probable that the biblical doctrine of hell does not entail everlasting conscious punishment."[44] Thus the outrage that sends many too far in the opposite direction, that of universal salvation, is needless. Hell is a temporary state ending in the annihilation of the condemned. The Church of England has also allowed for a similar view. *The Mystery of Salvation*, a 1996 report of the Doctrine Commission of the Church of England, says that perhaps hell "is not eternal torment" but might rather be "total non-being" and "annihilation."[45] Lane objects, "There is something incongruous about affirming God as a God of the living alongside a hypothesis about hell as annihilation of people. For this reason preference must be expressed for a view of hell as the possibility of a form of self-isolation and absolute aloneness resulting from a deliberate turning away from all communion with others and God. This possibility of turning away from communion with others and God must always be balanced by reference to the primacy of God's omnipresent offer of salvation to all in this life."[46]

A problem arises when a single system of meaning or frame of reference demands two incompatible positions or courses of action. Clearly in Christian soteriology there is and has been from the beginning an inherent tension between teachings of love of neighbor and universal divine grace, and belief in damnation. No resolution to this tension should be adopted that dispenses with moral accountability, even if we cannot now agree on what form an ultimate accountability may take. In all fairness it must be admitted that the same kind of tension exists in Buddhism and Hinduism as well as Native American traditions in which there is a recompense for evil in the life after death. While I am not in a position to say with any accuracy what Native American teachings on this may be (for example, whether a "hell" that may be real, is everlasting), the Buddhist and Hindu teaching of retribution through reincarnation and karma ("action" and its results) does not present the same soteriological dilemma that we find in Christianity. There are two reasons for this. First, in the worldview of Hinduism and Buddhism, no "hell" or other suffering determined by one's past evil karma lasts forever, even though there is a distinct danger of "just-world" and blame-the-victim thinking in karmic worldviews. Second, reincarnation means that all forms of life are capable of transforming into one another, and therefore no boundaries of exclusion can be absolute or permanent; rather, belief in reincarnation promotes a sense of the kinship of all life.

If our actions are motivated, as psychologists state, by the boundaries of our moral communities, then a restrictivist soteriology will not serve for environmental ethics, because soteriological boundaries are also moral boundaries. The not-saved are cast out of the moral universe. We are not likely to share the lesser goods of "resources" with those to whom the greatest good of "heaven" is denied. We are not much good yet at loving our enemies, and we will find it hard to love those who are sent by even an all-loving Creator to unending pain or annihilation, unless like the saints we are ready to take their destiny upon ourselves. Moral exclusion means that we seek to justify ourselves while distancing ourselves from the victims, who are guilty. The psychological—or spiritual and moral—difficulty here has been drawn to our attention. We cannot proceed by finding some human persons dispensable if we seek to establish a moral community that includes animals, trees, waters, and the land itself.

A reconstituted soteriology, now struggling to be born, may resemble some version of a modified *apokatastasis*, in which freedom and evil are not minimized, and the question of what happens after death is the subject to ongoing reflection and ecumenical, even interreligious inquiry with increased attention to private and "popular" belief and experience. For some, certain moral norms provide a way of drawing the boundary line between church and "not-church." A recent World Council of Churches study process on ecclesiology and ethics has concluded that

> there are boundaries, and it will always be the case that certain decisions and actions are in contradiction to the nature and purpose of the church and the central teaching of the gospel. Instructive past instances of this are those German Christians who uncritically pledged allegiance to the Nazi state, and those South African churches which supported apartheid. In both cases those concerned excluded themselves from the church of Jesus Christ. . . . Here the being of the church is at stake. It should be added that heavy caution is in order when the stakes of moral judgment are this high, since the boundary is one which draws the line between church and not-church.[47]

The church is a community of disciples called together and covenanted by God (not by themselves), formed in remembrance of Christ, based on gospel values, and living to proclaim the gospel in the world and witness for justice. Such an ecclesiology seems to bracket off eschatological individual salvation, and stresses ethical criteria for "church" and a common journey toward the kingdom. It leaves open the possibility that other faith communities may uphold the same moral norms as a gospel-based community.

It is possible in the light of Jesus Christ to look at forms of koinonia outside the church as movements of the Holy Spirit gathering people to serve God in ways they [people in general] may not fully understand. In humility, the church may seek to point to what the Spirit is doing outside its visible boundaries, as well as within, thus witnessing to the wider work of God in the world of creation.[48]

There may be many covenants, and invisible as well as visible boundaries of the "church."

David Burrell and Elena Malits in *Original Peace* also urge a creation-centered soteriology, which does not deny the need for redemption but understands redemption as "restoring the original order of creation." This restoration is accomplished by the grace of the One who freely created it, and our acceptance of creation as God's gift and participation in the work of restoration. In this the "natural" is not saved by the "supernatural"; Christ's mission of redemption must be seen in light of his role in the creation. In the beginning "through him all things came to be" (John 1:3) and in the end God will "unite all things in him, things in heaven and things on earth" (Eph. 1:9-10).[49]

THE ONRUSHING FUTURE

This restoration of the original order of creation is also a journey forward into the "onrushing future" Loren Eiseley speaks of. As a scientist, Eiseley asks, Since we know we are changing through evolution, what are we changing into? Psychologists who propose that the roots of moral exclusion are in each of us may regard evolution as self-interested and savage; "natural" processes hold out little hope of achieving moral inclusion. Morton Deutsch seems to hold this view:

> Evolution, through natural selection, has ensured that all living creatures have the capacity to respond positively to stimuli that are beneficial to them and negatively to those that are harmful. This inborn tendency to act positively toward the beneficial and negatively toward the harmful is the foundation on which the human potential for love and hate develops.[50]

Loren Eiseley was well aware of these kinds of evolutionary explanations of moral exclusion, but he was not convinced. He was always seized

by the mystery of the evolutionary process itself, and he tried, without resort to any formally religious analysis, to find the "unnatural" at work in
the "natural." Many others have appropriated evolution more theologically. Evolution as known by science has overshadowed the worldviews of
the religions and has been integrated with them, even with their narratives of "salvation." For many the "cosmic-earth" process, as Thomas
Berry calls it, and the process of ultimate human transformation are one
and the same. Teilhard de Chardin in the West and Sri Aurobindo in India
are most identified with formal philosophical statements of this pervasive
ecological and ethical vision. The vast Earth community is on this journey
with human persons, who have appeared as a particular self-conscious
manifestation of the cosmos.[51]

An emerging cosmic soteriology intends to achieve wholeness by opposing moral exclusion in all forms, and like the saints and Bodhisattvas,
by valuing the salvation of all above that of any individual. As Sri Chinmoy
has said, "We must regard the persons around us as limbs of our own body.
Without them we are incomplete. If we remain isolated . . . then the perfection that we achieve will be very limited. Unlimited perfection will
dawn only when we love humanity as a whole. It is only by accepting humanity as part of our own life, and by helping to perfect humanity with
our own illumination, that we can fulfill ourselves."[52] Our own "salvation" must be achieved through love for God's creation, or "the world,"
which includes not only humanity but all beings. Sri Chinmoy also states
that the greater the degree of illumination attained through meditative
practices, the greater one's ability to identify with beings not like oneself
but of any species.[53] In the positive moral restructuring now under way,
which will establish a wider and wider moral community, contemplative
disciplines play an indispensable role along with theological redefinition,
liturgy and sacrament, accurate knowledge of the natural world, and
committed action. We must practice using specific effective methods for
the expansion of moral consciousness, and train ourselves back into a
"subject-subject" relation with nonhuman persons, as many followers of
diverse religious teachings have begun to do as part of their environmental practice.[54]

As we face into the "onrushing future," we contend, as Loren Eiseley
says, "for a greater, more comprehensive vision of ourselves" that embraces and reconciles the different kinds of others within itself. Let us return to him for a last word, not in the valley where he found the snake

and the bird, but sleepless in a hotel room in Costabel.[55] "Upon that shore meaning had ceased. There were only the dead skull and the revolving eye. With such an eye, some have said, science looks upon the world. I do not know. I know only that I was the skull of emptiness and that endless revolving light without pity."

He had seen on the beach the dying of small sea creatures cast up on the shore by the turbulent waves. "Along the strip of wet sand that marks the ebbing and flowing of the tide death walks hugely and in many forms. . . . The tiny breathing pores of the starfish are stuffed with sand. The rising sun shrivels the mucilaginous bodies of the unprotected. The seabeach and its endless war are soundless. Nothing screams but the gulls." On that same beach he had met a man who looked for starfish and other living things and threw them back into the sea. Eiseley turned away saying, "Death is running more fleet than he along every seabeach of the world."

Later in his room the merciless eye in his skull senses another eye gazing at him from the darkness. This other eye changes from "something glaucous and blind," to the beautiful eye of a dead octopus he has just seen on the beach, to the bloodshot eye of a beaten animal, to the eye of his own mother as a child. As he thinks of "the long crucifixion of life," he remembers the words, "Love not the world, neither the things that are in the world." There is a waiting silence, as though he, as the human, is being asked to confront the universe itself. He answers, "But I *do* love the world. . . . I love its small ones, the things beaten in the strangling surf, the bird, singing, which flies and falls and is not seen again. . . . I love the lost ones, the failures of the world." He remembers, "It was like the renunciation of my scientific heritage. The torn eye surveyed me and was gone."

Out of the depths of a seemingly empty universe had grown an eye, like the eye in my room, but an eye on a vastly larger scale. It looked out upon what I can only call itself. It searched the skies and it searched the depths of being. In the shape of man it had ascended like a vaporous emanation from the depths of night. The nothing had miraculously gazed upon the nothing and was not content. It was an intrusion into, or a projection out of, nature for which no precedent existed. . . . Here at last was the rift that lay beyond Darwin's tangled bank. For a creature, arisen from that bank and born of its contentions, had stretched out its hand in pity.[56]

Loren Eiseley goes out from the room where he had lain in despair, and on the beach he finds again the man who throws the starfish back into the sea. As he throws with him, saving lives one by one, he thinks, "After us there will be others."

3

Fratricide and Ecocide: Rereading Genesis 2–4

Brigitte Kahl

THE APPLE THAT EVE ATE IN PARADISE WAS PURELY ORGANICALLY GROWN—yet it caused death, irreversibly. And when she took it, both God in heaven and the earth below wept desperately. They knew that from then on human beings would start to disrespect, mistreat, and abuse not only one another, but also the soil from which they were made: Adama, the earth.

Is this still the Genesis story? Presumably not. Facing the present ecological crisis, we are well aware that biblical traditions are more often seen as part of the problem rather than as pointing toward a solution. "Subdue and rule" (Gen. 1:28)—doesn't this crucial command to have dominion mark the beginning and very center of the destructive Christian-occidental relationship toward earth, water, air? In a way, hasn't the biblical God legitimated the ruthless exploitation and extermination of nature by being exclusively concerned about humanity?

History rather than nature, eco-imperialism rather than eco-justice, anthropocentrism instead of integral well-being of human and nonhuman species: Is this a fair description of what the Genesis stories tell us about the basic relations between God, humanity, and earth?[1] Or is this just what we were taught and are used to reading throughout the centuries of Christian interpretation within the framework of domination?

Is there a way to reinterpret and recultivate the biblical narratives for a non-ecocidal, non-imperial reading? Let us try to read one of the primeval biblical narratives (Genesis 2–4) from the perspective of the earth.

ADAM: SERVANT OF THE ADAMA (GEN. 2:4-15)

It is well known that the so-called second creation account (Gen. 2:4—3:24), commonly ascribed to the Yahwist source, describes how the first human being, Adam, is made by God out of earth, Adama. Interestingly enough, however, the story starts from a quite different angle. God doesn't enter the scene as somebody who is eager to create Adam, humanity, the crown of creation. First of all God has to deal with something like a universal climate catastrophe: dreadful dryness all over the earth, no rain, no water, therefore no vegetation. "On the day that YHWH, God, made earth and heaven, no bush of the field was yet on earth, no plant of the field had yet sprung up, for YHWH, God, had not made it rain upon earth" (2:4-5).[2]

The absence of bushes and plants, the state of the earth, seem to concern God here much more than the absence of human beings. In fact, Adam/human enters the story only as another remedy against the desert, the barrenness of the earth—after the rain. "No plant of the field had yet sprung up, for YHWH, God, had not made it rain upon earth, and there was no human/Adam to serve the soil/Adama." (2:5)

The Hebrew word 'abad, which is usually translated as "till/work the ground," in fact means servitude, slave labor. The same type of work Israel will be forced to do in Egypt later. Humanity receives its original definition as "servant to the earth," being in a clearly dependent and subordinated position, which is expressed in the very naming: Adam-of-Adama. God doesn't create the Adama for Adam, but the other way around: He creates Adam to serve Adama. To get her green. Therefore, before turning to Adam God has to solve the water problem. "But a surge would well from the ground and water all the face of the soil/Adama; and YHWH, God, formed the human/Adam, of dust from the Adama" (2:6-7).

Like the animals to come, humanity is made out of Adam's substance: dust from the Adama. "She" (a female noun in Hebrew) provides the matter and appears in a kind of mother position. By calling the humans Adam after Adama, the earthly origin, kinship, commitment, and destination is inscribed into the body of humanity. Of course, they are mutually dependent, earth and humankind, "she" needs "him" as "he" needs "her," but the primary emphasis is on the earth. "She" is the reason humankind came into being: to end the desert and help the earth bring forth the life that is in her, seed-bearing plants and fruit-bearing trees (1:11). The second creation account is not anthropocentric, but earth-centered and oriented toward mutuality.[3]

But God also seems to be fond of the earth in an unusual way, when compared with other Mesopotamian creation myths. Not that the gods of Babylon didn't like gardens and tasty fruit, but they certainly hated the manual work related to it. In the Atrakhasis Epic (1800–1600), for example, the junior gods have to dig the irrigation channels and provide food and drink for the other gods. They get so tired of it that they go on strike. As a result, they decide to create slave laborers, so that the gods can rest forever. This is how humanity comes into being, as substitute workers, slaves to the gods to work in place of the gods.

In this Genesis creation account humanity is created for servitude as well, but there aren't any divine or human masters—just the earth who needs service. This seems to be quite an odd definition of slavery. The Biblical paradise is meant for work, but it is not meant to be a place for slave labor in the ordinary social sense. There is a kind of "earth slavery," however.

And God obviously doesn't mind doing slave labor for the earth as well. This is weird again. We meet a God who really gets God's hands dirty! First when God forms Adam out of Adama: the Hebrew verb describes a potter working with clay. And what happens after Adam finally is there, to serve the earth? We might expect God to lean back and watch his creature taking up the spade to start digging and planting. God now would be in a position of leisure to do the higher work adequate for free men, like philosophy or astrology or theology. But instead we see God taking the spade and planting the trees in the garden, definitely hard and dirty manual work. Only then does God put the human being there, making sure that the trees are beautiful to the eye and and bear fruit already, so there is an abundance of food. Bread and roses, both are there, and Adam's task is simply to serve and preserve the garden. Wherever humans will touch the soil, God's footmarks and fingerprints are already there.[4]

YHWH, God, planted a garden in Eden/ Land-of-Pleasure, in the East, and there he placed the human/Adam whom he had formed. YHWH, God, caused to spring up from the soil/Adama every type of tree, desirable to look at and good to eat . . . (2:8-9)

Now a river goes out from Eden, to water the garden . . . (2:10)

YHWH, God, took the human and set him in the garden of Eden, To serve/*'abad* and to preserve it (2:15).

After there was universal desert in the beginning, God now has created a wonderful greenhouse. All that the earth/Adama needs to flourish is in place—Adam, trees, water—plenty of water: A whole river, which after that divides into the four mighty streams of the world, waters the garden. This is another thing Adam doesn't have to take care of. There is no need to dig irrigation channels, not even some modest watering cans to carry around in the evening . . .

THE FIRST BIBLICAL COMMANDMENT: A HOLY TREE (2:16—3:24)

The world was meant by God to be a flourishing garden, with God as the chief gardener and the human as an assistant. And the garden had only one rule: Eat and enjoy everything, but don't touch the one tree, for then you will die. "YHWH, God, commanded the human/Adam, saying: From any tree of the garden you may eat, yes, eat, but from the tree of the Knowing of Good and Evil—you are not to eat from it. For on the day you eat from it, you must die, yes, die" (2:16-17).

Have we ever noticed that the first commandment God gives to humanity deals with trees? That the first word of Torah, Law, is a life-preserving instruction as to how humanity can live on the natural resources? And how it can't—or it will turn all into destruction?

We know how the story went on: Humanity didn't observe the first commandment. They took from the tree they were not allowed to touch. They didn't respect its holiness. They thought it was all theirs. Subject to the logic of consumption, usefulness. They wanted to set the rules themselves, to know and decide good and evil, like God. Therefore they both ate from the apple Eve had picked. And God, when coming to enjoy the garden, has to ask the famous question: *Adam, where are you?* (3:9). And Adam, hidden amid the trees of the garden now, starts to complain about the female counterpart God gave him, and to claim that it was all her fault. And then God tells them what will happen: Domination of one human being over the other, first of male over female, will enter human history. Life-giving, natural fertility will get difficult, both on the side of Eve and of Adama. And Adama, cursed because of Adam's disrespect of the tree, will start to bring forth thorns and thistles next to the nourishing plants in the field.

> To the woman he [God] said: I will multiply, multiply your pain from your pregnancy, with pains shall you bear children. Toward your man/*ish* will be your desire, yet he will rule over you. To Adam he [God] said: Because you have obeyed the voice of your woman/*ishsha* and have eaten from the tree about which I commanded you, saying: You are not to eat from it! Cursed is the earth/Adama on your account, with painstaking labor shall you eat from her, all the days of your life. Thorns and thistles let it spring up for you when you eat the plants of the field. By the sweat of your brow you will eat your bread until you return to the earth/Adama, For from her you were taken. For you are dust, and to dust shall you return (3:16-19).

Until you return to the earth. For from her you were taken. Throughout the centuries, the "back to earth" of Gen. 3:19 has been almost exclusively remembered at the tombs of the dead. Its challenge to Christian life practices was seldom heard. But the text very explicitly talks about a change of direction, for the Hebrew word for *return* implies also the theological dimension of repentance, turning back to God. Taking the fruit of the forbidden tree has damaged the relationship not only between God and Adam, but also between Adam and Adama, as the *thorns and thistles* demonstrate. When Adam is sent out from the garden, his task to serve the earth is repeated by God. It sounds as if Adam, God-like in a sense now, could have easily forgotten his primary link and liability to the earth. "YHWH, God, said: Here, the human/Adam has become like one of us, in knowing good and evil. . . . So YHWH, God, sent him away from the garden of Eden, to serve the soil/Adama from which he had been taken" (3:22-23).

But the difficulty about Adam, servant of the Adama, isn't only that he has acquired God-like knowledge of what is good and evil. The problem is also that man will achieve a master position over woman (3:16). One wonders what effects this new structure of domination will have on the other male/female relationship of the text: Will the man/*ish* who rules over his wife/*ishsha* still accept his position as servant of the Adama/earth? How does the story go on?

Does it go on? We are hardly used to reading Genesis 2–3 as an earth story. But we are completely unfamiliar with following the storyline of Adama-Adam-Eve further into chapter 4. Even ecological and feminist reinterpretations of the Genesis narratives usually stop at 3:24.[5] Probably the dogmatic issues of original (female) sin and fall attached to chapter 3 have absorbed so much attention throughout the centuries of occidental Christian interpretation that chapter 4 as final part of the garden story was ignored. The dogmatic Christian narrative has frozen Adam and Eve under the tree of knowledge. And Eve, with the deadly apple in her hand, became forever trapped in a discourse about sin and inevitable disaster, human corruption and punishment, sexuality and the nature of women.

In the biblical narrative, however, the final word about Adam, Eve, and Adama is not said in 3:24. Specifically not about Eve, who reenters the stage together with Adam, when the curtain opens for the post-paradisiacal scene "East of Eden." And again Adama and the earth-minded God of chapters 2 and 3 will play a crucial role.

CAIN AND ABEL: LORDSHIP AND BROTHERHOOD (GEN. 4:1-9)

> And Adam knew Eve, his woman/*ishsha,* she became pregnant and bore Cain/*Kayin.* She said: I have got/created (*kaniti*) a man/*ish* with/as YHWH! She continued bearing—his brother, Abel. And Abel was a keeper of a flock, and Cain was a servant of the earth/Adama.
>
> And it happened after some time that Cain brought from the fruit of the earth/Adama an offering to YHWH, and Abel, he too brought, from the firstborn of his flock, from their fat-parts. YHWH had regard for Abel and his offering, for Cain and his offering he had no regard (4:1-5).

The story has remained a theological riddle until today. Why does God prefer Abel and his gift to Cain? Isn't Cain treated in an extremely unjust and unfair way? Is it God who, in the last analysis, causes the first murder? But why? Why does God provoke Cain's natural jealousy against his brother? Because God all of a sudden prefers nomadic herdsmen to gardeners and land-possessing servants of the earth?[6] Beef to grain? Bloody sacrifices to vegetarian ones?[7] Contrariwise, does Cain represent the tribe of the Kenites, who were smiths and metalworkers and therefore important for the manufacturing not only of tools, but also of weapons (compare 4:22; 4:23f)?[8] Or is it just God's omnipotent power to choose and reject whomever God wants?[9] Or does the story make a point about the well-known inequality among human beings, which is beyond understanding, but came into existence right at the beginning?[10] "Life is unfair. God is free."[11] But what would it mean for the concept of God's justice if God is the one who originally has created this basic "unfairness"?

The text leaves us with no direct information as to why Abel is elected by God. But before we try to fill the lacuna with theological, sociohistorical, or psychological speculations, we have to look a bit closer at the text itself.

We are used to reading the Cain-and-Abel narrative as a brother story and a narrative about the situation of humanity after the fall. But there aren't really two brothers. And there are no humans-in-general. *I have created/got a man together/equally with God,* is Eve's proud proclamation at the birth of Cain (4:1). This initial exclamation can be translated in different ways, particularly regarding the (cocreative?) position of Eve vis-à-vis God and Adam/male (compare 2:7, 23).[12] Regarding Cain, however, it is rather clear that he is on the one hand put into a close relationship to God like Eve[13]— and on the other hand described as a man/*ish*.

Nowhere else in the Bible is a newborn baby called and celebrated as a man/*ish*. Therefore it is somehow striking to see that this maleness of Cain, which the text emphasizes so strongly, rarely played a significant role in the history of interpretation. Whereas Eve in the paradise story was always and "naturally" perceived in distinctly female categories, her son Cain without much debate has been transmuted into "the" human being as such. But the story of Genesis 4 cannot be properly read without gender categories. It doesn't speak about the abstract human condition after the primary (female) fall, rather it confronts us with the male counterpart of the fall account and as such has a widely parallel and even climactic structure.[14]

Cain, the firstborn of humanity and head of future generations comes into being as a strong male close to God. The notion of rule attributed to this extraordinary *ish*/male is not only related to the special status of firstborn sons in biblical law (compare Deut. 21:15-17, Gen. 27:29), it is also derived from the definition of male/*ish* as a ruler in 3:16. *Toward your man/ish will be your desire, yet he will rule over you.* There is no doubt that Eve in 4:1 considers Cain to be definitely *her man* and that all her *desire*, joy, and pride is focused upon this man of hers.[15] Nothing indicates at this point that he could become her ruler one day, as foretold in 3:16.

And then there is "his brother." Whereas Cain is born as a man, Abel is defined as a relational, dependent human being right from the beginning, by the semantics of the birth order. Abel is just another one (*she continued to give birth . . .* 4:2), not the number one child. Eve even forgets to name him. A second-born who gets his name in a seemingly self-understanding way, expressing his social position: the Hebrew term *Abel* (*hevel*) means vapor, nothingness, meaninglessness. Nothing is mentioned about any exclamation of joy or affection at Abel's birth, nothing about his relationship to his mother, his father, or God. All the social meaning he gets is taken from Cain, to whom he is born as *his brother.* Throughout the story Abel will be identified as Cain's brother not less than seven times. Abel is a dependent by birth, the small brother nothingness of Cain, Eve's man-with-God.

Cain is born as a lord, Abel as a brother. This becomes the hermeneutical key for the interpretation of the whole story, which does not call Cain *his brother* a single time. It deals with a man/*ish* and his brother.[16] And with a birth order that in a "natural" way has created social hierarchy and inequality, making it impossible for the man to become a brother. It is within this precisely defined framework that God, acting in absolute autonomy, turns out to have a special regard for the one who is nobody and meaningless in the eyes of his fellow human beings. Haven't we met elsewhere the biblical God who shows a preferential option for the small and neglected rather than the powerful?

Sacrificing the Firstborn Order?

We could also have a look at the different sacrifices. The text states that Abel just follows the example of Cain—*Abel, he too, brought . . .* (4:4). Again Cain, not Abel, is the first. The firstborn male initiates humanity approaching God in cultic ways. And no breakthrough to brotherhood happens on the way to the "altar" (compare Matt. 5:23-24). The cultic order just reflects and reaffirms the social order.

Abel, however, in contrast to Cain, doesn't bring only the best, fat-parts, but also the firstlings. According to Exod. 34:19 he is supposed to do so. Of course Abel was not present at Sinai, but he obviously knows and respects the special rank of the firstborn. He knows also that they belong to God, including the firstborn sons (compare Exod. 34:20). Symbolizing fertility, future, and life as such, the firstlings of earth, animals, humanity are under God's specific command just like the one tree in paradise, the tree of life. Nobody else should dispose of it. Does Abel, the second-born, have a special sensitivity to how vital it is that the firstborn stay under God's decree?[17]

Cain, on the other hand, doesn't bring the firstfruit of the Adama, he just brings *fruit of the earth*/Adama. Should this be read as an indication that Cain's sacrifice is of inferior quality?[18] Cain thus would appear less "faithful" than Abel (compare Heb. 12:4) or, more precisely, as somebody who doesn't accept God's ultimate right of disposal, God's commandment regarding the fruits of the earth, her fertility. Does Cain think that he himself can decide on the future of life, and that there is no sacred part and realm to be absolutely respected? Has he deliberately taken the part of the fruit that belongs to God just as Eve and Adam did in paradise—or did it maybe not even come to his mind that not everything is his? Then we have finally reached the point where Cain, designated both as *man with God* (4:1) and *servant of the earth* (4:2), claims God-like, unrestricted power in dealing with the earth: to become her ruler as he is the ruler of his brother.

But God doesn't accept. God refuses Cain's ritual gift, counteracting the almighty man. Which doesn't mean that God rejects him. On the contrary.

> Cain became exceedingly enraged and his face fell. YHWH said to Cain: Why are you so enraged? Why has your face fallen? Is it not thus: If you intend good, bear-it-aloft. But if you do not intend good, at the entrance is sin, a crouching-demon, toward you his desire—but you can rule over him (4:5-7).

The actual "fall" occurs only here. It is Cain's face that falls, closing him away both from Abel and from God. Cain, the man-with-God, doesn't accept a God-with-the-brother. But God wants him to raise his face again, to do good: to see his brother and listen to God, rather than deciding good and evil for himself. The dialogue between God and Cain, which practically comprises the whole section 4:6-15, is profoundly moving. God talks to Cain, wrestles with him, tries to convince and to convert him to brotherhood. It is the first time anybody in the Bible explicitly talks about sin: God trying to teach Cain that sin is not inescapable, but can be mastered. God talking not about human sin in general, but about the concrete, male sin of isolation and domination. Even after the paradise is lost, God wants to save Cain from the murderous demon sitting on his threshold. The God in favor of Abel is in favor of Cain as well. Unfortunately, Cain has a clearly opposite expectation of what a favoring God should be like.

That's why God fails. And Cain wins. He kills his brother. And this happens, not incidentally, in the *field*. We have to remember that the field is the very place where, at the beginning of the story, bushes and plants were to grow (2:5). Water and Adam-servant-of-the-Adama were necessary for that. Now we are again in the field. But the place doesn't remind Cain of his task. Cain, the son of Adam and a servant of the Adama as well, is ready for rule, no longer for service.

> But then it was, when they were out in the field that Cain rose up against
> Abel his brother and he killed him (4:8).

Cain has demonstrated that it is he who sets the rules. He hits back if he feels offended and doesn't allow anybody to question his power position: neither Abel, nor God—and not even Adama.

When God asks Cain, "Where is Abel your brother?" (4:9), echoing the "Adam, where are you?" in the garden (3:9), the reply will be, "I do not know. Am I my brother's keeper?" The first and only time Cain talks about *my brother,* he renounces him. He refuses any positive relationship of watching, protecting, taking care of him. Cain makes clear once again that he is a strong, independent man, no nurse, no baby-sitter. The Hebrew word for *keeping* used here is exactly the same that originally had described Adam's task with regard to the garden: taking care, preserving next to serving. Rule and kill rather than serve and preserve is the new definition of man/*ish.* This is how Cain, the firstborn male of humankind, bangs into history.

Cain turns all other characters into the losers of his story. Not only Abel. Also God. What a ridiculous, unmanly God is this, who doesn't "naturally" take Cain's side! Or at least remain neutral, thus preserving the status quo of privilege and power. A God who interferes, gets related, compassionate—but then is too weak to protect his favorite one.

"Am I my brother's keeper?" also reads: Why didn't *you* take care of him if you liked his offering so much? Why did you upset me rather than confirm my number one position, why did you refuse to be God how I expect God to be—God with me, God in the image and likeness of the powerful male?

BEATING PLOWSHARES INTO SWORDS: CAIN AND ADAMA (4:10-24)

But the defeat of Abel and God is the defeat of the earth as well. And this is the point where the story according to the narrative logic must return. The Adama cannot live with this murderously successful and powerful son of Adam. He has spilled blood, but she is dependent on water.[19] He exercises rule where she needs service and caretaking. It seems quite "natural" that her fertility stops.

> Now he [God] said: What have you done! A sound—your brother's blood—cries out to me from the earth/Adama. And now, cursed be you from the earth/Adama who opened up her mouth to receive your brother's blood from your hand. When you wish to serve the earth/Adama she will not any longer give her strength to you! Wavering and wandering must you be on earth (4:11-12).

Adam, who was there as one of the main characters of the story since it began, ultimately becomes an active player. She opens her *mouth* to receive blood, that is death, rather than life-giving water and seeds from Cain's hand.[20] As a result, the communication between the two is irreversibly destroyed and Cain is driven away from the *face of the earth* (2:14). She expels him, she refuses him her strength and fertility, she spits him out. Abel's blood crying to God from the *mouth of* Adama has made her cursed, barren, and resistant to Cain. The first death in human history is not a peaceful receiving of dust returning to dust, but a desperate rearing up of the blood-soaked earth on behalf of the slain victim.

And again God shares the perspective of the violated, revolting earth.[21] Cain is not driven away from the face of the earth alone, but has to conceal himself from God's face as well (2:14). A new configuration has emerged: Cain is on the one side, God, Adama, and Abel are on the other. Nobody knows where Eve is.

Cain has to leave the Adama and live in Nod, meaning *wandering*. There is no more servant of the Adama, and we anticipate the desert growing again. Fratricide has produced ecocide, but ecocide was where it started: when Eve transgressed the holy borderline protecting the *one* tree. Cain, her favorite son, now has turned the cornfield into a battlefield, plowshares into swords. It is no wonder that among his children and grandchildren not a single farmer turns up, but the first city builder foreshadowing Babel (4:17), and also the first smith, Tubal-Cain, producer of metal tools and weaponry (4:22). And that finally at the climax of his genealogy Lamekh will sing his famous "song of sword," celebrating unlimited, murderous violence and power.

> Ada and Tzilla, listen to my voice,
>   women of Lamekh, give ear to my saying:
> Aye—a man I kill for wounding me,
>   a child for bruising me!
> Aye—if sevenfold vengeance be for Cain
>   then for Lamekh seventy-seven fold (4:23-24).

What a contrast between Eve's initial adoration of her first baby as "her" man/*ish -with-God* (4:1) and Lamekh boastfully addressing his two silent wives, when he declares death on anybody opposing him, whether man/*ish* or child/*yeled*. Or does the one just echo the other? The term *yeled* can also mean lad, young man, but in the presence of the two mothers— Lamekh has three sons and one daughter so far—its basic connotation of *child*, derived from the verb *give birth, beget,* seems important. Male power to take life has gained victory over female and earthly power to give life. As predicted in 3:16, man/*ish* has become ruler over woman/*ishsha*.

The roaring of Lamekh's voice (4:23) doesn't only silence his wives' voices, it also makes the other voice inaudible, which must be still crying to God from the Adama: the "voice of the blood of your brother" (4:10). Lamekh wipes out the voice of mourning violent death; his language speaks about retaliatory strikes, genocide, and mass destruction as the self-understanding, legitimate right of the powerful, whenever they feel *wounded* or *bruised* (4:24). It sounds as if he was talking about a glorious basketball game. The discourse on good and evil finally has got rid of Abel, earth, God.

No future, it seems, for Adam and Adama. Cain has survived as the strong, the lucky, the only one who made it. Humanity on earth will be derived from him and from his great-grandson Lamekh. Their genes are ours. Their male strength is the origin we all come from—and the reason we don't have a chance to survive, realistically speaking. Seven generations after Cain human life multiplies death seventy-sevenfold, social death, military death, ecological death. The cry of Abel and Adama has been swallowed by the noisy rhetoric of victory, power, success, and boundless growth, which produces the dead-end genealogy of self-destruction. Fratricide has lead to ecocide and finally must produce suicide.

EVE-ABEL-ADAMA: REBELLIOUS RECONCILIATION (4:25-26)

Is there any hope left? Can the earth, can humanity, can life be restored? And where, by the way, is God?

God. We have to take a closer look at the story. It was not quite correct to assume that Cain survived by his strength and virility. Rather it was God, God alone, who let him survive by giving him a sign of sevenfold protection (4:15), which only later on gets perverted into seventy-seven fold aggression by Lamekh. But at first Cain, the merciless, gets a chance to learn that he lives by only the mercy of God which he had ignored, ridiculed, defeated.

And God acts once more, merciful again. Seven generations beyond Adam and Eve have come and gone. Both should have died long ago. Lamekh sings his murderous song, with his two wives respectfully, or rather fearfully, listening, and nobody is there to stop him. Human history rushes into disaster. And there, just at the point of no return, Adam and Eve get a second chance. They are allowed to reenter the scene. The beginning of 4:25 reads like a repetition of 4:1. "Adam knew his wife again, and she bore a son . . ." Eve gets pregnant and gives birth. Another son. And like the first time she will name him. But everything else is different now. "She called his name: *Shet/Granted-One!*" Meaning: God has granted me another seed in place of Abel, for Cain has killed him.

For the first time Eve pronounces the name of her second-born, Abel. He was not worth mentioning for anybody before, except God: *Where is Abel your brother? I do not know . . .* (4:9). Ignored by Eve, silenced and denied by Cain, Abel finally had found intercession by the Adama—before both of them had been made voiceless by Lamekh again.

Now Eve speaks for Abel. She remembers him. She takes his side. She confesses the murder Cain has refused to confess. Eve is no longer the woman in 4:1 who had celebrated her own procreative strength to produce powerful masculinity close to God so exceedingly that no space was left for the smaller brother. If we take 4:25 seriously as an integral part of the story, Eve by implication in the meantime must have seen the earth drenched with blood, a skyscraping, earthless city mentality growing, invincible iron-made arms built. She must have watched Cain's male descendants propagating an ideology of relentless power that doesn't mind destroying the earth, subduing women, and murdering children. It was a long and torturous way to go. Seven generations long Eve was not allowed to die, but had to witness and suffer seventy-seven-fold death in her sons and daughters.

And then she is back at the point where it started, giving birth again. Has all this just been a nightmare, an apocalyptic vision? Can she act as if nothing had happened? She could, of course. We always can. Repeat our mistakes. Forget about Abel and raise another son. But Eve doesn't. From the moment she has named her third-born, a counter-voice against Lamekh's song is there: *another seed in place of Abel, for Cain has killed him* (4:25). Right into the face of the proud victor she dares to talk about a victim. To call Lamekh's heroic forefather, her favorite son Cain, a killer. By publicly mourning for Abel-the-loser, Eve interrupts the discourse of domi-nance—and the dreadful silence of Lamekh's two wives.[22]

This time Eve doesn't praise her fertility. It is God who out of grace be-yond understanding has granted her another son. Her knowledge of good and evil, once linked to a beautiful fruit and a powerful, promising male, has been matured, transformed, reinformed by tears and grief. She has come to know that the future of her children can be "good" only to the extent the evil done to Abel is not forgotten. That's why she inscribes Abel's name and memory into the story of her third son.

That's why she has to return to Adama as well. For seven generations Abel's blood has been crying from the mouth of the earth, seemingly un-heard. Nobody in Cain's line is mentioned to have served the earth either. Now Eve, wife of Adam, has joined the earth's solidarity with Abel and her resistance against the murderer. It is not only Abel and Eve, but also Eve and Adama who get reconciled in Seth. When the earth had become pol-luted by Abel's blood, her life-sustaining capacity was turned into infertil-ity and curse. Eve's naming of Seth takes up the cry of Abel's blood, out of the mouth of the earth. It restores justice. One could imagine that this should have a cleansing and restoring effect on the earth as well. Eve's conversion purifies and decontaminates what has been the source of curse and paralyzed fertility. She replants the seed of blessing and hope into the mistreated soil of the Adama to whom she has returned (compare 3:19).

It hardly comes as a surprise that after all this has happened, humanity (re-)starts to worship YHWH, God, in 4:26 with Enosh, Seth's son. Enosh means *human* again, but has a stronger compound of weakness, fragility, and mortality than the original Adam/human (compare 2 Sam. 12:15, Ps. 103:15). *Calling out the name of YHWH* in 4:26 is in many ways different from the initial sacrifice that led to murder. Eve has recognized and redefined God now as YHWH, the ONE WHO S/HE IS (compare Exod. 3:14): A God with a preferential option for Abel and for the earth/Adama. The self-centered, power-driven religiosity and ideology of Cain/Lamekh finally is unmasked as male idolatry. Both the first and the last verse of Gen. 4 in the Hebrew text close with the name of God. But whereas in 4:1 this name is attached to the dominant man/*ish*, it has been redirected toward the earth/brother/other-related human/Enosh-son-of Seth in 4:26. This is the decisive theological lesson taught in Gen. 4 about God, earth, gender, humanity. Eve is the first human who learns and prophetically proclaims it as rebellious "good" news to disturb and subvert Lamekh's power hymns.

EPILOGUE

When the genealogical tree of humanity from Adam to Noah is developed in the following Priestly chapter (5), Adam's son from whom humanity is derived will be Seth. Seth, who represents and remembers Abel, is the basis for the future and survival of humanity—not Cain. Seth-pro-Abel is installed as Adam's firstborn against the logic of primogeniture, which divides brothers into winners and losers. The last become first. This reversal of the "natural" birth order from now on will be one of the most striking and pertinent features of the Genesis narratives. From Ishmael to Esau, Reuben, Serah, Manasseh—none of the firstborn sons will get his birthright to be the dominant one . . .[23]

Seth means the survival of the "unfit," God's "counter-natural" selection of the endangered and excluded, the memory of the exterminated and slaughtered. Seth also forever embodies Eve's conversion, her turning back to God and to the earth through a knowledge of good that ripened in the midst of evil. With the seed of Cain and Lamekh still being there, reimplanted also in the "new" genealogy,[24] Eve's reconciliation with Adama, Abel, and God has to stay a continuously critical, resistant, and repentant one.

The new and painful wisdom Eve acquired long after taking the apple has never been acknowledged throughout centuries of Christian inter-pretation, which have been obsessed with tying her to the tree and to dogmatic constructs about sin and sexuality, regardless of her ongoing story. Eve's narrative comeback in 4:25 marks the climax and reversal of the whole garden story. It is as if we had read the passion narratives con-stantly without the Easter stories. The account on Abel, Eve, and Adama in Gen. 4, in fact, contains powerful elements of a "resurrection pattern." It talks about conversion in the midst of perversion, rising after the fall—restoration of life after death has entered human history.

At the beginning of a new millennium we are more than ever alien-ated from the life-saving knowledge and courage that enables Eve in Genesis 4 to finally deconstruct and resist the "good" propagated by the powerful, thus bringing about the (re-)birth of humanity as well as the revival of the earth. It is time to rediscover the unread story of Eve and to return to this highly critical and post-naive knowledge that makes her finally the mother of all life and all hope for humanity-on-earth until today.[25]

PART 2

OVERCOMING ECO-INJUSTICE

IN EARTH COMMUNITY

4

The Muslim World: Globalization and Ecology

Ibrahim M. Abu-Rabi

IN RESPONSE TO THE CONFERENCE on "Ecumenical Earth: New Dimensions of Church and Community in Creation," this paper examines the social, economic, intellectual, and ecological impact of globalization on the contemporary Muslim world. Far from examining the Qur'anic position on nature and ecology, which has been discussed by a variety of authors, I will limit my discussion to globalization and its attempt to create a new socioeconomic, political, and, ultimately, ecological structure in the Muslim world.[1]

It is almost impossible to give one simple definition of the term *globalization* because it carries a number of implications in the economic, social, political, ideological, and intellectual realms. Globalization is not a brand-new phenomenon, since it emerged after the triumph of laissez-faire capitalism in the post–industrial revolution era and the expansion of Europe overseas during the age of imperialism. In other words, triumphant European imperialism created deep structural, economic, political, cultural, religious, and ecological transformations in the so-called Third World and led to a permanent interaction between South and North.[2] Imperialist domination was double-edged: on the one hand, it led to the modernization of some leading institutions and segments of the colonized world, such as the army,

the police force, the educational system, and the subjugation of natural resources for the benefit of modernization. On the other hand, however, it
created social and economic disequilibrium, opening major gaps between
the countryside and the urban centers, which in turn led to the flight of the
poor to the city. This social and economic situation had its impact on the
environment in the Muslim world.

NATION-STATES

The nation-state, emerging in response to the penetration of bourgeois
capitalism and emphasizing an autonomous national economic and cultural independence, sought to create new structures and foundations for
the new state that aimed at bypassing the traditional dependence created
by defunct imperialism. The existence of the Soviet Union and the ensu-
ing Cold War after World War II gave the new nation-states some room to
maneuver. Two major events, however, shifted the balance in the 1970s
and the 1980s in favor of the capitalist West: first, the conquest of the huge
Chinese market by American capitalism; and second, the collapse of the
Soviet system and the end of the Cold War, which signaled the triumph of
the capitalist West over the Socialist East.[3] These two major events, without parallel in the history of mankind, left the nation-states easy prey to
the challenges and dangers of the new geopolitical and economic realities
of the New World Order.[4] The above change proves once again the importance of economic decisions in the direction of world politics and the future. Profit-motivated and highly competitive capitalism begins a new
drive: the conquest of space after the conquest of the terrain.[5] Enter the
multinational companies that see the future of capitalism in conquering
new space and new immaterial territory. To do that, they aim at creating
a global climate that allows competitiveness without the controlling
hands of the nation-state. This tendency of "aggressive capitalism" to go
amok, so to speak, is all the more dangerous in the absence of an international economic and political system and only meager international
coordination in protecting the environment. The monosystem of neo-
liberalism, as one author notes holds sway:

> In this era of generalized liberalism, the mission of promoting abundance
> and well being is entrusted to private firms, in collaboration with states
> and the international organizations charged with the responsibility of

assisting them. Companies which produce goods and, increasingly, services, do so, in the case of the most highly performing ones, without regard
to borders. Given that their sole driving force, their only *raison d'etre* is
profit, one must recognize that an immense chasm separates the assigned
goal from the capacity for action. And, without in the least denying the existence of the "losers" of the North, it is necessary to emphasize this fact:
the South is not in the race.[6]

Creating a globalized climate that is amenable to a new type of international profit has had negative impacts on indigenous economies and
ecology in general. In a sense, it creates new sets of rationales and values
that are not in tune with the cultures, traditions, and histories of indigenous peoples and nation-states. The logic of capitalism is not to maintain
or develop a healthy social, economic, and ecological system, but to gain
profit in the shortest period possible.[7]

The last thought raises the questions about the newly gained relationship between the multinationals and the nation-state; the role of the state
in society; the deep changes in power relations, not just between South
and North, but also with the countries of the South; the nature of civil
society; and the implications for democracy in the Third World.[8]

Globalization challenges the nation-state to open up its space and borders for a novel type of competitiveness free of any control.[9] The political
elite of the nation-state are expected to cooperate fully with the economic
enterprises, and the accumulation of national capital is very often impossible in view of the fact that many nation-states in the Third World
suffer from burdens of debt to the advanced world or the International
Monetary Fund. The rules of the game change here: national development and growth in the Third World is hampered by the accumulation
of capital on an international scale. According to Samir Amin, in the
1950s and the 1960s globalization was somewhat controlled by three international factors: the intervention of the capitalist state in the process
of capital accumulation; the Soviet project of socialist economy; and the
Bandong project of the nonaligned world formed under the auspices of
Sukarno, Nehru, and Nasser.[10] With privatization mushrooming in the
countries of these leaders, now deceased, the nationalist/socialist project
of self-sufficiency, the empowerment of the poor, and the protection of
the environment has come to a deadly halt. In the case of the Arab
world, for example, the Gulf region was forcibly cut off from the rest of

the Arab world by the capitalist West that intensified its hegemony, both economic and military, in the wake of the military defeat of Iraq in the 1991 Gulf war. The result, in the words of Samir Amin, is that the states of the Gulf have been turned into "protectorates that are devoid of any freedom to maneuver both economically and politically."[11] They do not even control their own ecosystem. In the words of Immanuel Wallerstein, the Third World was able to win the political battle in the 1950s and the 1960s, whereby decolonization "had been achieved almost everywhere. It was time for the second step, national development. . . . The second step was never to be achieved in most places."[12] In the age of liberalization and integration, globalization does not permit the local economies to breathe on their own.[13]

The failure of the nationalist economies in such countries as Indonesia, India, Egypt, and Algeria is proof of the triumph of rational technology in the advanced West. However, as some economists have pointed out, the spread of "financial liberalization" or "technological globalization" cannot be determined by technological factors alone; politics have a lot to do with the spread of rational technology and globalization. It is the political desire of the center to subjugate the nation-states, except perhaps Israel, to the exigencies of the capitalist market.[14]

The advocates of globalization envision a kind of "global village economy" that facilitates the spread of modernization and technological rationalization to every corner of the world. They propose that globalization has led to the integration into the world market of those societies that had been hitherto marginalized and impoverished. In their view, globalization did not just result in the creation of millions of new jobs, and the improvement of social and economic conditions of the poor, but also led to an opening in the cultural and mental space of the poor nations.[15] Even if one is to accept the above views of the advocates of globalization, which has become an inevitable process in many Third World countries, one must turn a blind eye to other no less significant processes accompanying globalization: the "globalitarian regimes" that are more entrenched than the "totalitarian regimes" of yesteryear.[16] The global oppression of the nation-state has created new forms of oppression of civil society by the already "oppressed" nation-state, broken down social cohesion in the Third World, and whittled down the democratic space in society. Civil society is suffocated as a result of the new shifts in power boundaries in society; freedom of expression becomes a rare commodity; and the environment goes unprotected.[17] Also, one astute author observes,

> As the industrialized nations are gradually figuring out, the new world order imposed by the globalized economy means a race to the bottom for everyone, as jobs are eliminated in the name of global competitiveness or exported and the transnational corporations assume a level of power above any government. Even in a country like India, where 10 percent of the 980,000,000 residents comprise a new middle class that has benefited from the globalized presence of transnationals, the other 90 percent are simply not in the plan for the dazzling future. The 10 percent with disposable income constitute a large enough market to cause salivation among the global players: India is called a great success story.[18]

In the new nation-state since the 1980s, democratic space has been challenged to the core. One would expect that the advanced Center that has carried the slogan of democracy for a long while would promote real democracy in the South. This is far from true. Under globalization a new relationship is forged between the political elite and the economic powers, especially the multinationals.[19] In the case of the Muslim world, the tribal, quasi-constitutional state, controlled by the same family or clan, gains additional repressive powers. Civil society suffers from additional loss of freedom, and the working people and women are disempowered.

The gradual penetration of the multinationals in the Third World economies, far from eliminating poverty and alleviating the misery of the urban and rural poor, has led to four intertwined phenomena: increase in the number of the poor and the unemployed; concentration of wealth in the hands of the political elite, a deepening ecological crisis, and an increase in the repression of the state.[20] Indonesia is one prime example of this state of affairs. With the onslaught of modern technologies under the guise of globalization, the old mission of the West, that of *mission civilisatrice*, is reaffirmed in the new/old god of money, technology, investment, and prosperity.

In the Third World, the image of the intelligentsia gets transformed radically in the age of globalization. In the colonial era, the indigenous intelligentsia played a leading role in both political and cultural independence.

Although these intellectuals were, according to Benedict Anderson, "lonely, bilingual, and highly anxiety-ridden intelligentsia," they were nevertheless in a position to reflect the anguish and suffering of their people.[21] They fought for independence from their colonial masters, whose schools they had gone to. The new intelligentsia of "Third World globalization" does not share the anxiety of the colonial intellectual elite. Scientists, technocrats, engineers, and researchers all have something in common: preoccupation with business and investment, all expressed in a new mode of English, that of the London School of Economics or the Harvard Business School. According to Pierre Bourdieu, those new technocrats tend to favor economic profit at the expense of social and mental dislocation in Third World societies. The technocrats support what he calls a "structural violence" in these societies, that is, an increase in the number of the unemployed and marginalized in society.[22]

As seen above, the New World Order did not come out of the blue. With the collapse of the Soviet system in the early 1990s, after many decades of severe struggle, the Third World became easy prey to the hegemony of the only remaining superpower.[23] Whether or not it was the intention of Iraq to challenge the hegemony of the West in general and the United States in particular by invading Kuwait in 1990, the amassing of Western troops under the banner of the United Nations in the Gulf sent shock waves through the nerves of the modern Muslim world. The military defeat of Iraq by the West did in fact preserve, if not enhance, the national interests of the West, which, in clear historical irony, further strengthened the authoritarian political regimes in the Gulf states and obliterated any real chance to achieve democracy for many years to come. In addition to signaling major shifts in world alliances and the rise of the United States as the only major superpower in the world today, these two events—the collapse of the Soviet system and the defeat of Iraq—have raised once again, and perhaps in a much more acute fashion than before, the issue of Western, especially American, cultural hegemony and its impact on Third World cultures. The American impact on the Muslim world in the post-Cold War era is not limited to the economic and political. It is primarily intellectual and conceptual. The ruling elite in the Muslim world take the functioning ideas in the capitalist West as their ideal model.[24]

Postcolonialism ensued from neocolonialism and is its twin brother. It is the product of the New World Order.[25] As a historical event of tremendous importance to the lives of Muslims and non-Muslims alike, colonialism very often entails a military occupation of one country by another (that is, a military occupation by a European country). Colonialism also entails direct control of natural resources, which makes a difference in the strategic interests of the colonizer.

IMITATING THE WEST

The political elite of the new nation-states have sought to modernize their countries by blindly imitating the West. These elites have benefited from political and military protection by the West that permitted them to stay in power. In some of these countries, the West has never raised the issue of human rights or the absence of democracy. What mattered was preserving the strategic interests of the West while easily sacrificing principles.

The basis of neocolonialism is a new form of economic domination that allows other discrete forms of domination—political, cultural, and intellectual. During the Cold War between the Soviet Bloc and the Western capitalist world, Third World countries felt somewhat relieved from cultural and political pressure by the West since the balance of world power permitted them to function with some freedom. However, the status quo changed with the collapse of the Soviet system and the military defeat of Iraq. These two events left both the Arab world and Arab culture defenseless in face of the hegemony of the United States. With the emergence of the United States as the leading superpower, a number of states, such as Cuba, Syria, and Libya, were, and still are, accused by the center of supporting terrorism.

Since the colonial era, the periphery has been dependent on the center, and the diffusion of ideas through satellites instituted a new relationship between the Muslim world and the West. The center practices what one may call a hegemonic "imperialist culture."[26] Most of the thinkers of the Muslim world who grew up in the shadow of colonialism draw our attention to the major conclusions of European, and even some American, thinkers about the rise of America in recent years and its cultural impact on the whole world, including Europe: "The American empire is the only empire in the world; it is an exclusive hegemony. This is the first time in the history of humanity that this strange phenomenon has occurred."[27] The United States is a unique empire. It is a major producer of all sorts of goods; however, it is also an avid consumer. The history of America, from the very beginning, is marked by an extreme tendency toward expansion: thirst for land, thirst for power, thirst for the new, thirst for greatness— all needs which can be met on their own."[28]

According to the famous American literary critic Edmund Wilson, American expansion overseas in the wake of the defeat of Nazi Germany in World War II was not by coincidence.

> We thought we were liberating Europe and fending off the imperialism of feudal Japan, but we turned up after [World War II] occupying or control- ling foreign countries all over America, Europe, Asia, and the Middle East, and sometimes as unwelcome as the French in Algeria, the British in Cyprus or the Russians in central Europe. After years of being shocked by the imperialism of others, we are developing a new kind of our own, and we find ourselves scowling at the Soviet Union and spending billions for weapons against it—and weapons even the testing of which is dangerous to our own population—without any real provocation and for the simple sub-rational reason that we are challenging the Soviet Russians for dom- ination of large sections of the world.[29]

The recent manifestation of globalization, in the view of many Third World intellectuals, is triumphant Americanization that has advocated a new kind of cultural and economic model, "Besides being an economic system, globalization is an ideology that serves this system. American- ization and globalization are highly intertwined."[30]

The information gap between North and South has been com- pounded in the contemporary age of globalization by what is called "soft power," that is, the power of cybernetics and the launching of technolog- ical warfare from a distance. According to Richard Falk of Princeton Uni- versity, the current thinking of the elite in the West and the United States predicts that the cybernetic potential is of unlimited nature:

> In the United States there are strategists who dream of taking control of the cybernetic networks and the fabulous wealth that the industries of "virtual" knowledge and know-how apparently will produce. These strategists want to build the new empire of the electronic era, at the cen- ter of which will be a global market totally activated by the technologies of the future.[31]

A country as powerful and as young as the United States is still fasci-
nated by the early immigrants' experience of conquering the prairies in
the American heartland. That land conquest seemed unlimited initially.
But then by the end of the nineteenth century, all came to a halt. The
American mind had to grapple with new frontiers. The new frontiers of
the New World Order are the conquest of space and the total subjugation
of the ecological system to the exigencies of the new capitalist order.
With the brain drain from the poor countries continuing, and the migration of not an insignificant number of high-tech experts from the former
Soviet Union, the United States possesses enormous resources of technology. American globalization has begun in earnest.[32] One must note,
however, that the advanced center encourages the migration of skilled
professionals from the Third World and that it has begun to enact laws
that make it difficult for nonprofessionals to immigrate.[33]

This important fact has resulted in: a Western superiority in economic
and political affairs, the spread of Western ideas by acquiring Western technology, the brain drain from the Third World to the advanced center, and
the gradual infiltration of Western cultural and intellectual values, as well
as the scientific values, into the domains of the Third World. This leads to
an absence of a real cultural dialogue between South and North: "In return, it is the absence of communication and of cultural tolerance that
risks putting peace in peril during the coming years."[34]

In spite of the "information superiority" exhibited by the West, however, the people of the center still know very little about the people of the
Third World and the challenges facing them. The mass media in the triumphant center are no better than twenty years ago, still wages a war of
ignorance about the real problems affecting the South. This double face of
globalization (too much information on the Third World but too little
knowledge of its problems) becomes all the more dangerous when the
new capital forces penetrate every corner of the world and fashion it according to the demands of the new global economy.[35] The advanced West
uses its superior technology of research in order to make more profit at
the expense of the Third World, especially as the unequal conditions between North and South seem to persist.[36]

Globalization has also accelerated the brain drain from the Third
World to the advanced center. The place of preference for many Third
World intellectuals and professionals is the United States. This process has
been rightly called "intellectual hemorrhage," since it depletes the poor

countries of much-needed expertise in all fields of science. Many emigrate, not just in search of better economic and social standards, but because the development process in their native countries lacks the appropriate vision to incorporate them productively. Very often, this lack of vision is complemented by blind imitation of the modernized North, leading to a transfer of technology with no creative contribution from the South. In other words, the South can purchase technology but it must create its own forms of modernity and modernization. Yet these forms cannot be created in the context of the continuous exodus of its skilled professionals. As a consequence of this unfortunate state of affairs, the Muslim world and the rest of the Third World countries suffer from the following interdependent problems: illiteracy, absence of rigorous scientific research, and lack of democratic values.

Although this bleeding of "mental resources" from the poor countries is an alarming phenomenon, it has led to some positive results, especially in the advanced center, where a dialogue about competing cultural and religious values is taking place between people of different religious and cultural communities.[37] The North was also in need of labor from the Third World. Europe has imported skilled and nonskilled labor from many Muslim countries, most notably Morocco, Algeria, Tunisia, Turkey, and Pakistan. The continuation of this exodus is an indication of underdevelopment in the native countries. "Underdevelopment is the inability to develop or make reasonable use of competent human resources."[38] Skilled migrants do not leave for financial reasons alone, but because in their new adopted country, they have a better chance to obtain further education in their profession and more opportunities for advancement.

Scientific knowledge is one of the major landmarks of development and progress in contemporary society. Because of the rapid advance in science and technology, the world of knowledge is going to double its scientific information in the next decade or so. This is tremendous in view of the fact that we are learning more in a decade than did our ancestors in a thousand years. But the West and Japan control most of this knowledge and the best brains of the Third World migrate to the center. What this means is the creation of fundamental "knowledge" gaps between North and South and, coupled with the North's feeling of cultural superiority, very little effective cultural communication between South and North: "It is ethnocentrism that makes the introduction of true cultural communication difficult."[39] The West, which constitutes 22 percent of the world's population and is going to be only 16 percent of the world's population thirty years from now, consuming 70 percent of total world resources, has three major obsessions: the demography of the Third World, the Judeo-Christian ethic, and Japan.[40]

Globalization is constructing a new world that will, in a few decades from now, look much different than the one we are accustomed to. Different major transformations are already under way: (1) the collapse of socialism and the spread of privatization to such countries as China, India, and Egypt; (2) the rise of regional powers, such as the European community, in the wake of the rise of the United States to the position of supreme power; (3) the widening of social and economic gaps between rich and poor within and between countries; (4) the globalization of exploitation, which is a natural consequence of privatization and multinational investment; (5) the rise of ultra- nationalism, ethnic cleansing, and creation of new refugee problems; (6) the internationalization of crime, especially Mafia-related crime; (7) the destabilization of the nation-state; and (8) full subjugation of the ecosystem for the sake of capitalist profit and competitiveness.

FINAL THOUGHTS

The Western mind-set, which has shaped the socioeconomic and intellectual destinies of the world since the Industrial Revolution, centered on the notion of progress.[41] To some, the potential for progress is unlimited.[42] The physical and mental terrain of the Third World is there to occupy and colonize. In the modern worldview, "a salvational sense of progress places economic expansion and technological innovation at the center of importance." The phenomenon of progress has indeed posed a major challenge to traditional cultures, their socioeconomic bases, and their ethical worldviews. Globalization has not given up on progress, even the most damaging forms of progress: those leading to a new form of colonization. Hannah Arendt observes that the classical notion of progress led to a "process of never-ending accumulation of power necessary for the protection of a never-ending accumulation of capital" shaping the "progressive" ideology of the late nineteenth century and foreshadowing the rise of imperialism. Globalization is leading already to a new form of colonization that is more subtle and destructive than the classical one. Furthermore, globalization, the latest manifestation of the modern mind-set, has created

confusion as to what is important in life. The traditional notions of prosperity, connectedness, community building, and aiding the poor have
been displaced by new aggressive notions of what life means.

Before the dawn of the twentieth century, the religious intelligentsia
of the Muslim world considered European progress to be devoid of any
ethical foundations. Some, however, argued that the Western mind-set
had been for many centuries intent on building an ethical foundation that
did not subscribe to the worldview of the monotheistic revelations.

Under the aegis of globalization, the ethic of the Western mind-set encourages fast accumulation of wealth and power, and an absence of respect for natural laws. Extravagant consumerism is the rule of the day. In
the view of Richard Falk, "At present, it is mainly the consequence of the
globalization of Western cultural influence, including its commitment to
modernization, that has produced a world order crisis of multiple dimensions: nuclearism, industrialism, materialism, consumerism."[43]

In view of the colossal consequences of globalization, a new popular
consciousness has to evolve in order to understand and resist the negative
tendencies of globalization and protect the environment. The Muslim
world must work hard at reviving the social, financial, and economic
ethic of Islam, as a monotheistic phenomenon, in order to combat these
dangerous inclinations.[44] It is important to create equilibrium between the
demands of nature and those of humans and to revive a sense of community that withstands the attacks of individualism that have become the
rule of the day in advanced industrial societies and their satellite societies
in the Third World. With increasing gaps between North and South, and
within most countries in the South, between the countryside and the city,
and with the increasing number of the marginalized and impoverished in
the cities, there is no escape from reviving the Islamic communal ethic
that "commands the good and prohibits the evil." According to Fazulr
Rahman, "The purpose of man's creation is that he do good in the world,
not substitute himself for God and think that he can make and unmake
the moral law at his own convenience. This is the difference between
physical laws and the moral law—the one is to be used and put to service;
the other must be obeyed and served."[45] This would be one effective way to
safeguard the environment.

5

Affirming Life
for the Disregarded Many

*Martin Robra with Deenabandhu Manchala
and Sarah Anderson-Rajarigam*

THE CHALLENGE OF GLOBALIZATION

For some it is synonymous with salvation, for others a new expression of
hell: globalization. The debate on globalization reflects the asymmetrical
and unjust distribution of power and wealth on planet Earth. Those who
benefit from economic globalization want to convince people that there
was and is no alternative to a globalized market economy and the spread
of Western civilization around the world.[1] But people in South and
North, East and West know that fragmentation and destruction of the social fabric of societies characterize the reverse side of increasing richness
for the "chosen few" and the growing power of corporate business. Those
who are made dispensable, the "surplus people," are excluded, but they
do not vanish. Street children, homeless people, youth gangs in the ghettos are visible even in the United States of America, the most powerful
and richest country in the world.

Globalization has led to an unprecedented concentration of power in
the financial centers of the global market that contributes to the weakening

of the nation-state, to fragmentation and exclusion on a global scale, and to a merciless attack on the integrity of creation. While globalization universalized aspects of modern social life, it also created reactions that again focus on the local and on ethnic, cultural, and religious identities. Resisting the project to globalize the neoliberal version of the market system, communities have rediscovered the hidden sources of their identities and have begun to revitalize ethnic, religious, and cultural traditions, often reviving old and potent symbols of belonging and solidarity. But this has not in itself led to new forms of cooperation, or created the alliances and coalitions necessary for the badly needed process of "globalization from below"—that is, new social and religious institutional arrangements. Sometimes the reactions to globalization from above have even degenerated into fundamentalism and ethnocentrism.

The Eighth General Assembly of the World Council of Churches (WCC) held in December 1998 at Harare, Zimbabwe, stated in response to this situation,

> The challenge of globalization should become a central emphasis of the work of the WCC. The vision behind globalization includes a competing vision to the Christian commitment to the oikoumene, the unity of humankind and the whole inhabited earth. . . . The logic of globalization needs to be challenged by an alternative way of life of community in diversity. Christians and churches should reflect on the challenge of globalization from a faith perspective and, therefore, resist the unilateral domination of economic and cultural globalization. The search for alternative options to the present economic system and the realization of effective political limitations and corrections to the process of globalization and its implications are urgently needed.[2]

This chapter cannot entertain the details of the debate on globalization, but it does assume that any discussion of new initiatives at the global level needs to take into consideration the accelerated process of globalization that marks the present context.[3] This applies to both the Earth Charter Initiative (discussed in another chapter in this volume) and the Theology of Life Program (TOL) of the WCC (on which we focus here).

Steven Rockefeller's excellent contribution to the Ecumenical Earth Conference expressed high expectations about the possible impact of the

Earth Charter Process on the United Nations (UN).⁴ The Charter's hoped-for endorsement by the UN General Assembly will give a desperately needed renewed emphasis to the sustainability agenda in the UN system. Although strongly affirmed at the Rio Conference on Environment and Development in 1992, the goal of sustainable development has been over-shadowed in international negotiations by the preoccupation with eco-nomic growth and the increase in world trade, not least because the process of globalization itself is almost exclusively driven by economic forces and corporate interests.

This means that equal in importance to the hoped-for endorsement by the UN of the Earth Charter itself is the charter's own process, a con-trast to globalization dynamics. The crafting of the charter represents a promising method in that people from different contexts representing different worldviews and value systems have been interactive with one another at various stages of the document's development. Via regional meetings and global consultations, they have had a fair chance to influ-ence the development of the Earth Charter in successive drafts. This kind of process has value in itself and is necessary to the future role of civil society at the global level and in the UN system.

Indeed, there is a need for a number of similar processes. The task be-fore us is not less than changing the course of history for the sake of the disregarded while reconciling humankind with creation, a task that will not be achieved by only fine-tuning current economic and political processes and adding another set of institutions to care for environmental concerns. A socially and ecologically sensitive cultural dimension at the global level is needed, a shared global ethos and ethic. Previous attempts at a global ethic—influenced by Enlightenment idealism—were developed by a small minority of concerned people and were inherently elitist and provincial. The moral communities and moral formation, however, that would provide a viable environment for the kind of universalized ethic the Enlightenment dreamt of and we certainly need, do not yet exist. At best, these base communities for a genuine earth ethic are in the making and the Earth Charter process, like the developing institutionalization of human rights, aids their cause.⁵

From another angle, globalization has not only brought about the homogenization of certain institutions and cultures, it has also helped create new local cultural environments and cross-cultural alliances.

Communication technologies—electronic globalization—strengthen linkages between peoples and cultures. Easier and efficient accessibility across and between regions facilitates solidarity among social movements and networks. There is potential here for greater participation by more people in matters that vitally affect their well-being and shape their common future. In every region of the world, issues of power, land, community, and identity are basic aspects of life at the center of energetic relationships with persons in diverse cultures and with nature in all its biodiversity.

The reality of unequal distribution of power and wealth, of exclusion and poverty, however, challenges any cheap language of a shared global community. The often-used image of the "global village" is thus very misleading insofar as the new global culture disrespects diversity and fails to work from it. The new situation is lacking the sense of community, belonging, and mutual accountability that is typical of village life.

It was exactly for this reason that the Theology of Life Program was designed as a tool to learn, in a theologically self-conscious mode, more about processes of community building and the social and religious institutional arrangements required in the present situation. This is reflected in the method of the program and its primary theological-ethical focus on the concept of "ecumenical Earth."[6] The following statement in a background document to the Recommendations on Globalization by the Harare Assembly of the WCC shows the relevance of "ecumenical Earth" for the work of the WCC:

> It is now even more necessary than before to call for a fundamental reshaping of the economic system and to affirm God's gift of life that is threatened in so many ways. Sustainable development, a concept prominent in international fora, still leaves powerful forces of globalization in command and does not question the underlying paradigm of continuous and unlimited progress and growth. Affirming God's gift of life to all creation in the midst of the pain, suffering, and destruction caused by economic globalization, it is imperative to discern a life-centered vision.[7]

Jesus came so that all may have life and have it more abundantly (10:10). God's salvation in Jesus Christ means not only fullness of life for the human community, but the restoration of all creation to its goodness and wholeness. God's Holy Spirit comes to renew the whole creation.

According to the creation stories of the Bible, Earth was meant to be home for all living creatures, existing in different spaces but linked to each other in a web of relationships. The human community is placed within the wider community of Earth, which is embedded in God's household of life. This vision of a truly ecumenical Earth challenges the ecumenical movement: to search for new ways of revitalizing and protecting the communities of indigenous peoples and of the marginalized or excluded, to participate in resistance against the growing domination of economic globalization, and to engage in the building of a culture of peace and just relationships, a culture of sharing and solidarity.[8]

THEOLOGY OF LIFE AND GLOBALIZATION

The TOL process articulates a vision of ecumenical Earth as a complex web of relationships, and the TOL process provides an opportunity to learn more about strengthening the ecumenical dimension in the life of the churches and building community from the bottom up. In recognition of the destructive consequences of unjust global structures and relationships, special attention has been given to the experience of people in those contexts who are oppressed by dominant cultures of white European or North American origin. Their perspective provides new insights and impulses for criticizing the present global context and relating the local to the global in a different way.[9] For too many centuries, theological reflection was part and parcel of an imperial paradigm supporting the quest for territorial control and domination. Theology of Life in turn starts from the question of how to build community from the bottom up when the local space is contested and marked by discrimination on the basis of class, race, and gender.[10]

From the point of view of ecumenical history, TOL builds on decades of WCC reflections on "Just, Participatory, and Sustainable Society" and on "Justice, Peace, and the Integrity of Creation" (JPIC). The objective is to ground this work again in the concrete struggles of people, to learn from contextual theologies in different regions of the world, and to bring them into interaction. The term "contextual theologies" as used here includes liberation, feminist, womanist, and indigenous theologies. The TOL process is based on concrete experiences of life; as an attempt to do theology from below, it has the ability to offer relevance and credibility to an activity—theological reflection—that is often accused of being too Western, cerebral, and removed from the realities of life.

The program started in 1994 with twenty-three case studies of churches and movements undertaken in different parts of the world. The Ten Affirmations of the JPIC World Convocation at Seoul were chosen as entry points for the case studies. Several of the case-study groups had the opportunity for mutual exchange. The case studies were complemented by a historical study of ecumenical social thought in the WCC. The method of the process was based on the assumption that theological commonalties and differences, when raised up in local, regional, and worldwide interconnected struggles, can deepen understanding in each place and for all involved.

The TOL process has followed a narrative, community-based approach. The narrative approach shows how faith is practiced by those who are marginalized and excluded, what symbols of faith mean to them, and how those symbols contribute to the life of the community. The stories of the poor in the experiential study of their predicament and in their perceptions of life help us to understand better the meaning of life. This means trying to listen and to learn what the poor have to say about their problems, feelings, disappointments, fears, suffering, tragedies, losses, anxieties, aspirations, and vulnerabilities. Not least, it means learning how they experience the "God of Life" in the midst of all these. What are the life-giving forces that nurture and build up communities? How are the symbols, the narratives as expressions of identity, the practices, and the life of the community linked to each other? How do they influence and shape each other? How do people embody their theology and live their faith in community? Following this narrative approach and its inductive style of theological reflection, the Theology of Life Program moved into a mutual process of sharing. How do we receive what others share? Are we willing to enter into relationships that lead into new dimensions of life?

AN ECUMENICAL SPACE

TOL case-study coordinators met twice during the process before the culminating event took place in January 1997 near Nairobi, Kenya. One was

an orientation meeting in May 1994 in Geneva was followed by a conference in September 1995 at Brasov, Romania. Here participants underlined:

> We need theological and ethical tools to deal with fragmentation, to tap
> into the creativity and resources of the people of God and their traditions,
> to understand sources of spiritual growth and social survival.
>
> TOL . . . can be envisioned as an open space, a theater for the presen-
> tation of the gifts and contributions of others. It is a safe arena, though not
> without risk. It is a space of acceptance, of understanding, of affirmation.
> Such a context or space is a necessary precondition to dialogue. Dialogue
> marks out the conciliar space. Such a framework opens up exciting possi-
> bilities for ecumenical dialogue and ecumenical social thought and ac-
> tion. TOL must revive and learn from ecumenical memory, to be aware of
> common processes that are at work as that common space is sometimes
> contested, to understand the elements of that contestation, and, at times,
> that space is the arena of convergence.[11]

The coordinators encouraged each other to trust the language of life
and resist the common division between intellect and emotion, usually
devaluing the latter in favor of the former. The open space, or better, the
safe space, where repentance, reparation, reconciliation, and forgiveness
can take place became a key metaphor for the approach. It is necessary to
underline *safe space* because the program also made visible how asymmetrical power relationships easily destroy the community and hurt those
who make themselves vulnerable when they begin to share. Sharing is
often conflictual by nature and those involved need to be prepared to
work through conflicts that emerge on the way. Shared commitment to
the vision of justice, peace, and integrity of creation is also crucial; in tense
situations, it provided a sense of solidarity among participants in the case
studies and the conference that followed.

To show how this process worked, some of the results from TOL studies in India are briefly indicated here, followed by a description of the culminating conference in Nairobi that reflected on case studies from every
continent. Finally, some conclusions will be drawn about the process as an
alternate method of doing theology and creating global/local community
from the bottom up.

LEARNINGS FROM INDIAN CASE STUDIES

The poor of India are not nameless and faceless people. They are the *dalits*, "backward" castes, indigenous people, in some cases, ethnic, linguistic, and religious minorities, women, and many other such marginalized communities and people. [12] The Indian case studies were from different parts of the country with reflections and stories of people such as agricultural laborers, released bonded laborers, migrant workers, skin tanners, unemployed tribal youth, weavers, urban poor, and domestic workers. [13] Most of these were dalits, tribals, and women.

Dalits comprise 27 percent of the total Indian populace and 90 percent of the Christian population in India. Poverty in India is not a mere economic phenomenon but a sociocultural one, an essentially systemic evil that legitimizes marginalization and oppression of the weak and the powerless. Even after half a century of "positive discrimination" (where the government grants certain basic privileges which are otherwise denied to the scheduled castes and tribes), dalits suffer every day at the hands of "upper caste" people because of their economic dependence. More than their "insufficient and inadequate" participation in development, it is their enforced and asymmetric participation in it, by which they bear the costs but are excluded from the benefits, that has reduced them to something like donkeys bearing the burden of development. Globalization as "development" in fact excludes the lives of dalits and dispossesses them of their land and rights, further aggravating and deepening the colonial/neocolonial processes of social injustice and ecological degradation.

The complexity of this phenomenon reveals that poverty in India is not only a denial of basic necessities. It is a denial of dignity and the right to live. Dalits are marginalized people who bear the brunt of the caste system and the worst of the consequences of globalization. Their case in fact underscores the need to recognize "the other," to understand the common bond of "earth" and "earthiness," and to contribute to a meaningful future for a presently dying planet. The need to relate to one another despite differences and in the face of numerous obstacles has been exemplified over and again by the base communities of the dalits. Furthermore, their earthiness—being connected directly to the resources of life—can best be understood as a continuous living relationship with the earth. This links them up with their fellow human beings in similar situations of oppression. But it also provides an alternative basis for solidarity. It need not be oppression alone that unites people. The fact that we derive our life and sustenance from the same earth can also become the binding force. This entails or assumes, as it does for dalits, an understanding of the universe as a web of very complex relationships and nature as a tissue of subtle connections.

"God Opts for the Poor" was the affirmation that guided the study process as it attempted to define the contours of an Indian "theology of life." The studies affirmed that this is not humanitarianism but a call for justice, and that justice is a value in which all other values are subsumed. The absence of justice in relationships at both personal and structural levels is perhaps the main cause for much of the malaise in the world today, as well as the present eco-crisis itself. The poor in India, as elsewhere, are the victims of injustice and consequently also of environmental disasters. The ecological question is inextricably bound up with the question of justice. Nature and history are inseparable. The option for the poor is an option for a safe and just world for all.

Today the poor in India are an awakened lot. They are becoming aware of their oppression and marginalization and are able to identify their causes and organize their resistance. They have developed tools of analysis and strategies for combat. The growing number of grassroots movements of the dalits, indigenous people, women, and agricultural laborers, and the movements against the multinational corporations, eco-destruction, big dams, and so on, testify to this spirit of resistance and the clamor for justice. A theology of life in the Indian experience is a theology of struggle and of change.

The churches need to have constant interaction with these awakened communities if Christian faith is to be a liberative and transformative power in these struggles. This requires trans-religious forms of fellowship and witness rooted in Christ, just as it means an inclusive and egalitarian theology. Yet this inclusiveness is qualified in that the criterion is commitment to the affirmation of life for all, with social transformation as a necessary means.

Church participation in this liberative process will draw from its own story, amid trans-religious forms of work together. The Bible is, after all, a story of God's continuous presence to change and transform everyday realities. Change is a sign of life. That "God Opts for the Poor" means God changes situations on behalf of the poor who are victims of power and dominance. The prophetic cry for justice and kindness toward the weak are thus strong motifs in the biblical tradition. And the gospel is a danger in history; it can "turn things upside down." This revolutionary dimension of biblical faith needs to be reclaimed by the churches in the present hermeneutical context of the poor and disregarded.

Historical study of the "Responses of the Indian Churches to Poverty and the Poor" found, however, that many churches were and are preoccupied with traditional forms of response—running orphanages, boarding homes, homes for the aged and the disabled, schools and colleges, hospitals and health services, and community development projects. These efforts are commendable, given the limitations within which the churches are placed. Yet they have ended up institutionalizing mission as something needing social-service expertise; and the churches, in spite of their long avowed concern for the poor, end up serving the victims of poverty rather than attacking poverty and its causes. Moreover, they maintain an urban, middle-class, elitist image despite the fact that the majority of Indian Christians are predominantly poor (dalits and tribals). Tendencies of class, caste, and gender domination have thus led the churches themselves to be less than Christian in faith, culture, and practice. Consequently, the church has not succeeded in leavening the social order. To be sure, many evangelical organizations have opted to work among the poor. But the content of the gospel they preach is deplorably insensitive to the crucial issues of life and its systemic evils. The results are often reactionary, helping the poor at best to survive poverty rather than to fight it.

Understanding the stance of many Indian churches means recognizing that by and large they have been guided by theological positions and scriptural interpretations influenced by politically, economically, and culturally dominant Western Christian society. These have a completely different value orientation and have proved to be nonpersonal, contemplative, and status quo-ist (tacitly supporting and justifying certain political and economic ideologies) while simultaneously promoting an individualistic pursuit of salvation, narrow denominationalism, and social indifference within the body of the church itself. Intensified environmental degradation and the ruthless destruction of people and cultures have accompanied these ideologies and theologies.

The experience of those who are struggling for life against powers and structures points to the need to develop nonhierarchical methods of doing theology, beginning with people and their predicaments. From there one goes on to understand God in relation to them—and not the other way. Such an approach can be a corrective to the strong anthropocentric element and the limited view of sin and salvation in traditional Christian theological thinking. Dalit and tribal realization of the sacramentality of the earth and earthly realities help to inculcate reverence for all life forms. The struggles and aspirations of those who are denied life call us to realize that life is a gift of God and no one has a monopoly over it. Earth and all that it holds constitute one great household or family of God.

The church, which claims to be concerned for the poor in the present context of increasing poverty, has to address the causes of poverty. Many other religious groups, social and political organizations express "concern" for the poor. What is expected of the church's solidarity with the poor is its ability to present itself as a concrete model of an alternative community the poor are looking for and are a part of. It is a Eucharistic community signifying the promised world in which all are equal, and in which nobody is denied.

The earth too is a Eucharistic reality. Like the Eucharistic bread, the earth too needs to be seen as the bread of life that God breaks for the whole world. The church within ecumenical Earth is essentially an alternative community of hope. This community character, which has been lost owing to the kind of institutionalization the church has taken in India, has to be reclaimed. To that end, the Indian TOL case studies show the following areas as those needing special attention: First, our ecclesiological notions are bathed in Western anthropocentrism, individualism, institutionalism, and denominationalism. The increasing fragmentation and polarization of society further necessitate the task of rediscovering what it means to be "church" in a country like India. Second, traditional theological education on the subcontinent is geared to training an individual to be the leader of a religious community. This notion of ministry is obsolete. The church is a community of people called together for witness and service. Concentrating all efforts and energy on individual leaders is a serious contradiction of the essence of the church as a community of people. Lay training, extension education, training for special ministries, and clerical training should each have its place. Third, denominational identities and theologies are irrelevant for the poor, particularly in a pluralistic society like India. Moreover, the primary concern of denominational theologies is to inculcate loyalty to church traditions and obedience to authority. A trans-denominational form of ecumenical Christian existence is urgent and necessary to identify and combat all forms of marginalization, or the abuse of power, as well as to discover afresh the meaning of "ecclesia" in relation to the vision of the kingdom counter to the increasing fragmentation of the human community and threats to life on earth.

Sokoni

The design for the culminating event of the TOL process was inspired by *sokoni,* the Swahili word for the traditional African market, which still is a lively place not only for the exchange of goods, but also for communication and sharing of information and ideas. [14] The aim of the culminating conference was to create a truly ecumenical space that would help participants listen to the stories of others, learn through experiencing commonalities and differences, and grow together across boundaries, sharing life with life. Unlike most international ecumenical gatherings, the setting itself—a circle of thatched huts without walls near Nairobi, Kenya—encouraged interaction and reminded the participants of the "circle of life" as a powerful symbol for the life-giving and life-sharing energy of the Holy Spirit.

Even more important, the majority of the participants were Kenyans. Their expectations, participation, and culture provided a coherent framework for the process of sharing. It was this presence and influence of the best traditions of African culture that informed and shaped the spirit of the meeting, and made all the difference. Instead of decontextualizing the individual experiences in order to compare them on an abstract level, those coming from abroad were asked to recontextualize their contributions, making them relevant for the Kenyan context. The local became the lens for discussing and interpreting the global.

Too often global structures and, in consequence, the dominant processes that are shaped in and by the North, attract all the attention and carry all the weight. Too little space is given to vital alternatives that exist in different parts of the world, and there is too little energy to move beyond concepts and really engage in common practices grounded in local cultures that are meaningful and convincing to the people.

Sokoni became the symbol and clearest expression of the TOL process and spirit. There it became obvious how much the World Council of Churches depends on a vital web of churches and ecumenical groups, committed to serve and to proclaim God's compassionate love to all humankind and the whole creation. The strength of the ecumenical movement depends on functioning linkages between churches all around the world, ecumenical groups, and others who are concerned about just relationships between human beings and sustainable ways of living on earth. So far, these linkages form a thin and fragile web. It is, therefore, paramount that the WCC continues to develop and strengthen its capacity to nurture, sustain, and expand this web. Sokoni served this purpose.

Margot Kaessmann, reporting on sokoni to the Central Committee of the WCC in September 1997, said:

> Ecclesiologically the Sokoni has been a powerful symbol to me: a church where you cannot close the door. We were in a round house! The minister sitting next to the street child, the refugee women from Africa next to the professor of theology from the USA. All sitting in an open circle, no hierarchy possible and anybody can join. The circle has no limits and no possibilities of exclusion. The experience was so deep because people did not present papers but talked about their lives. It was a living theology, theology of life. . . . There is an ecclesiogenesis when people talk about their pain, about poverty and violence, about denial of human rights, about war and destruction. There is the vision of the church being the place for their stories, their experience and in sharing, new energy for life would grow. In telling and re-telling the stories of the God of Life; of Jesus giving his own life so that all may live—the biblical message as the foundation of that church . . .[15]

This vision is a direct challenge to the churches themselves. Their community, their being the body of Christ, their essence is threatened:

- if they are not a true community of women and men
- if the poor are not at its center;
- if we cannot speak about those essentials of life;
- if children and youth are silenced;
- if violence occurs even within churches and Christian communities.

So it seems that inclusiveness, participation, truth as a precondition for reconciliation, a look at history that includes the marginalized, and mutual accountability are at the center of an ecclesiological approach like that. In the Study on Transnational Corporations of the '70s, the WCC once claimed to challenge the transnationality of companies with the transnationality of the ecumenical movement. Today I think we should challenge the globalization of economy and politics with the solidarity of Christians around the world, of people of faith around the world. The church of Christ overcomes all boundaries of class, gender, nation, ethnic group. It is a true community valuing life.[16]

AN ALTERNATIVE WAY OF THEOLOGIZING

Theology of Life is not a new theology. In response to the changing context of globalization, TOL develops an alternative way of theologizing—with experiences of the poor and marginalized at the center and with the goal of transformation.[17] This was emphasized by participants gathered from every continent at a consultation on Theology of Life convened in New York City in April 1998, jointly organized by the Union Theological Seminary (New York) and Unit III of the WCC. The choice of the place was guided by the awareness that faculty and students at Union are struggling with many of the same issues of inclusion, racism, economic inequity, and differences of interpretation and language within their own community. New York's radical polarities, from the communities of Harlem to the world's financial center at Wall Street, focus the tensions and asymmetries of the world at large like a magnifying glass in one spot. Summarizing the lessons learned in the Theology of Life Program, the participants in this consultation stated:

- Theology of Life de-centers Christianity and rereads Bible, theology, ecclesiologies, and church practices.
- Theology of Life entails a vision of ecumenical Earth (*oikos*) as an alternative to the project of globalization. The goal is the up-building of just and sustainable communities (*oikodome*).
- Theology of Life is attentive to the life-giving practices in the different communities. It emerges from the social and religious practices of communities and aims at deeper community. It is deeply rooted in a spirituality growing from the life of people.

Opportunities to listen to the stories of others and learn through differences in the ecumenical space are of high value in the present context of globalization. Such processes enable the laity and the clergy to discern their situation and understand the many complex ways in which different contexts are linked together and transformed by the influence of the prevailing economic system shaped by the political and cultural dominance of the most powerful nations, organizations, and groups.

In a situation where the economic and political systems dominate societies and colonize the everyday life of the people, cultural and religious narratives and symbols are in danger of losing their power to shape the relationships of the people and the basic aspects of their lives. They die or just survive in spaces gradually unlinked from or competing with global society. Our approach to such threatening economic globalization is to create safe spaces for sharing stories that affirm life, and to grapple with issues of patriarchal power, cultural domination, political oppression, economic injustice, or environmental destruction in ways that are inter-contextually, interculturally inclusive.

A process of transformation in the given global context depends on linking prophetic and visionary practices with cultural or counter-cultural narratives and symbols, so as to interpret the story of Christ and to embody the focal practices of Christian faith appropriately in each given locale. Transformation also requires the interaction of people representing different social and cultural contexts in order to get clarity about the common direction to go and how to move forward together.

Churches and ecumenical groups in different places need to challenge each other, to agree on a contract to journey together for a while (covenant), and to hold each other mutually accountable on the way. It is therefore understandable that the TOL program has emphasized the link between symbols, narratives, and practices in the life of a community. TOL case studies have explored the culturally specific configurations of these linkages and how they function in a given context, such as among dalits, women, and tribals in India.

Confronted—as an inescapable consequence of globalization—with a bewildering plurality of worldviews and values, an increasingly complex social life, and the hybridization of cultures and nature, the church's spiritual symbols are in danger of either being demonized or losing their power to interact in positive ways with narratives and practices of people and their communities. Religious symbols, stories, and practices are important for the formation and identity of a community that values cultural and natural diversity, transcending a homogenized environment. This is also a two-way process. An enriched cultural and natural context influences the interpretation of religious symbols, narratives, and practices and thus prompts a reexamination of the community's place and members' roles in the world. We are learning more about this in studies on gospel and culture and in contributions by feminist and womanist theologians.[18]

In their own 1997 evaluation of the Theology of Life program, the Decade of the Churches in Solidarity with Women and other areas of programmatic work, WCC Unit III commissioners highlighted the emerging style of ecumenical work:

> Essentially this style of ecumenical work is one in which churches, and movements, learn from one another, with the WCC as a vehicle for deepening and broadening their exchange and taking new or enhanced initiatives. . . . Most simply put this style of work is essentially *a space and a method* conducive to building up local and regional cultures of life and articulating theologies indigenous to them. The media may be storytelling, personal witness, Bible study and worship, analysis and reflection, drama, songs, music, dance, exhibits, or other forms. Substantively, the direction overall is a decentralized one that nonetheless includes global perspectives, that seeks a downward distribution of economic, social and political power, and that encourages a heightened status for all forms of life, in, with, and before God.[19]

In all of this, let us remember that the ultimate concern of Theology of Life is not the church as such but the kingdom to which the church witnesses. Discourse about the meaning of God's reign keeps us thinking in a "hermeneutic of the household" about the future of Earth and human beings.[20] The task amid the current fragmentation of human community is to identify and combat all forms of marginalization or abuses of power, and to discover afresh the meaning of ecclesia guided by the biblical vision of God's Commonwealth, which emphasizes God's liberating purpose and option for the poor. Toward this end, the TOL approach focuses on the experiences of marginalized communities and their life-giving practices, including new uses of symbols in liturgy and theology to affirm life. This fosters a reexamination of church life and witness in terms of how to live on earth with dignity in just and sustainable communities.

Boundary crossing to encounter peoples' stories from the underside of history is essential for learning to worship, work, and play in solidarity with the disregarded many. To practice faith and to do theology in new ways that address globalization's contradictions and embody community in solidarity with real struggles for life, church bodies of all kinds, from congregations to theological schools, must be closely linked with the places and people where they are based. They must seek a "secular *koinonia* in Christ" (M. M. Thomas's phrase) through social witness that is trans-religious, while remaining deeply rooted in Christian confession. The criterion for such inclusiveness is affirmation of life for all; the objective is to liberate theology, faith, and ethics for the liberation of the world.

6

Global Interdependence, the Earth Charter, and Christian Faith

Steven C. Rockefeller

THIS ESSAY EXPLORES THE SIGNIFICANCE OF GLOBAL INTERDEPENDENCE and the Earth Charter for the evolving self-understanding of the Christian church, with special reference to the church's relationship to the larger human family and the community of life as a whole. The essay begins with some brief general comments on the current world situation and the need for ethics and religion with a planetary consciousness. Over the past decade there has been considerable discussion about global ethics or what Pope John Paul II in his recent encyclical calls "planetary ethics."[1] It is also important to consider the meaning of the new emerging planetary consciousness for religion in general and for Christianity in particular.

After a ten-year worldwide conversation, a final version of the Earth Charter was approved and released by the Earth Charter Commission in March 2000. The remainder of the essay is a discussion of the nature and purpose of the Earth Charter initiative and its ethical and religious significance.

THE WORLD SITUATION, GLOBAL ETHICS, AND RELIGION

The Earth Charter project is part of the worldwide movement to create and implement a new global ethics. What drives the global ethics movement is the conviction that humanity has arrived at a critical moment in its evolutionary history when our survival and future well-being are dependent upon an ability to develop and to live in accordance with shared ethical values. The challenge is to build a world civilization of many nations, diverse cultures, and different races founded on common ethical principles, including, for example, mutual respect, justice, compassion, gender equality, participatory democracy, economic equity, tolerance, environmental protection, cooperation, and peace.

The urgent need for global ethics involves at least three interrelated factors. First, we live in a world today characterized by rapid change, increasing globalization, and growing interdependence. Our interdependence is ecological, economic, social, and political. Second, the problems we face threaten the foundations of world security. The future of the human species and the larger community of life on Earth is in doubt if human beings cannot address such problems as global warming, biodiversity loss, environmental degradation, depletion of resources, poverty, the growing disparities between rich and poor, violent conflict, the proliferation of nuclear weapons, and the rapid rise in human numbers. Third, the most serious problems we face are big, complex, and interrelated, and they can be managed only in and through worldwide cooperation with holistic thinking and integrated approaches. Partnerships must be formed that are interdisciplinary, cross-sectoral, cross-cultural, and international. Such alliances are needed at all levels of governance. Individuals, families, religious organizations, civil society, private corporations, governments, and multilateral organizations all have essential roles to play.

In a rapidly changing interdependent world where survival and well-being depend upon intelligent and compassionate collaboration, global ethics are required. Only with commitment to a planetary ethics that is inclusive and integrated can we fulfill our responsibilities to each other, the larger community of life, and future generations.

Global interdependence and the emergence of a planetary civilization present a new and difficult challenge for Christianity and the other religions. This can be briefly explained as follows. First of all, religion addresses fundamental human needs. Anthropologists find language, tool making, and religion to be universal characteristics of human societies. Modern secular societies that have tried to suppress religious concerns and to eliminate religion have not succeeded.

Second, every great civilization has produced its own distinctive forms of religious and ethical consciousness. Some might challenge this statement with reference to modern Western civilization. Yet a good argument can be made that the industrialized world is not fully developed, and it is made up of societies in search of a spiritual center. Third, the major world religions have their origins in different geographical regions of the planet and in separate civilizations. Each emerged as the predominant religious expression of a unique culture. In this sense, all religions are historically conditioned, each in a different way.

Now a new planetary civilization is beginning to emerge. The communications, transportation, and economic systems that are creating this global society are the product of the expansion and development of industrial-technological society. In order for the new planetary civilization and global consciousness to blossom forth and fully develop, it too must generate an ethical and religious awareness consistent with its geographical, intellectual, social, and economic situation. The global ethics movement and the Earth Charter are part of the quest for a spirituality and ethics adequate to the challenge of building a planetary civilization made up of diverse cultures in an age of advanced technology and increasing interdependence. The objective is to give to the emerging global consciousness the spiritual depth—the soul—needed to build a just and peaceful world community and to protect the integrity of Earth's ecological systems. In and through this process, the modern world created by science, technology, and industrialization has an opportunity to find its spiritual center and to realize its evolutionary potential and historical destiny.

In making these observations, the intent is not to recommend creation of a new religion. The hope is that each of the religions will adopt a planetary consciousness that involves awareness of global interdependence, acceptance of religious diversity, and commitment to promotion of shared values and interreligious cooperation in pursuit of world community. This requires that religious organizations will, if they have not already done so, abandon religious exclusivism and imperialistic religious ambitions. A religion transformed by a planetary religious awareness will embrace an ethic of respect for other traditions and an openness to learn from others while remaining faithful to its own particularity. It will seek the divine as the spiritual center of the greater community of life and the emerging global civilization. It will involve a world-affirming and life-affirming orientation as distinct from a world-denying otherworldly outlook. It will pursue spiritual disciplines that emphasize the quest for purity of heart. It will find expression in and through a practical ethic of respect for Earth and all life, love, compassion, justice, tolerance, environmental protection, and peace.

Most of the basic elements of such a pluralistic religious orientation can be found somewhere in the teachings and traditions of the major world religions. This is certainly true of the Christian tradition. The urgent need is to identify, elevate, and develop these ideas and values and to free them from ideas and values inconsistent with them. For example, teachings that support intolerance, religious exclusivism, narrow nationalism, racism, ethnic hatred, sexism, or the view that nature is merely a collection of resources to be exploited should be rejected as inauthentic whatever their source. In and through such a process of reflecting critically on its traditions and reconstructing them, each of the religions will in its own unique way move toward realizing the ideal of a fully evolved religion. The world will then be blessed with Buddhist, Christian, Hindu, Islamic, and Jewish forms of a planetary ethical and religious consciousness. The process is already well under way in many religious communities, but the resistance is also strong.

No religion can accomplish the task of transformation by itself. It requires engagement with the larger world, if for no other reason than that a major part of the task is identifying shared ethical values and cooperating in the work of building a world community beyond all the boundaries of faith and culture. This requires dialogue and collaboration with other faith traditions, the sciences, and secular culture. Becoming a religion with a planetary consciousness also means developing a new respect for and intimacy with Earth, our planetary home, and with the animals, plants, and ecological systems with which we are linked in the web of life.

THE EARTH CHARTER INITIATIVE, 1987–2000

The spirit of the Earth Charter initiative is consistent with the reconstruction of religious goals and ideals that has just been described. Moreover, the international Earth Charter consultation process and the Earth Charter document itself can contribute to the growth of religions with a planetary consciousness and pluralistic orientation. By way of introduction to the Earth Charter, it is useful to consider briefly the goals and history of the project.[2]

In recent years, the basic objectives of the international Earth Charter movement have been four:

- to promote a worldwide dialogue on shared values and global ethics.
- to draft an Earth Charter that sets forth a succinct and inspiring vision of fundamental ethical principles for a sustainable way of life.
- to circulate the Earth Charter throughout the world as a people's treaty that can be used as an educational tool and a guide to building a just, sustainable, and peaceful world.
- to seek endorsement of the Earth Charter by the United Nations General Assembly in the year 2002.

A brief historical account will explain how the Earth Charter initiative has endeavored to realize these goals.

The original proposal to create an Earth Charter that would clarify fundamental principles of environmental protection and sustainable development may be found in *Our Common Future,* the 1987 report of the UN World Commission on Environment and Development (WCED).[3] Representatives from government, nongovernmental organizations (NGOs), and religious groups worked to secure adoption of an Earth Charter during the United Nations Conference on Environment and Development (UNCED), the Rio Earth Summit, in 1992. The time was not right. Agreement was reached on the Rio Declaration, which is a valuable document, but it does not contain the breadth of vision required for an Earth Charter. In 1994, a new Earth Charter initiative was launched under the leadership of Maurice Strong, secretary general of UNCED and chairman of the Earth Council; Mikhail Gorbachev, president of Green Cross International, with the support of Jim MacNeill, secretary general of WCED; and Ruud Lubbers, Prime Minister of the Netherlands. Ambassador Mohamed Sahnoun of Algeria, a member of WCED, became the first director of this new Earth Charter project.

During the years 1995 and 1996, extensive research was conducted in the fields of international law, science, religion, and ethics in preparation for the drafting of the Earth Charter. The Earth Council, which had been formed after the Rio Earth Summit by Maurice Strong to advance implementation of Agenda 21, and many other partner organizations conducted

Earth Charter consultations throughout the world. The consultation process began with an international conference at the Peace Palace in The Hague in May of 1995. Representatives from thirty countries and more than seventy organizations participated in The Hague conference.

Early in 1997, the Earth Council and Green Cross International formed an Earth Charter Commission to give oversight to the process. The membership of the commission is representative of the different regions of the world. A secretariat for the commission was established at the Earth Council in Costa Rica under the leadership of the council's executive director, Maximo Kalaw of the Philippines. An international drafting committee was created and the drafting process began. In March 1997, a Benchmark Draft of the Earth Charter was issued by the commission at the conclusion of the Rio+5 Forum held in Rio de Janeiro. The Rio+5 Forum, which was attended by more than five hundred representatives of nongovernmental organizations and national councils of sustainable development, was part of a worldwide review of progress toward sustainable development since the Rio Earth Summit. Intensive consultations on the text of the Earth Charter were held during the six days of the forum. The Benchmark Draft provided a new focus for the ongoing international dialogue on the Earth Charter.

During the years 1997 and 1998, numerous conferences and meetings on the text of the Benchmark Draft were held in all regions of the world. An Earth Charter internet website was created by the Earth Council (www.earthcharter.org). National Earth Charter committees were formed in thirty-five different countries. In the United States, the secretariat for Earth Charter USA was established at the Center for Respect of Life and Environment in Washington, D.C. In December 1998, representatives from twenty-four national Earth Charter committees gathered for a six-day Earth Charter Continental Congress of the Americas in Cuiabá, Mato Grosso, Brazil. Some groups drafted national and regional Earth Charters as part of their contribution to the consultation process and the Earth Charter movement. Comments and recommendations on ways to improve the text of the Earth Charter were forwarded to the drafting committee, which circulated revised versions of the Earth Charter for further comment during 1998. Gradually Benchmark Draft II took form.

Early in 1999, a special international drafting meeting was held to complete work on Benchmark Draft II. This meeting included representatives from Argentina, Australia, Brazil, Canada, Costa Rica, Germany, the Philippines, Pakistan, Russia, and the United States with contributing members in India, Kenya, and The Netherlands. In April, Benchmark Draft II was formally released by the Earth Charter Commission. The commission also called for a continuation of the international consultation process throughout 1999. A two-week internet conference on the new text, which was organized by the Earth Council, attracted participants from seventy-eight countries and three hundred universities.

Numerous translations of the Earth Charter text were completed and Earth Charter dialogues involving both experts and representatives from grassroots communities were conducted in many countries. The number of national Earth Charter committees grew to forty-five. During October 1999, representatives from these national committees participated with the drafting committee in a ten-day online conference that focused on the text of the document. In December the drafting committee held a three-day meeting in Cape Town, South Africa, with representatives of national committees from Africa and the Middle East. Presentations and workshops on the Earth Charter were conducted at the Parliament of the World's Religions, which was also meeting at this time in Cape Town. In January 2000, another special international drafting meeting was held in an effort to finish the document. Meeting at the UNESCO headquarters in Paris in mid-March, the Earth Charter Commission carefully reviewed and refined the text in the light of the international discussion. The final version of the Earth Charter was issued on March 24. The Commission, however, has reserved the right to make adjustments in the text, if after four or five years there are very compelling reasons to do so.

Participation and collaborative decision making are Earth Charter values, and the Earth Charter drafting process was designed to be an expression of these values. It has extended over a ten-year period and has involved several hundred organizations and thousands of individuals. It is the most open and participatory process ever to have occurred in connection with the preparation of an international document. The leaders of the Earth Charter initiative considered the process to be as important as the final product. In and through it, more and more people have been involved in the worldwide dialogue on global ethics and Earth Charter values. In addition, by participating in the deliberations that were part of the drafting process, individuals and groups have developed a sense of ownership of the Earth Charter, which is essential if the document is to become an effective instrument of change.

As the formal drafting process began in 1997, there was general agreement on a set of criteria for the proposed Earth Charter. It was established that the charter should be: a declaration of fundamental ethical principles for environmental conservation and sustainable development; composed of principles of enduring significance that are widely shared by people of all races, cultures, religions, and ideological traditions; relatively brief and concise; a document with a holistic perspective and an ethical and spiritual vision; composed in language that is inspiring, clear, and uniquely valid and meaningful in all languages; and a statement that adds significant new dimensions of value to what has already been articulated in relevant documents.

The Earth Charter Commission made a decision to draft the charter first and foremost as a people's treaty rather than as an intergovernmental instrument for two reasons. First, during the 1990s most state governments were preoccupied with the promotion of economic growth, and they failed to meet the challenge of sustainable development as defined by Agenda 21 at the Rio Earth Summit. They were in no mood to embrace new and stronger ethical commitments. It was clear that an intergovernmental drafting process would not produce a strong document. Second, the end of the Cold War resulted in a renewal of civil society in many nations and the emergence of an increasingly influential global civil society, involving a worldwide network of NGOs linked together by the new communications technology. This global civil society can play a critical role in leading the world toward sustainable ways of living and can put much-needed pressure on governments and corporate leaders to cooperate in this endeavor. In order to be effective, however, individual citizens and civil society at large need a shared vision of fundamental values to guide planning, policy making, and action. With these considerations in mind, the Earth Charter Commission decided not to turn the drafting of the charter over to an intergovernmental process.

This decision has not altered the hope that the Earth Charter will be endorsed eventually by the United Nations General Assembly. The year 2002, which is the tenth anniversary of the Rio Earth Summit, has been set as the year for UN endorsement. If the Earth Charter is endorsed by the UN General Assembly, it will enhance the stature of the charter as a soft law document and increase its influence on governments and international law.[4]

In this regard, the Earth Charter has been drafted in coordination with a hard law treaty that is designed to provide an integrated legal framework for all environmental and sustainable development law and policy. This Draft International Covenant on Environment and Development is being prepared by the Commission on Environmental Law at the World Conservation Union (IUCN). The Earth Charter provides an ethical foundation for the covenant. The Draft Covenant was presented at the United Nations in 1995 and is being revised in the light of comments received from governments. The revised covenant will be presented to the United Nations again in the near future in the hope that it will generate the governmental interest and support required to start formal international negotiations on the document.

The ideas and principles in the Earth Charter are drawn from a variety of sources. The Earth Charter is influenced by the new scientific worldview and the discoveries of contemporary cosmology, physics, evolutionary biology, and ecology. It builds upon more than fifty international law declarations and treaties related to environment and development that have been adopted over the past twenty-seven years since the UN Stockholm Conference on the Human Environment. It also builds on more than 150 nongovernmental declarations, charters, and people's treaties issued in the North and the South since Stockholm. Many of these documents reflect the thinking and work of religious groups and the charter endeavors to give expression to a number of universal religious values.

The charter draws on the ground-breaking work done in the field of environmental and sustainable development ethics by contemporary philosophers and religious thinkers. It reflects the influence of the movements associated with human rights, democracy, gender equality, civil society, disarmament, and peace. It builds on the major UN summit conferences on the environment, children, human rights, population, women, social development, and the city held during the 1990s. The charter has also been developed in the light of the practical experience and insights of those groups that have successfully pursued sustainable ways of living.

As the broad range of sources upon which the Earth Charter is based suggest, the charter is not just a document about humanity's relations with the environment. It has been constructed with the understanding that humanity's environmental, economic, social, political, and spiritual problems are interrelated and can be effectively addressed only with integrated global solutions. All the principles in the Earth Charter are related to environmental issues, but they do not all deal exclusively with environmental issues. One of the distinctive characteristics of the Earth Charter in comparison with earlier environmental declarations like the World Charter for Nature (1982) is the breadth of its vision and its integrated approach. It provides a new framework for thinking about environmental protection, human rights, development, and peace as well as planning and decision making in civil society, business, and government.

THE STRUCTURE AND FIRST FOUR PRINCIPLES OF THE EARTH CHARTER

There are, of course, many different ways that one could draft an Earth Charter. Everyone involved has agreed that the preamble and principles should be as clear and succinct as possible. Yet there have been divergent views on just what this means.

Many people favor a very short text with a brief preamble and no more than twelve concise principles. Others strongly argue for a more substantial document like a UN declaration that includes guidelines for implementation. A very short charter would be more accessible to people and could be easily memorized. The problem with a short document is with what gets left out. The major challenges humanity faces are complex and interrelated and the ethical guidelines needed cannot in most cases be reduced to phrases of a few words like "think globally, act locally." In addition, many groups who feel marginalized and excluded from decision-making processes are particularly uncomfortable with the idea of a very short Earth Charter. They believe that those in positions of power will interpret the meaning of such a document as they will and there will be little if any opportunity for debate. These groups want the additional language and principles that qualify and clarify. There is another important consideration. Even though the IUCN Draft International Covenant spells out in considerable detail the practical implications of much of the Earth Charter, it may require many years of negotiation before governments reach agreement on the covenant. Therefore, the Earth Charter must be a document that can stand on its own.

In an effort to address these different concerns regarding the nature and length of the charter, a layered document has been designed with a Preamble, sixteen main principles, sixty-one supporting principles, and a conclusion entitled "The Way Forward." The sixteen principles with their supporting principles are divided into four parts so that the scope and structure of the Charter are easily understood. The structure is as follows:

Preamble

I. Respect and Care for the Community of Life (1–4)

II. Ecological Integrity (5–8)

III. Social and Economic Justice (9–12)

IV. Democracy, Nonviolence, and Peace (13–16)

The Way Forward

Part 1 contains four very broad principles that can be used as a short statement of the Earth Charter vision. (See the appendix for the text of the Earth Charter.)

- Respect Earth and life in all its diversity.
- Care for the community of life with understanding, compassion, and love.
- Build democratic societies that are just, participatory, sustainable, and peaceful.
- Secure Earth's bounty and beauty for present and future generations.

The drafting committee also prepared an abbreviated version of the Earth Charter that includes the preamble and the sixteen main principles only. It can be printed on one sheet of paper, front and back. A commentary on the Earth Charter is being prepared for those who may wish an in-depth interpretation of the text.

The first paragraph of the preamble introduces the major themes of the document. It affirms that humanity stands at a critical juncture in history, a time of both danger and new creative possibilities, when we must make choices that will have profound long-term consequences. The Charter is presented as a declaration of global interdependence and universal responsibility. In an interdependent world, everyone shares responsibility for the future well-being of the human family and the larger living world. Our responsibilities as human beings extend to the greater community of life of which we are a part, as well as to one another and future generations. This expanded sense of community and inclusive moral vision lie at the heart of the Earth Charter.

Paragraphs two through five of the preamble offer a rationale for the opening statement in the first paragraph. They briefly describe humanity's cosmological and ecological situation, the grave environmental and social problems facing the world, the choices before us, and the need for a new sense of universal responsibility or global citizenship. The concluding paragraph is a call for development of a vision of shared values that will serve as an ethical foundation for the emerging global community. The interdependent principles of the charter are introduced as a response to this need.

In the preamble, the Earth Charter principles are described as "interdependent principles for a sustainable way of life" that should function as "a common standard" by which the conduct of all individuals, institutions, and governments is "guided and assessed." The Earth Charter principles are to be viewed as providing a conception of sustainable community and sustainable development, and of what must be done to achieve it. This involves both promoting human development and well-being and protecting the integrity of Earth's ecological systems. This is consistent with the IUCN definitions of sustainable development as "improving the quality of human life while living within the carrying capacity of supporting ecosystems" and as "improving and maintaining the well-being of people and ecosystems."[5] The reference to a common standard by which conduct is to be "assessed" indicates that the Earth Charter can and should be used to measure and evaluate the progress of organizations and communities in achieving sustainability. It can be used to promote accountability.

The term *human development* has been used by the United Nations Development Programme to make clear that the goal of development is not economic growth as an end in itself.[6] The goal is full human development, which involves ecological, social, ethical, cultural, and spiritual as well as economic dimensions. Economic activity is to be seen as a means to human development in this wider sense. In many parts of the world, especially in the South, economic development that is equitable and sustainable is urgently needed.

With these considerations in mind, the Earth Charter embraces an integrated understanding of sustainable living and sustainable development that includes commitment to respect for human rights and fundamental freedoms, justice, gender equality, economic equity, eradication of poverty, human empowerment, participatory democracy, transparency in governance, and peace as well as environmental protection. Sustainability requires implementation of all the Earth Charter principles. So conceived, sustainable development is a vision of a better future for all and a universal goal. Moreover, without such a broad integrated understanding of sustainability, there is no possibility of achieving it.

The title of part 1 underscores the fundamental ethical significance of the attitudes and values associated with "respect and care." The first principle of the Earth Charter, "Respect Earth and life in all its diversity," is the foundation principle for the other three general principles that follow and for all the other principles in the Earth Charter. Protecting the vitality, diversity, and beauty of Earth and building just, sustainable, and peaceful communities begins with an attitude of respect—for oneself, other persons, other cultures and religions, other life forms, Earth, and the larger cosmic whole of which we are a part.

A good argument can be made that the most fundamental cause of the environmental problems that afflict the planet is the lack of respect for nature at large that pervades modern industrialized cultures. The nonhuman world is commonly treated as merely an object or a thing to be used—a collection of resources to be exploited. It is viewed as having utilitarian value only. In order to address this problem, a profound attitudinal change is required. This involves recognition and affirmation of the interdependence and the intrinsic value of all beings.[7] The first principle of the Earth Charter highlights and addresses this fundamental issue.

By affirming respect for "Earth" as well as "life in all its diversity," principle 1 invites respect for the planet as a whole and for all the different systems that sustain the biosphere, including those that make up the geosphere, atmosphere, and hydrosphere. Oceans, rivers, grasslands, and mountains as well as trees and wolves warrant respect. In addition, the principle of respect for life applies to relations with persons as well as to relations with other life forms. The sense of ethical responsibility in relations between persons and peoples flows from respect. An attitude of respect is the foundation upon which human-rights law is built.

Some religious thinkers prefer to use the word *reverence* rather than *respect,* and they call for reverence for life.[8] A good definition of reverence is respect tinged with awe. Respect for life becomes reverence for life when there is an awakening to the sacredness of life. A reverence for life is fundamental to a religious planetary consciousness. The concluding sentence of the Earth Charter makes reference to "the awakening of a new reverence for life."

The second, third, and fourth principles deal with the three major spheres of relationship and ethical responsibility. These three spheres involve relations between human beings and the larger community of life, relations among human beings in society, and relations between present and future generations. Principles 2, 3, and 4 develop the meaning of the declaration of responsibility in the last sentence of the preamble's first paragraph: "It is imperative that we, the peoples of Earth, declare our responsibility to one another, the greater community of life, and future generations."

The Earth Charter understands human beings to be interdependent members of the greater community of life and principle 2 asserts that we consequently have a responsibility to "care for" the larger living world with "understanding, compassion, and love." In emphasizing "caring for" the community of life as humanity's fundamental responsibility in relation to it, the Earth Charter follows the IUCN World Conservation Strategy published in *Caring for the Earth* (1991). In harmony with the teachings of the world's great spiritual traditions, the Earth Charter recognizes the fundamental importance of love and compassion for the healing of Earth and social renewal. The reference to "understanding" as well as "compassion and love" is an expression of the realization that in order to care for Earth and one another effectively, our thinking and action must reflect an integration of the head and the heart. Feelings of love and compassion are essential but not sufficient. They need to be joined with and informed by intelligence and knowledge.

TWELVE ADDITIONAL MAIN PRINCIPLES

The twelve main principles in parts 2, 3, and 4 seek to set forth the major values and goals that follow from affirmation of the first four broad principles. These twelve organizing principles, numbers 5 through 16, deal with interrelated ecological, economic, social, political, and cultural issues.

Part 2 on ecological integrity contains four principles that set forth ethical guidelines and strategies for protecting and restoring Earth's ecological integrity and constructing systems of production and consumption that are environmentally sustainable. Principle 5 with its six supporting principles highlights the critical importance of preserving the natural systems that sustain life and Earth's biodiversity. Principle 6 combines in an innovative way the principle of prevention and the precautionary principle. The principle of prevention emphasizes that the only sound method of environmental protection is avoidance of serious harm rather than attempts to remedy or compensate for harm. Two international lawyers,

Alexander Kiss and Dinah Shelton, have appropriately called the principle of prevention "the Golden Rule for the environment both for ecological and economic reasons."[9] They explain: "It is frequently impossible to remedy environmental injury. Even if the damage is reparable, the costs of rehabilitation are prohibitive." The precautionary principle is designed to ensure prevention of serious or irreversible harm. Principles 6.a and 6.b clarify its meaning and link it with the polluter-pays principle, which is the best way to ensure compliance.

Principle 7 focuses on safeguarding Earth's regenerative capacities by developing sustainable patterns of production, consumption, and human population growth. The Earth Charter deals with the issues of economic development and population in the same principle because this approach provides a balanced way of addressing two fundamental issues that often receive differing emphasis in the North and the South. Representatives from the North often stress the urgent need to stabilize population in the South in the face of unprecedented increases that are putting extraordinary pressures on ecological and social systems. Representatives from the South point out that Northern patterns of production and consumption are the major cause of environmental degradation. Both unsustainable economic development and ongoing growth in the global human population threaten the foundations of world security and must be harmonized with Earth's carrying capacity. Addressing these critical issues together in one principle has won wide international support and is the approach used in the Rio Declaration and the IUCN Draft Covenant. Principle 8 focuses on the critical role of scientific and other forms of knowledge in designing systems for producing goods and services in a sustainable fashion.

Some further discussion of how the Earth Charter deals with population concerns may be helpful. In addressing the issue of sustainable patterns of human reproduction, the Earth Charter does not refer to population control or population stabilization. There are reasons for avoiding this language. The UN conferences on population and women held in Cairo (1994) and Beijing (1995) concluded that an emphasis on population stabilization focuses attention on women's fertility, which is not helpful, because it does not get at the real root of the problem. At these gatherings a consensus was reached that the most effective way to address mounting population pressures is to focus on gender equality and equity and on the empowerment of women through education, access to health care, and economic opportunity. Cairo and Beijing also emphasized the special importance of universal access to reproductive health care and the right of all women and men to reproductive health.

The Earth Charter's approach to the problems created by population growth follows the Cairo and Beijing consensus. Principle 7.e addresses the universal need for reproductive health care and responsible reproduction. Principle 7 also makes clear that societies should design policies pertaining to human reproduction that respect human rights. Principle 11 in part 3 affirms the need for gender equality and should be read together with principle 7 as part of the Earth Charter strategy for dealing with concerns about population.

The use of language about reproductive rights and health is strongly opposed by some conservative Protestant and Roman Catholic groups, because they believe this language involves an endorsement of abortion. In the Benchmark Draft Earth Charter issued in 1997, there was a principle that read: "Secure the right to sexual and reproductive health, with special concern for women and girls." This is consistent with the language developed at Beijing. Yet its use in the Earth Charter was strongly opposed by some conservative religious groups. At issue is the way "reproductive health" is defined in the Beijing Platform.[10] Some groups argue that any use of the word *reproductive* in connection with health, health care, and rights implies acceptance of abortion. The problem was made more complex because some individuals and religious groups, who were not themselves opposed to the Earth Charter wording on reproductive health in the Benchmark Draft, were deeply concerned that their support for the Earth Charter might pull them into a fight over abortion. Therefore, they recommended deleting the principle on "the right to sexual and reproductive health," and they threatened to withdraw their support for the Earth Charter if this was not done.

There never has been an intention to insert in the Earth Charter a principle that takes a position for or against abortion. The language used in the Benchmark Draft was modified in an effort to avoid misunderstandings on this matter. The new language simply states: "Ensure universal access to health care that fosters reproductive health and responsible reproduction." Different cultures and communities may interpret the principles in the Earth Charter in different ways, but the principles focus attention on critical issues and frame the debate.

Part 3 focuses attention on social and economic justice as a fundamental dimension of sustainability. Principle 9 affirms the urgent need to eradicate poverty, which involves a dehumanizing condition that denies individuals and groups their fundamental human rights and freedoms. More than one billion people are trapped in poverty, which is both a cause and a consequence of environmental degradation. For all these reasons, the struggle to overcome poverty must be a major component of the effort to build a just, sustainable, and peaceful world in the twenty-first century.

Principle 10 calls for an economic system that promotes human development in an equitable as well as sustainable manner. The creation of an equitable global economy is fundamental to the prevention of poverty and a basic requirement of justice. If human development is to be equitable, major changes are required. Current patterns of production and consumption continue to widen the gap between rich and poor. Roughly 20 percent of the world's population consumes 86 percent of the benefits of development and the poorest 20 percent consume only 1.3 percent.[11]

Consistent with the conclusions of the UN Cairo and Beijing conferences on population and women, principle 11 affirms gender equality and equity as prerequisites for sustainable development. This principle has generated many debates in the course of the consultation process. Representatives of societies and religious groups with enduring patriarchal traditions often oppose inclusion of references to gender equality in the Charter. For example, a debate broke out on this subject during an Earth Charter dialogue at a conference on Islam and ecology, held at the Center for the Study of World Religions at Harvard Divinity School, with Muslims arguing both points of view. In addition, some women and men have opposed a principle on gender equality on the grounds that the Earth Charter should include only the most general principles and that it should avoid principles that focus on particular groups.

The Earth Charter Commission, however, firmly supports the international consensus reached at the recent UN conferences on population, women, and social development that gender equality and equity are a prerequisite for sustainable development and environmental protection. It has become clear that the success of any effort to mobilize people on the local level to care for the environment and to live sustainably depends to a significant degree on the empowerment of women and their full participation in the decision-making processes that shape economic, political, social, and cultural life.

Principle 12 addresses the most fundamental aspect of environmental justice, and it includes a call to end discrimination in all its forms. The principle recognizes that the quality of the environment has a major impact on the physical health and spiritual well-being of a people. Special recognition is given to the rights of indigenous peoples, whose fundamental human rights have been grossly violated for centuries and whose traditional practices often reflect a respect for Earth and other values consistent with sustainable living. Over the past decade wide support for such recognition has developed within the international community. Examples of this support may be found in a number of international declarations such as the Rio Declaration.

Part 4, which is entitled "Democracy, Nonviolence, and Peace," addresses concerns related to governance, education, and the building of a culture of peace that treats all living beings with respect and consideration. Principle 13, as well as principle 3, affirms political and social democracy as a universal human value. In this regard, the United Nations Commission on Human Rights adopted a resolution on "Promotion of the Right to Democracy," which affirms that "democracy, development, and respect for all human rights and fundamental freedoms are interdependent."[12] Principle 13 also highlights the importance of transparency and accountability in governance, the meaningful participation by all interested individuals and organizations in decision-making processes, and effective access to administrative and judicial procedures. Implementation of these principles is essential to the protection of the environment and human rights.

Universal education is fundamental to a healthy democratic society and to a genuinely liberating process of social transformation. Principle 14 calls for the creation of schools and other educational programs that provide all citizens with the knowledge, values, and skills required to live sustainably.

Building on principles 1 and 2, principle 15 makes clear that the Earth Charter extends respect and moral consideration to all living beings. It goes beyond existing international law, which recognizes in documents such as the World Charter for Nature (1982) and the Biodiversity Convention (1992) the intrinsic value of nonhuman species and the moral responsibility of people to protect endangered species but is silent on the moral standing of individual living beings apart from humans. In the spirit of nonviolence and a culture of peace, the Earth Charter emphasizes prevention of cruelty to animals and the minimizing of harm to other living beings.

In affirming humanity's moral obligations to other life, it must be kept in mind that the ethical responsibilities a person has in relation to other human beings are far more extensive than those a person has in relation to animals and plants. When these responsibilities conflict, hard choices have to be made, using intelligence and compassion as a guide. The Earth Charter does not use rights language to describe the responsibilities that human beings have in relation to nonhuman species, because there is no international consensus on the use of rights language in relation to animals and plants. The charter focuses on the more fundamental issue, which is the extension of ethical responsibility to the greater community of life.

Principle 16 is concerned with building a culture of peace, which has become a major theme of UNESCO and the worldwide peace movement. The Earth Charter views peace both as a goal of a sustainable society and as the way. The goal of peace is listed last in principle 3, and the principle on peace is the final main principle because achievement of enduring peace requires environmental protection, respect for human rights, democracy, and economic justice. It is also true that environmental protection, justice, and human development depend upon building a culture of peace that nurtures a spirit of compassion, tolerance, nonviolence, and solidarity. The values of respect for nature, freedom and justice, equitable human development, and peace are interdependent.

The last principle of the Earth Charter, 16.f, provides a definition of peace that is similar to the biblical understanding of *shalom*: "peace is the wholeness created by right relationships with oneself, other persons, other cultures, other life, Earth, and the larger whole of which all are a part." The Earth Charter principles begin with a call for respect for all life and culminate with a vision of a culture of peace in which people are able to become whole persons and develop liberating and healing relationships with each other and the larger living world.

The conclusion of the Earth Charter, entitled "The Way Forward," is a call to commitment and action. It envisions a new beginning made possible by both inner change—a change in attitudes and values—and a new partnership of civil society, business, and government in support of major social and economic transformations.

From the outset, the organizers and leaders of the new Earth Charter initiative have been in agreement that the Earth Charter should recognize the spiritual as well as ethical dimensions of humanity's environmental, economic, and social challenges. In line with this objective, the Earth Charter recognizes certain widely shared spiritual attitudes and values that support a sense of universal responsibility and that can sustain the human spirit in times of testing and trial. Among these attitudes and values are: reverence for the mystery of being; a sense of identification with and belonging to the larger whole; reverence for life; gratitude for the gift of life; hope; humility; caring, love and compassion; commitment to equity; appreciation of beauty; a concern for being more, not just having more; and a quest for peace.

A document like the Earth Charter cannot, of course, use the word *God* or refer to "the Creator" because there is not an international consensus regarding this language, even among religious people. Those who believe in God and a Creator, however, can give a theological interpretation of some of the language used in the charter. For example, the idea of "reverence for the mystery of being" (preamble) and the concept of "the larger whole of which all are a part" (principle 16.f) can refer to God as well as the cosmos and nature.

During the Rio+5 Forum in Brazil, a Christian newspaper reporter objected to the absence of a reference to God in the charter. A participant in the Forum responded by pointing out that the charter calls on everyone to be an instrument of peace and then asked: "Would not a person who pursues right relationship with the world along the lines of the Earth Charter definition of peace enjoy a good relationship with God?"

CONCLUSION:
CHRISTIANITY WITH A PLANETARY CONSCIOUSNESS

The effort to identify and define shared ethical values and to give them expression in a document like the Earth Charter is all part of the quest for what this essay has identified as religion with a planetary consciousness. The Earth Charter can be used as a valuable educational instrument by Christian communities exploring the ethical meaning of this new religious orientation. Moreover, the search for an authentic Christian expression of this outlook is leading the church to ask anew some fundamental questions.

Where is the living Christ, the Divine Logos, encountered today? Is the encounter limited by the boundaries of the institutional church? Is it wherever healing, wholeness, liberating relationships, and community are being realized?

Nowhere in the New Testament is the face of Jesus the Christ described. Do we not catch a glimpse of that face in the countenance of our brothers and sisters in moments of authentic relationship? Do we not behold something of the divine beauty in the wind and the waters and in the miracle of life revealed in plants and animals when we encounter the world with our whole being?

Where is the true universal church? Is it defined primarily by creeds and rituals? People do need concrete forms of worship that meet their special needs as historically conditioned persons. But is not the universal church and body of Christ found also in partnerships with all women and men of goodwill who seek purity of heart, justice, human empowerment, and peace? Are trees, wolves, and rivers part of the body of Christ?

Is the goal of the Christian life salvation as an individual separate from the world, or the healing and liberation of the one world of which we are all a part? Various brands of liberation theology, including ecotheology, have been encouraging adoption of the latter approach. The selfish individualism often encouraged by capitalism is in part a secularized version of doctrines of salvation that emphasize an atomic individualism and a dualism of self and world. There is an urgent need for a theology that affirms global interdependence and understands individual salvation to be closely linked to universal responsibility and ecological and social liberation. The work of many eco feminist theologians is a good example of theology moving in this direction. One could call it Christianity with a planetary awareness. Some may prefer a different name. The label is not important. What is critical is adoption of life-affirming spiritual attitudes and ethical values such as those being expressed in the Earth Charter.

The questions raised in this essay about planetary ethics, the living Christ, the universal church, and the meaning of salvation and liberation have far-reaching implications for the church's understanding of what it means to be a Christian and a religious person. Thinking through these questions in the context of the current world situation is a challenging task, but it is essential if the churches are to help individuals find wholeness and the world find justice, sustainability, and peace in the next century.

PART 3

ENVIRONMENTALLY ENGAGED

CHURCH AND COMMUNITY

7

Climate Change
and Ecumenical Work
for Sustainable Community

David G. Hallman

INTRODUCTION

The churches' involvement in the issue of climate change stems from our belief that God created and loves this world. We believe that God intends that humans, as an integral part of creation, should live in a wholesome relationship to the rest of creation so as not to cause such destruction that species, ecosystems, and indeed large numbers of people are threatened. The churches also see climate change as a profoundly ethical issue. It is being caused largely by the polluting emissions from rich industrialized countries that have accumulated in the atmosphere over the past 150 years, whereas the consequences will be suffered disproportionately by the poor of developing nations and by future generations. It is a problem of eco-justice.

The engagement of the ecumenical movement in the issue of and negotiations about climate change provides a model of churches working toward the realization of sustainable community. In particular, this ecumenical engagement:

- benefits from and contributes to a rich ecumenical history of conceptual stimulation and pragmatic action on sustainability;

- represents an integrative approach connecting theological reflection and action, ecclesiology and ethics, social and ecological justice, and the church at global, national, and local levels;
- demonstrates a credibility in its collective witness that goes beyond the modest scale of the church engagement;
- depends on collaborative and challenging relationships with secular organizations such as scientific bodies, nongovernmental organizations, and the United Nations; and
- provides a new opportunity for interfaith reflection and action.

OVERVIEW HISTORY OF ECUMENICAL ENGAGEMENT ON SUSTAINABLE COMMUNITY

More than a decade before the term *sustainable development* became popularized through the 1986 Brundtland Commission (World Commission on Environment and Development) the concept of sustainability was being articulated at a World Council of Churches (WCC) consultation of scientists, theologians, and economists in Bucharest in 1974.[1] This 1974 consultation was convened in response to the Club of Rome's report, *The Limits to Growth,* which sounded an alarm about how natural-resource depletion, pollution, and population growth was placing an intolerable strain on the Earth's resources.[2] What emerged out of the Bucharest discussion on the role of science and technology in the development of human societies was the articulation of "a concept called 'sustainability'—the idea that the world's future requires a vision of development that can be sustained in the long run, both environmentally and economically."[3] The consultation led to the WCC adopting a program on "just, participatory, and sustainable societies" (JPSS). The JPSS framework demonstrated the awareness of the need to link socioeconomic justice and ecological sustainability. This has been a recurring theme within the ecumenical community and has been a gift to the broader global community.

The just, participatory, and sustainable society framework was expanded in 1983 at the Vancouver Assembly of the WCC with the inauguration of the conciliar process on "justice, peace and integrity of creation" (JPIC). Though the churches have done quite a good job in stressing the linkages among these various global problems, we have had our share of debate within the ecumenical community about the relationship of socioeconomic justice and ecological sustainability. The 1990 WCC World Convocation on Justice, Peace and Integrity of Creation in Seoul and the lead-up to it stands out as one of the points in our history where this discussion was particularly vigorous. There were criticisms, particularly from persons involved in economic-justice work, that the rising priority on environmental concerns was a Northern and largely middle-class diversion of the churches' attention from the more critical concerns of hunger, poverty, and racial injustice. The Seoul JPIC Convocation did nonetheless take a significant step forward in the articulation of the ten affirmations that, together with the analyses on which they are based, provide a clear elaboration regarding, on the one hand, the interrelatedness of economic inequity, militarism, ecological destruction, and racial injustice and, on the other hand, the theological, ethical, and spiritual basis for affirming and sustaining life in its fullness.[4]

The UN Conference on Environment and Development (UNCED) held in Rio de Janeiro in June 1992 intensified ecumenical involvement in issues of sustainability and in interaction with the broader global community.[5] Along with representatives from other faith groups, the WCC was able to provide a substantial profile of religious communities at UNCED witnessing to our belief that the issues being addressed by the Earth Summit had ethical, spiritual, and theological dimensions that could not be ignored. (UNCED provided the initial conception of a theological resource that later resulted in the WCC book *Ecotheology: Voices from South and North*).[6]

More explicit work on the theme of sustainability was done in 1993 when the WCC-related Visser 't Hooft Memorial Consultation sponsored *Sustainable Growth: A Contradiction in Terms?*[7] That endeavor and the resulting booklet focused on the destructive and inequitable impact of a global economic system that emphasizes economic growth at all costs. The participants suggested that the term and concept of "sustainable development" was at risk of being eviscerated of its transformative potency by being expanded to include sustainable economic growth. In fact, this is precisely what we have seen in the documents that governments adopted at the Rio Earth Summit and most of the UN conferences since.[8] More recently, the WCC has begun using the concept of "sustainable community," seeing it as a more helpful image because of its focus on the nurturing of relationships within community which should be the intent of economic and social policies and practices.

Within this historical context, the ecumenical work on climate change has emerged as a specific focus for the broader concerns about the links between economics and environment. The WCC work has included support of regional workshops in regions around the world, consultations and resources that seek to analyze the issue from a theological and ethical perspective, advocacy at national levels and within the UN negotiations on climate change treaties, etc.[9]

AN INTEGRATIVE APPROACH

Ecumenical engagement with the issue of climate change began in 1988 at a consultation cosponsored by the World Council of Churches in cooperation with an environmental organization which brought together scientists, economists, politicians, environmentalists, development workers, and church representatives. Over the past ten years, this approach has become a pattern of integration with a number of dimensions.

Theological Reflection and Action

Theological reflection has been a regular element linked to education and advocacy work. Throughout the ecumenical community, there has been an exciting development of ecological theology and ethics over the past decade. My book *Ecotheology: Voices from South and North,* which brings together articles of twenty-five theologians and ethicists from around the world, demonstrates the richness of the conceptual reflection and action in developing countries as well as in industrialized nations.[10] The WCC work on climate change has drawn on this theological reflection in our consultations, resources, and advocacy statements made at national and UN levels. Not only has our advocacy and education been enriched by theology but conversely, we have been able to provide an opportunity for theologians to deepen their reflections by engaging them in consultations on climate change.

Ecclesiology and Ethics

For the most part, denominational divisions have not inhibited active cooperation on climate change as an issue of applied ethics. The participants in the international, regional, and national consultations have come from many Protestant and Anglican churches. Orthodox churches have been actively engaged in particular through a representative of the Ecumenical Patriarchate on the WCC core group directing the climate change work. The Ecumenical Patriarch himself endorsed the WCC-initiated petition campaign leading up to the 1997 UN Climate Conference in Kyoto and raised the churches' concerns about climate change with U.S. President Clinton during the Patriarch's U.S. visit in October 1997.

The major disappointment has been our inability to involve significantly the Roman Catholic Church. Because the Holy See is represented within the UN as a state, it has more direct access to the climate change negotiations than does the WCC, which participates in the category of nongovernmental organizations (NGOs). However, if my memory is accurate, the Holy See has not made any statement over the past ten years of UN negotiations, while the WCC has made numerous interventions as an NGO. Repeated approaches to the Vatican eventually led to a letter from the Vatican to national conferences of bishops in industrialized nations encouraging them to support the pre-Kyoto petition campaign in their country. At national levels, some Catholics have been engaged, particularly members of religious orders.

Social and Ecological Justice

Climate change connects ecological concerns with many aspects of socioeconomic justice. Responding to climate change raises major economic issues in terms of the impact of industrialization and development patterns. The international negotiations initially recognized that the responsibility for reducing greenhouse gas emissions lies primarily with the industrialized countries and that action on climate change should not limit the capacity of Southern countries to develop in order to meet basic needs of their people. This understanding is captured in the wording of the 1992 UN Framework Convention on Climate Change that refers to all parties having "common but differentiated responsibilities." Over the past few years, however, it has become increasingly clear that industrialized countries are not making significant progress in limiting emissions and the United States in particular has been actively and publicly pressing for larger developing nations such as India, China, and Brazil to also agree to commitments to limit emissions.

Ecumenical involvement in advocacy and education on climate change has reflected a strong solidarity position with peoples of the

South, particularly as represented through Southern churches and NGOs. The Pacific Conference of Churches (PCC) has issued some important statements on the dramatic implications of climate change for their countries, and the WCC has promoted the PCC statements widely, as well as supporting the intergovernmental organization, the Alliance of Small Island Countries (AOSIS). An Indian NGO, the Centre for Science and Environment, has produced some very critical analyses of aspects of the international negotiations (such as emission trading) that have been used by both the WCC-supported ecumenical consultations in India and by the WCC.

The Church at Global, Regional, National, and Local Levels

Ecumenical engagement on the issue of climate change has allowed for a dynamic interrelationship among churches at global, regional, national, and local levels. The WCC has been represented at all of the climate change negotiating sessions within the UN since 1989 monitoring the debates, participating in NGO strategy sessions, advocating with delegates from various countries, making statements in the plenary, and hosting ecumenical and interfaith religious services. The information and analysis garnered through this involvement has been shared with WCC member churches through educational resources, press releases, mailings to denomination offices, and nurturing a network of church activists around the world.

Regional ecumenical organizations in Africa, Latin America, Asia, and Europe have played a role by sponsoring consultations that have utilized WCC print, audiovisual, and human resources. The All Africa Conference of Churches (AACC) has organized creative, experiential workshops on environmental stewardship related to climate change using ecological issues of most relevance to local churches as the focus for practical training, environmental education, and theological reflection.

National ecumenical councils and networks in twenty-three industrialized countries responded with varying degrees of enthusiasm to the WCC-initiated petition campaign leading up to the Kyoto Climate Summit. The petition campaign provided an occasion for educational programs among churches in each country, linking to national environmental NGOs, advocacy directed toward national governments, and finally a joint event at a UN negotiating session in March 1996 when representatives of all the national campaigns presented the results of the petition to the UN Secretariat on Climate Change.

Climate change is one of the programs of the ecumenical community that lends itself to intensive local church activity particularly in industrialized countries of the North. Most of the action that needs to be taken on climate change is to reduce greenhouse gas emissions in industrialized nations through individual lifestyles as well as among larger-scale economic actors. Local congregations have utilized educational resources and programs developed by national denominational and ecumenical offices that give practical advice to members, encouraging them to reduce energy use in their own homes, opt for public transportation over extensive use of the individual automobile, and participate in tree-planting projects that contribute to capturing carbon dioxide. An increasing number of congregations are also examining their church buildings to reduce energy use as a contribution to addressing climate change.

This dynamic interrelationship on the climate change issue among the various levels of the church is only limited by the resources available to continue building and nurturing ecumenical networks internationally, nationally, and locally.

MODEST SIZE BUT CREDIBLE COLLECTIVE WITNESS

There has probably been more widespread engagement throughout the ecumenical community on the issue of climate change than any other single environmental concern. This is likely a result of the coordinated WCC program on climate change in collaboration with member churches and regional ecumenical organizations in many different countries.

Yet we must acknowledge that the level of ecumenical activity on the climate change issue is modest. While many Christians are committed to discipleship, it is probably true that only a minority of church members and congregations are actively involved in social justice concerns generally and environmental issues specifically. In many ways, climate change is difficult to raise as an urgent concern within congregations because of the long-term nature of the problem, the perceived scientific debate, and the overwhelming nature of the issue.

Given the limited scale of ecumenical and denominational activity on climate change, the credibility of our collective witness does seem to be greater than one might have expected. The petition campaign is a case in point. Organizational inadequacies and innocence on the part of the churches resulted in smaller initiatives than many had hoped. Nevertheless, the impact on national governments and the UN was considerable. Political representatives in many countries indicated to the churches that they were impressed that the churches considered the issue of climate change important enough to organize such a petition campaign. Though the results may have been modest, political leaders appear to have taken the initiative as indicative of a broader public concern about climate change beyond the expected members of civil society such as environmental groups.

Ritual and symbolism are also strengths in the ecumenical tradition that have proven to have potent impact in the climate change program. On several occasions during major sessions of the UN negotiations, the WCC sponsored ecumenical and interfaith events. The most dramatic to date was the Inter-religious Gathering on Climate Change held during the 1997 UN Climate Conference in Kyoto. The event drew participants from the negotiating session as well as many local Japanese representing a wide variety of religious groups, including Christians, Buddhists, Shintos and new religions. Held in the Catholic cathedral in Kyoto, the service began with the ringing of prayer bells by Buddhist and Shinto priests and traditional Japanese music, and included prayers in many languages and an address by the chairperson of the UN negotiations. The event concluded with a candlelight march from the Catholic cathedral to a major Shinto shrine.

Participants in the negotiations have expressed great appreciation for these ecumenical and interfaith events, which seem to give them an opportunity to step back from the intensity of the politics and touch a deeper level of commitment. The delegates, UN officials, and NGOs who attend the services, as well as the local people who participate, appear to be spiritually nurtured by the rituals, prayers, and music. One particular example that stands out was the large public event in Bonn in March 1997 at which we presented the results of the petition campaign. We had children present the booklet that summarized the campaign to the chairman of the negotiations along with a bouquet of cherry blossoms to symbolize our hope for a fruitful result of the negotiations in Kyoto six months later and to emphasize the sustaining of creation for these children and their children. The chairman was so moved by the event that he had the cherry blossoms sitting on the head table when he opened the next session of negotiations the following morning and spoke at some length about the WCC event and the urgency of the task that faced the delegates.

New Partnerships

The WCC program on climate change has been critically dependent on existing networks within the global ecumenical community and the development of new partnerships with many secular organizations.

The regional support programs, through which we have cosponsored workshops in Africa, Asia, Latin America, and the Pacific concerned with climate change in a broader environment and development context, have relied on regional ecumenical organizations. Though their resources are limited, they have seen the issue as a significant enough priority to organize events in their regions. The future of that work is dependent, however, on continuing financial assistance from the WCC.

The advocacy work in industrialized countries as well as at the UN negotiations has relied on support from the many environmental NGOs that have considerably more technical expertise on the issues of climate change than is resident within our ecumenical network. A very collaborative relationship has developed in which they provide us with analyses of current issues under negotiation and allow us to participate in many of the NGO strategy sessions. Conversely, they appreciate the work that the churches have done to raise public awareness through our own ecumenical and denominational networks and to make our voices heard on ethical dimensions of the issues during the negotiating sessions.

There has also been a vital interrelationship with members of the scientific community. The WCC was represented at the second World Climate Conference in 1990 which provided the impetus for the beginning of intergovernmental negotiations. We were also invited to present a paper at a workshop in Nairobi in 1994 on social and ethical dimensions organized by the Inter-governmental Panel on Climate Change (IPCC), the official scientific body advising the UN. A senior member of the IPCC has participated in a WCC consultation and advised us on the science section of our recent study document, *Climate Change and the Quest for Sustainable Societies*. The American Association on the Advancement of Science also invited the WCC to make a presentation at an October 1998 science-religion dialogue on global climate change. Each of these exchanges has provided an occasion for deepening our level of engagement with the scientific community—both challenging them and being challenged by them.

INTERFAITH CHALLENGES

As noted above, there have been a few opportunities for significant interfaith collaboration, most significantly at the Kyoto Climate Summit in December 1997. Still, this remains an area of considerable challenge for the ecumenical community.

There have been interfaith events over the past number of years that have focused on broad questions of faith, spirituality, and ecology. Most of these have underlined the considerable degree of consensus that can be articulated across the faiths on the need for active engagement in caring for creation. There have been fewer initiatives that seek to translate this general consensus into specific advocacy initiatives.

There are several difficulties to be addressed. All religions must wrestle seriously with the issue of faith and culture. In particular, how can religious faiths, which espouse concern for the well-being of creation, have a positive impact on the economic, political, and social context of the countries in which they exist? A survey of the global situation quickly reveals that ecologically benevolent sacred texts, rituals, and theology do not automatically translate into an environmentally benign economic system. A particular challenge for the WCC with its involvement in the intergovernmental negotiations is to find opportunities for dialogue with Islamic representatives, since that is the dominant religion of the Middle Eastern OPEC countries that have played a fairly obstructionist role in the negotiations. A few attempts have been made to open a Christian-Islamic dialogue on climate change, but the results have been very minimal to date.

CONCLUSION

Ecumenical engagement in the issue of climate change will be long-term, given the nature of the challenge. The history to date augurs well for a creative involvement that could have a significant impact on the response of the global community, as well as an enlivening effect upon the church itself.

8

Seeking Eco-Justice
in the South African Context

Ernst Conradie, Charity Majiza, Jim Cochrane,
Welile T. Sigabi, Victor Molobi, and David Field

WE BEGIN IN CAPE TOWN, where, some three and a half centuries ago, the Dutch East India Company established the first European settlement on this part of the African continent. Our route takes us on a mental tour of four specific places, each of which symbolizes something important about our reality, and the meaning and scope of eco-justice in our context.

Our tour commences at the statue of Cecil John Rhodes, the grand imperial agent who sought British rule "from Cape to Cairo." The statue stands in the former gardens of the Dutch East India Company. Rhodes is raising his arm, eyes staring North with an intensity that projects him as the great visionary anxious to bring the blessings of British rule to the entire African continent. The inscription at the foot of the statue reads: "This is our hinterland." Rhodes is also reputed to have said: "I am of the opinion that we are truly the best race in the world and that the more of our world we inhabit, the better it is for mankind." Underlying this statement are three fundamental ideological assumptions: (1) that unlimited space and scope for colonial and imperial expansion is accorded to the members of an allegedly superior race; (2) that the rights of indigenous peoples in the different countries have to give way and be subordinated to interests and potential of this allegedly superior race; and (3) that the natural resources of the continent and the cheap labor of its people are available to foreign colonial powers and immigrant settler communities for the implementation of this vision.

Our second stop is the national parliamentary building. This was the symbol of colonialism and apartheid. Here the dispossession of land was legalized, apartheid was institutionalized, and resistance against apartheid was criminalized. This same parliament—reborn, now belonging to all South African citizens, and remarkably open to the public—has become a symbol of the new democratic political order. A corner has been turned, though the road ahead remains long.

Next we board the ferry to Robben Island, seven miles off the mainland in Table Bay. From here one may stare back at the city, at the parliamentary complex, at the gardens where Rhodes looks stonily ahead. This island, since early colonial rule, has been a symbol of dehumanization, exclusion, and repression. It stands for the attempt to break the spirit of resistance against colonial domination. For a while it was a leper colony, and then once more it became the prison that held those who challenged the dominating powers. But it broke fewer spirits than anticipated. Known during the years of struggle against apartheid as "the university," because of the unceasing, often surreptitious debate and self-run education programs of its prisoners, Robben Island became a powerhouse of the liberation struggle and a potent symbol of the strength of the human spirit.

From Robben Island, looking across the bay, we see Table Mountain, our fourth stop. Other monuments are all overshadowed by the majestic bulk and presence of this mountain, sacred to our Khoi ancestors and to many others who still live under its shadow. Walk reverently up the mountain and you will be struck by the incredible variety of vegetation and the beauty of the coastline and of the mountain itself.

Once at the top we are able to look over the Cape metropolitan area—if the layer of urban smog permits—to see the city center and its industries, the affluent northern and southwestern suburbs and the vast areas of the Cape Flats, where millions of impoverished people live in squalid houses, shacks, and on rubbish dumps. We look down upon a sea of contradictory representations in geography and architecture: They represent injustice and the struggle for justice, poverty and the struggle for well-being, dehumanization and the search for a fuller human being, degradation and the desire for a clean and whole environment.

These four stops on our mental journey capture the ambiguities, the fragility, the pain of a context within which any attempt to tackle issues of eco-justice must be placed. They also point to vistas that are inhabited by hope and energy, faith and commitment. It is this paradox of actuality and possibility that defines our response to the challenges presented to local communities, and the ecclesial community in particular, by the vision of an ecumenical Earth.

FROM POLITICAL TO ECONOMIC LIBERATION

The past decades in the history of South Africa have been dominated by the struggle for political liberation. During the past twenty-five years liberation theology has spelled out the gospel in the context of the suffering of marginalized people. It addressed the cries of the victims of discrimination, humiliation, land dispossession, forced removals, oppression, tyranny, torture, rape. It insisted that God is to be encountered among the victims of injustice. The scope of a concern for liberation from political oppression now has to be extended—not only to economic liberation but also to the liberation of the earth and all its creatures.

Since the miracle of a peaceful transition to democracy in 1994, the focus of the public debate in South Africa has indeed shifted, at least to some extent, from political liberation to economic liberation. This is born from the realization that justice is still to come.[1] Even more acutely, it arises from the cries of the poor, the hungry, the homeless, the sick, the abused, the unemployed, the aged, the illiterate. In that respect South Africa is a low-income, highly indebted, developing country with insufficient resources to deal with its problems and needs, and considerable vulnerability to international markets and financial speculation. In the struggle for economic and social justice, the issues of poverty, employment, education, housing, health services, crime, and AIDS demand our attention and consume our energy. The combination of these factors has led to a marginalization of a concern for the environment.

The environment as such means quite different things to different people, reflecting different social locations and cultural experiences within our complex and fractured society. Some think that "the environment" refers to nature conservation. Others experience it in the form of air and water pollution that affects their daily lives and health. Some focus on the proper management of natural resources under their control. Others are concerned with inadequate health and safety standards in the working environment. Some think about it only when there is news about an environmental catastrophe. Yet others are anxious about somewhat remote global issues, such as the melting of the ice caps, which may have great consequence, but which are difficult to locate clearly within our own context.

An Emerging Environmental Awareness

Despite the marginalization of the environment as a focus of concern, there is an emerging awareness that care for economic and social justice cannot be separated from the environment. This emerging awareness has two important aspects.[2]

On the one hand, there is a broad recognition that human well-being is dependent on the well-being of the land. Most informed people, including a great many South Africans of all kinds, are well aware that the destruction of a healthy environment will necessarily affect human dignity. We are rooted in the soil of Africa, our "mother." This is the home (*oikos, ikhaya*) where we belong.[3] The notion that we have to care for the earth so that the earth can care for us is integral to traditional African wisdom. The mindful husbanding of land and cattle that was part of traditional practices has not entirely disappeared, notwithstanding a century of industrialization, modernization, and urbanization. This is true even for those in urban areas who no longer have cattle and land, but whose vision of well-being draws on traditions of the past.

On the other hand, there is a realization that the problems poor people experience on a daily basis are essentially environmental problems. This has both urban and rural dimensions. People living in urban townships are often the victims of environmental degradation caused elsewhere—by nearby industries, for example.[4] Townships were often located precisely on environmentally degraded land that was therefore not in demand. We may list the following as some of the typical health hazards of township life:

- air pollution—either through nearby industries or through the use of braziers and coal stoves (even in electrified houses);
- pollution of water supplies by broken sewerage pipes, stagnant pools, or people doing their washing next to water taps to avoid

walking characteristically long distances to reach a decent washing place, if one exists at all;

- the visual ugliness of pollution, leading to a lack of basic human dignity;
- typically very high population densities—a localized form of over-population;
- inadequate sanitation;
- a high incidence of contagious diseases;
- regular floods or landslides;
- a lack of basic infrastructure;
- cutting of trees for firewood in the neighborhood, where any are left; and
- the struggle for political control over ever scarcer resources.

In rural areas, the scarcity of clean drinking water and firewood, which has serious human and economic consequences, is an environmental problem at its very roots. Deportation or removals under apartheid forced many South Africans to live in overcrowded conditions on land unable to support them effectively, resulting in extreme poverty. This process has reinforced environmental degradation: through overgrazing, soil erosion, and the exhaustion or depletion of water supplies. Many people have resorted to poaching and forms of deforestation as a survival strategy. These forms of environmental degradation are seldom deliberate but an increasing number of humans in a limited area inevitably exacts an environmental toll. This environmental damage increases poverty, leading to a vicious circle in which people are damaging the very fabric on which they depend for their survival.

Women and children often bear the brunt of coping with these environmental problems. As soil deteriorates, women have to work longer hours in backbreaking toil to harvest food from barren soil. Children suffer most, from diseases like diarrhea owing to a lack of drinkable water and inadequate sanitation. In deforested rural communities, girls and women expend increasing energy and time to collect firewood. Women are often forced to work in environmentally hazardous conditions for low wages. Women receive fewer financial rewards, work more hours, have less access to education, do more of the household caretaking, and have to bear and provide for their children. Typically, mothers sleep last and rise first.[5]

The middle-class and elite members of South African society enjoy First World standards of water, energy, sanitation, health care, and education.[6]

Their lives display the consumerism and wastefulness that is characteristic of most of the First World with its devastating effect on the earth. Inadequate environmental legislation does little to mitigate this impact at this point in our history.

The Social Location of the Struggle for Eco-Justice

From this analysis it becomes more than clear that to address poverty is to address this range of environmental hazards: The quest for economic justice is a quest for environmental justice. The struggle for eco-justice has to challenge the abuse of power that results in a situation where poor people suffer the effects of environmental damage caused by the greed of others.

In South Africa, this vision for eco-justice is beginning to emerge in the context of civil society. It is the focus of the Environmental Justice Networking Forum, a loose alliance of more than five hundred nonprofit, community-based, and nongovernmental organizations. This vision suggests that the environment has to be "marginal" in a second important sense of the word: The struggle for eco-justice has to affect the lives of those on the economic periphery of society. Indeed, we may go further and say that the extent to which the struggle for eco-justice effectively addresses this reality is, in important respects, the measure of its purpose and value.[7] This is possible only if the struggle for eco-justice can be rooted practically in local black communities under black leadership among the poor and deprived. Unless this is achieved, we will be falling far short of what is required in South Africa.

Furthermore, it is crucial to recognize that poverty is also a strongly gendered reality, that women generally bear the bulk of the burdens of poverty, and that effective development work must take much more seriously the constraints upon and potentials of women in this context. One may say, therefore, that eco-justice needs to take root not only among black communities under black leadership, but also among black women under the leadership of black women.

The capacity to deal with environmental dimensions of poverty rests as much on the people themselves as it does on structural and systemic interventions by government or other external agencies. The emphasis on the role of local marginalized communities has to be understood within the context of the tendency (in South Africa and elsewhere) in state organs, in government, and in business toward macro-solutions and "expert"-driven policy processes on the one hand, and a consonant downgrading of, if not hostility toward, micro-initiatives on the part of ordinary citizens on the other. A strong sense of participatory democracy accompanied the initial transition in South Africa, carried on the back of about fifteen years of struggle deeply rooted in "illegal" civic associations, youth groups, women's organizations, street committees, and a host of other forms of civil society. This has begun to dissipate in the face of policy processes, which all too frequently seem not to prize local initiatives and policy interventions very highly. Eco-justice will be achieved only through particular ways of conceiving democracy and particular kinds of democratic practice.

It is therefore clear that any adequate discussion of eco-justice must be grounded in the context of the challenge of poverty and a vision of democracy if it is to have an impact on South African society.

Policy Implications

A moral vision for eco-justice clearly has to be effective in marginalized communities. If it is to be sustained, however, it must also be expressed in the form of public policy, accompanied by appropriate budgetary allocations to enable policy to be carried out. The need for a policy framework is in part met, in the first instance, through a section of the new South African constitution. Clause 24 of the Bill of Rights states that everyone has the right (1) to an environment that is not harmful to his or her health or well-being; and (2) to have the environment protected, for the benefit of present and future generations, through reasonable legislative measures that (a) prevent pollution and ecological degradation, (b) promote conservation, and (c) secure ecologically sustainable development and use of natural resources while promoting justifiable economic and social development.[8]

Implementation of this constitutional goal involves confronting the central dilemma of the struggle for eco-justice in South Africa: How are we to promote desperately needed social and economic development without compromising ecological integrity? Current economic and political dynamics in South Africa indicate that this will prove to be an excruciatingly complex task.

Given the resources of the state and of markets in a "globalizing" framework, which has a direct, heavy, and frequently negative affect on emerging economies such as South Africa, citizen-oriented programs, actions, and agencies may well be swamped. It is imperative, therefore, that all available positive resources be harnessed in synergy with each other—an appropriate vision for the ecologically minded person. It is here that the churches have a significant role to play as they seek to bear witness to God's commitment to the earth and to act as a voice for the voiceless. This is particularly important in rural areas, where churches are often the only (or the chief) organ of civil society and the clergyperson may be one of the few members of the community with a tertiary education and access to needed resources (human, organizational, informational, and material resources).

The real question is whether churches and Christian agencies can meet such a challenge, recognizing the interlinked character of justice and ecology in the context of poverty. They are, in fact, severely pressured at the moment, with depleted resources, massive new demands for which we have no deep thinking or adequate practice, a sense of loss of identity and purpose in the absence of a clear common enemy, and a secular polity environment that tends to push them to focus on narrow moral concerns or to drift into privatized religious practices.

AN ECUMENICAL CONTRIBUTION

The Christian faith has to do with an awareness of a calling. This, however, differs fundamentally from the nationalistic visions of Western states and empires:

- God calls people from the ranks of those who are enslaved and considered outcasts.
- God liberates God's people, not for dominating other people, but in order to become a blessing to humankind.
- God wants God's people to serve God's purpose to recover creation from the forces of destruction that have been unleashed by humanity's refusal to act as responsible stewards of creation.
- Through the Holy Spirit the crucified and risen Christ is present in the midst of the fellowship of believers and shares in the suffering not only of humans but also of the whole creation. At the same time the Spirit empowers believers to contribute to the liberation of creation.

The churches played a crucial role throughout the years of struggle against apartheid in seeking to address the dispossession of land and other resources. This activity set a precedent for a continued activism to promote the restoration and healing of the land. The churches supported the resistance of communities threatened by dispossession of their land by the apartheid regime. A particular case is the Mogopa community. In cooperation with other organizations, the South African Council of Churches (SACC) succeeded through its ecumenical links in raising such an outcry that the apartheid regime had to refrain in the time that followed from using bulldozers to remove people from their land.

The ecumenically based Covenant Program did a lot to strengthen communities affected by removal measures, by conducting ecumenical worship services, and by linking them with Christian groups in other countries who pray for them. These international ecumenical groups then lobbied their own governments demanding that they intervene.

In 1984 the SACC sent an ecumenical delegation to partner churches to challenge them to draw the attention of their governments to the forced removal policy of the South African government. It also drew the attention of member churches to the challenge they face as owners of land in a country in which the majority of people have been dispossessed of their land. Church leaders were asked to commit themselves to promoting measures that aim at responsible use of the land, which would restore it to its fullness.

After the transition to democracy, churches are faced with the task of raising awareness in the South African public of the obligation to redistribute land and resources, and to heal the land. Even if land is restored to its original owners the question has to be solved as to how it can be used to the benefit of all the stakeholders concerned. Could it be that people in this region—which is considered to be the cradle of humankind—have been endowed with special possibilities to contribute to the rehumanization of humankind and the liberation of creation? This remains an ambiguous question with a fragile footing. It is likely to be answered in the positive only if a far greater level of engagement with the issues of eco-justice follows, based on practical foundations and with material consequences through an integrated, holistic vision of an ecumenical Earth.

Eco-Justice: Blind Spot or New Vision?

In 1991 Jacklyn Cock, a South African sociologist, published a report titled, "Towards the Greening of the Church in South Africa."[9] In this report she investigated the environmental awareness of church leaders and official church publications, and resolutions on the environment. She concluded that there is a "blind spot" and a "deep silence" within Christian churches in South Africa on environmental issues.

The reasons given (and defended!) by her informants for the silence of the church on environmental issues tend to confirm the earlier suspicions of Lynn White that Christianity bears a huge burden of guilt for the environmental crisis.[10] These reasons include the following: a preoccupation with human salvation, the doctrine of divine transcendence, the emphasis of the Judeo-Christian tradition on human domination over nature, the dismissal of environmental issues as "new age" concerns, and even the perception that the ecological crisis confirms apocalyptic prophecies in the Bible. By contrast, Cock's interviews with environmental activists in South Africa revealed a striking absence of any religious affiliation!

Since 1991 this discouraging state of affairs has improved somewhat. This is evident from the following five indicators:

- Several Christian communities are beginning to respond to environmental concerns in their local contexts (some case studies are mentioned below).
- Some Christian denominations as well as the South African Council of Churches have recently passed resolutions on the environment, symbolically indicating an awareness of the need to attend to environmental degradation.
- An acknowledgment of environmental agendas is beginning to creep into the dominant discourse and rhetoric of theologians, church leaders, and Christian communities. Still, such discourse is characterized predominantly by notions of conservation and stewardship and not by a concern for eco-justice.
- Several recent theological conferences have specifically addressed environmental issues.[11]
- A growing number of academic articles on Christianity and the environment are being published in theological journals in South Africa.[12]

Despite these indicators, it has to be acknowledged that the church is not (yet) an important role player toward eco-justice in South Africa and that some degree of resistance against environmental agendas remains prevalent. Nevertheless, the potential of local Christian communities to make a significant contribution toward eco-justice should not be under-estimated. There are three important sociological reasons for this.[13]

1. According to several important studies, the church is one organ-ization in South Africa that can make a real difference. Local Christian communities enjoy the trust of people at a grassroots level beyond any political party, labor union, or community or-ganization, and, taken together, Christian churches form the largest, most influential, and most active organized civil body in the country with a demographic reach second to none.

2. The church is a unique source of moral leadership. It has often provided people with moral vision and courage who have played a vital role in the country's well-being (for example, people such as Desmond Tutu, Beyers Naude, and Frank Chikane, to name but some of the more prominent figures who have provided a rich legacy of engaged Christianity).

3. The biblical roots of the church and the history of Christianity are full of examples that can be retrieved to support the kind of eco-logical vision required today to face the ecological crisis.

Churches can respond to the challenge of eco-justice at several levels. Through preaching and teaching, Christian churches can encourage their individual members to make a difference where they live and where they work. Further, and perhaps most important, they can set in place con-crete examples of ecologically sensitive communities. This may be done through Christian worship, Christian education, the formation of people of moral vision and character, the creation of a climate in which children can learn to appreciate and love creation, and through sustainable and creative practices on the land and property owned by the church. In these ways Christian communities may become a sign of hope for the world (see the case studies and reflection below).

The churches may also encourage members to cooperate with and support numerous other organizations concerned with the environment (among them, numerous examples of projects initiated by Christians). In this respect, it will not be helpful, nor is it necessary, for Christian churches to duplicate the work of other environmental organizations. Churches should, instead, support the work of these organizations as much as possible, establish the necessary channels and networks of com-munication, and encourage their members to participate in the work of these organizations. While Christians may ultimately have a distinct ecological vision, they could share the "penultimate" goals of many other environmental activists.

In the past church organizations often felt the need to establish schools, hospitals, centers for the disabled and elderly people, and agricultural projects, wherever such projects were necessary. More recently, several examples of environmental projects initiated by Christian communities have emerged throughout South Africa. They represent a range of theological and practical approaches to engagement by Christians, illustrating:

- prophetic annunciation and denunciation, the verbal addressing of pressing eco-justice issues of a particular context;
- didactic action aimed at educating congregations and the broader society;
- transformative action challenging ecological degradation and building healthy, eco-just community;
- restorative action directed at healing the earth, including efforts to clean up pollution, to remove alien vegetation, and to establish recycling programs; and
- enhancement programs aimed at enabling the earth to be fruitful in a sustainable manner.

CHRISTIAN PROJECTS FOR ECO-JUSTICE

The Khanya Programme is a ministry designed by the Methodist Church of Southern Africa for rural people. This model is "culture-creation-and-people-friendly" and can be pictured as a ship's wheel. The hub of the wheel represents revitalized worship. Emanating from this hub are five spokes representing development programs: permaculture design, livestock distribution, "serv-fari" adventures, appropriate housing, and micro-industries. This model is already assisting the church to steer a new approach in rural ministry. It uses available church land for the benefit of the poor by way of empowering people to overcome unemployment and hunger. It empowers rural communities to prepare for their own future.

The Hub—Revitalized Worship. The concentration here is upon: blessing of the seeds, firstfruits ceremonies, harvest festivals, combined worship with animals, land produce, and people.

In the blessing of the seeds, people are reminded of the time for planting and about our responsibility for our own food production. They take
part in this ceremony by bringing their seeds and by reading a pledge that
commits them to planting and caring for their gardens. For the firstfruits
ceremonies, they offer thanks for God's act of leading our country away
from apartheid while marking our responsibility to shape our country
and our future (Deut 26:1-11).

During the harvest festivals people are encouraged to celebrate God's
provisions and to commit ourselves again to making use of our gardens.
The final liturgical activity consists of combined worship with animals, land
produce, and people with the goal of linking worship of God with the lives
of the rural people, their animals, and gardens. An integrated worship center is in the pipeline, planned to be a triple, concentric, connected structure
with an altar at the center. The first circle is the church for the people; the
second is the *kraal* for animals; and the third circle consists of gardens. The
idea is to link worship with animals and the garden produce that we live
upon. Through these worship ceremonies and festivals, the word of God is
linked to the daily lives and experiences of the rural people.

The Five Spokes. (1) Permaculture design: In Genesis 41 we are told that
Joseph encouraged the Pharaoh to fend off the pending famine in Egypt
by constructing granaries. Through permaculture design, rural people
are taught to combat hunger and poverty by planting vegetable- and
fruit-producing "garden granaries" around their homes. Permaculture
design teaches a sustainable way of integrated food production that
cares for God's creation. It also encourages those who are involved in it
to teach others design skills. According to Australian specialist Bill Mol-
lison, "Permaculture is a system by which we can exist on earth by using
energy that is naturally in flux and relatively harmless and by using food
and natural resources that are abundant in such a way that we don't
continually destroy life on earth."

(2) Livestock distribution: The Khanya Programme provides poor
people with domesticated animals and training in animal care. This is
done through close working with Heifer Project South Africa. These animals benefit their owners in a number of ways, providing manure for
vegetable gardens and food for their tables. Recipients of animals pledge
to "pass on the gift" by giving the first female offspring to another family
with no animals.

(3) Serv-fari adventures: Combining the challenge of Christian service with the excitement of an African safari, the serv-fari program offers visitors a rare experience. They work at one of the Methodist Mission Stations in the Eastern Cape while being able to experience the beauty of Africa at nearby game reserves. They also work with the local people at their home places and thus gain firsthand information about and experience of their culture.

(4) Appropriate housing: The Khanya program seeks to equip the people to build affordable yet attractive and durable houses of mud bricks. (Housing is one of the major problems of a liberated South Africa.)

5) Micro-industries: With the assistance of KSM Milling, rural people are taught baking skills and how to run a micro-bakery. Ovens are made from recycled 40-gallon steel drums that are provided at cost. Ongoing customer service is also provided. Fresh bread is baked and sold from these micro-bakeries daily. Both operators and the community living nearby benefit from this project.

The Faith and Earthkeeping Project was founded in 1995, functions under the auspices of the World Wide Fund for Nature—South Africa, and is managed as a project within the Research Institute for Theology and Religion at the University of South Africa. Three staff members run the project. The principal aim of the project is to help raise consciousness of, empower, and support communities and individuals at a grassroots level to create and implement their own activities and policies for local, regional, and national environmental protection, conservation, and sustainable resource use, with a view to help improve their quality of life. This is done through the promotion of a religious engagement in ecological and development issues.

Three specific objectives follow from this, that is, research, consciousness raising, and mobilization. Research is primarily done with regard to what has been published locally and abroad in the fields of environmental philosophy, theology, and ethics, in order to promote an understanding of local and global environmental problems and the role that religious practices have played in this regard. It also investigates the role that religious communities can play in creating a lifestyle compatible with the ecological realities of the world in which we live, and it produces relevant educational material for schools, colleges, universities, and at a grassroots community level. Courses in religion and ecology are already offered in various institutions and at a grassroots level to equip and enable people to participate in environmental action.

Conscientiousness raising is a process that aims to develop an awareness of environmental problems and associated threats to local communities. It nurtures a senses of responsibility and urgency with respect to these problems and strengthens social values existing within local communities toward environmental stewardship. It is accomplished through presentations, workshops, projects in communities, discussion groups, retreats, tours, conferences, articles, lectures, the publication of a quarterly newsletter, and a series of degree, certificate, and personal development courses.

Wherever a particular need is identified, the Faith and Earthkeeping Project aims to mobilize people in those communities through their networks to address that specific need in an environmentally sensitive way. Local environmental conditions and priorities are at all times taken into consideration in the planning of projects. The aim is to achieve site-specific conservation objectives and projects. This leads to various kinds of initiatives, for example, tree planting, preservation of water resources, veld management and land use, cleanup operations, urban greening and agriculture, nurseries, and recycling projects. Overall, this work in seven of the nine provinces in South Africa covers multidimensional urban projects, rural sustainable agriculture projects, and semi-urban agriculture and greening projects.

Abalimi Bezekhaya ("Planters of the Home") is an organization that promotes an urban agriculture and greening program. Its aim is to provide opportunities for the poor, especially women, in the townships of the Cape Flats, to support each other, to grow food for themselves and their families, and to gain self-respect by creating home food security. Low-cost resources and skills training are the means by which this support is offered. More than ten thousand people are already involved as small-scale vegetable farmers in this project. Abalimi Bezekhaya is a non-denominational organization, independently managed and funded, but affiliated with Catholic Welfare and Development.

The associated Cape Flats Tree Project promotes the greening of local neighborhoods, schools, and public parks. It establishes well-maintained models to inspire others to follow. By establishing these models, a greater environmental awareness and understanding of biological organic methods for the healing of both the earth and her people is encouraged.

The Struggle against Toxic Waste Near Philadelphia. In August 1994, a large waste-disposal company explored the possibility of a hazardous-waste dump ("gifgat" or "poison hole") two kilometers from the small rural town of Philadelphia, near Cape Town. The company offered a huge amount to an absentee farmer in the area for a suitable piece of land and promised employment for many workers. The farming community was soon up in arms about the dangers of highly toxic waste infiltrating the groundwater system of the area. One semi-employed farm worker responded to the offer of a well-paying job: "No, not if it will bring death to my children."

The local Dutch Reformed congregation facilitated a series of meetings, and a long and intricate battle ensued. The Department of Environmental Affairs, legal experts, environmental monitoring groups, and the local newspapers soon became involved in the process. The company used everything in its considerable power to enforce its plans—from bribery to clandestine scare tactics. After numerous meetings, telephone calls, peacemaking efforts, and prayers, the owner of the land unexpectedly withdrew his offer to sell the property. David had managed to deter the mighty Goliath.

"Wikkel, Woeker, Werk" Recycling Project. A congregation of the Gereformeerde Kerk in Alberton-West started in 1991 with a project to collect iron, tin, aluminum, glass, paper, and plastics for reuse and recycling. Enormous quantities of material have been collected since then. In this way the congregation helped to clean the environment, manage waste, give young and old in the congregation a sense of purpose, and encourage a spirit of community and cooperation, and this also helped to earn a considerable income for the congregation. It also published two booklets providing advice to other congregations on how to manage such a project.

The Diocese of Umzimvubu in the rural region of the Eastern Cape faces numerous environmental challenges. Many of these are a legacy of the homeland system. The Anglican Diocese of Umzimvubu, under the leadership of Bishop Geoff Davies, has attempted to address some of these issues as well as to raise the church's consciousness of environmental issues. This work is symbolized in the development of the Glenthorn Training Centre outside Kokstad. The Glenthorn farm, the residence of the Bishop of Umzimvubu, is in the process of being transformed. Efforts are being made to reverse the ecological degradation that has taken place. Part of the estate is being set aside and developed as a nature reserve. A training center has been set up where various conferences and training courses are held within the context of an awareness of the goodness of God's creation.

The work of the diocese is not confined to Glenthorn. The diocese appointed an agricultural officer, Bob Thelin, to teach and equip farmers within the diocese to engage in sustainable agriculture. It is envisaged that this project will not only contribute to providing food for many poverty stricken families but will also counter the effects of the ecological degradation of the past. The diocese also acted as a voice for the community in recent debates concerning the development of a toll road and holiday resorts along the Wild Coast. While the project was abandoned for financial reasons, Bishop Davies had become a spokesperson for the opposition to the development because of its environmentally destructive character and its failure to empower and develop the local communities.

A few examples from our Southern African Neighbors of church-based environmental projects were collected during a tour of the region in 1997. They are representative but not in any way comprehensive.

Tree-Planting Eucharists in Zimbabwe, initiated by African Instituted Churches in Zimbabwe, have become quite famous throughout the world. Since the formation in 1988 of ZIRRCON (Zimbabwe Institute of Religious Research and Ecological Conservation), churches in the country have been challenged on the basis of their Christian faith to engage in tree-planting activities. In 1991 the Association of African Earthkeeping Churches (AAEC) was established. These organizations promote massive programs for afforestation, wildlife conservation, and the protection of water resources. Several nurseries have been established from where trees are planted for fuel-wood, for nutrition (fruit trees), for commercial use and building operations (for example, blue gums), to protect and clothe the soil, and to provide for future generations (for example, red mahogany).

Tree-planting ceremonies are often linked to eucharistic services. These innovative liturgies are introduced to integrate environmental ethics and church praxis. In this way Christians are "proclaiming a widening message of salvation which encompasses all of creation, and in their services of worship they are dancing out a new rhythm which, in its footwork, spells hope for the ravaged earth" (Inus Daneel).

The Heritage of the Mission in Zambia. Since the 1890s mission stations have been built all over Zambia by the Catholic Church, the London Missionary Society, and the Dutch Reformed Church, often owing to requests from the local (Angoni) chiefs. The early missionaries set an example of enhancing the fertility of the land with their water projects, the planting of numerous fruit trees, and various small-scale agricultural projects. These examples still encourage people in local villages to plant and protect trees, to care for the environment, and to create a source of nutritional food in the process.

Projects for Sustainable Agriculture in Zambia. The Christian Council of Zambia is involved in numerous development projects all over Zambia. In some respects, it seems to provide infrastructure and training where the government is unable to fulfill its responsibility. One of these projects is based on a hundred-acre farm in Lusaka West that serves as a model and training center for sustainable agriculture. On this farm a system of rainwater harvesting and the building of small water tanks or wells has been developed. Other activities include fish farming, tree planting, the use of indigenous plants for fertilization and pesticides, etc. This project serves as an example to the government and local villages of what can be done regarding food security and sustainable farming with limited resources.

In Madzimoyo, the Reformed Church in Zambia has established a Church Lay Training Center. The emphasis of this center has shifted from a predominant emphasis on spiritual training to a more holistic approach. One of the projects is a demonstration plant to offer a model of sustainable agriculture to local farmers, to provide for basic nutritional needs (also for the training center), and to earn some additional income through selling the surplus produce. This project encourages the use of natural forms of fertilization and pesticides. This is not only more environmentally sustainable but also reduces expenditure and financial risks.

A Center for Appropriate Technology at Mindolo. The Mindolo Ecumenical Foundation is located at Kitwe, in the Cobberbelt region in Zambia. It provides training programs emphasizing self-employment to students from all over Africa. This includes a Center for Appropriate Technology (with an emphasis on carpentry and metalwork), a Pottery School, and a Small Holdings Farm. The emphasis in these courses falls on community-based self-employment that would be sustainable within a rural context. This requires less sophisticated forms of technology that would not be expensive to acquire or maintain. The farming project enables the Mindolo community to feed itself. In these ways a self-sustaining use of water, energy, and food is encouraged.

Animal Orphanage at Mua in Malawi. Deforestation has taken place on an enormous scale in Malawi. One of the consequences of this process is that the natural habitat of a large number of animals has been destroyed. At the Catholic mission at Mua, near Lake Malawi, an animal orphanage has been started to provide shelter for a wide variety of these homeless animals. This has helped local parishioners to develop a relationship with these animals instead of viewing them only as a source of meat.

Mua is perhaps best known for the Kungoni Arts and Crafts Center, which was developed there under the leadership of the local priest, Father Boucher. This center explores the relationship between Christian symbols and traditional symbols in the Chewa, Yao, and Kungoni cultures. The creation stories in these cultures are told through art in order to draw attention to the intrinsic link between culture and the environment and the threat of human insensitivity to the preservation of natural resources.

ECCLESIOLOGICAL REFLECTIONS

The case studies discussed above remind us that people and earth are thoroughly interrelated, either thriving or being oppressed together. The cases also suggest fresh ways in which a new vision of the church can be concretized within an African context. They help us to visualize what it means for the church to be the eschatological new creation amid the brokenness of the present creation.[14]

In the biblical image of the church as the "firstfruits" of the new creation, it is portrayed as the first installment of the renewal of creation. In the exuberant harvest celebrations of numerous sustainable agriculture projects this image receives a new context. The firstfruits of the vegetable gardens are presented before God in gratitude for the harvest and for a new avenue toward self-sustenance and human dignity. The church thus becomes the firstfruits (and vegetables!) of the new creation.

To identify the church as the firstfruits of the new creation is to confess not only that the redemption that has begun with the church will extend to the entire earth, but also that through the church the earth will be sanctified and cleansed.[15] It is the presence of the Spirit that constitutes the church as the firstfruits of the new creation. "The Spirit is the pledge and guarantee, the 'down payment' of the coming redemption, which is designed to reach the whole creation."[16] The Spirit empowers and equips the church to engage in a praxis of transformation as it looks forward in hope to the redemption of all things. Thus when churches and other Christian groups become involved in the struggle for eco-justice, as is seen in the case studies that have been presented, they are giving expression to the nature of the church as the firstfruits of the new creation.

In 1 Cor. 15:20 Christ is described as the firstborn of a new dispensation. This image may be extrapolated to the church as the body of Christ and the firstborn of the new creation. The image of the firstborn has a rich heritage in the Bible. All believers participate as newborn people in a new creation. Those who have received a cow or a goat through the Khanya program—and thus a new livelihood for themselves—pledge to give the first female offspring to someone else in need. In this way concrete and visible signs of the new creation are established on Earth.

The eschatological vision of Isaiah 11 projects peace between God and animals, and not only between human beings and God. In the envisaged sanctuary of the Khanya program (where a *kraal* for animals forms one of the three circles in the building structure) something of this harmonious coexistence between God, humanity, and the animals becomes visible and concrete. The animals may also come into God's presence.

A further image of some potential is that of the church as a tree of life. Tree planting is a crucial aspect in the work of AZTREC (Association of Zimbabwean Traditional Ecologists), Abalimi Bezekhaya, and numerous others. Especially in rural areas this is a crucial form of earthkeeping in light of the problems of deforestation and the daily task of collecting ever more scarce firewood. In biblical imagery, trees are a symbol of the good life that God intended for creation in the beginning (the tree of life). The tree of life also appears as an eschatological symbol in the last chapter of Revelation, where it bears fruit twelve months of the year and where leaves of the tree bring healing for the nations. This rich imagery is concretized in the praxis of tree-planting eucharists. The church is a tree-planting community and therefore functions as a "tree" (source) of life for the whole creation.

There are numerous other eschatological symbols for the church that may be explored in a similar way (for example, the church as the communion of the saints, the river of life, a banquet for the poor, etc.). The direction is clear. The earthkeeping practices of these African case studies help to concretize and renew the meaning of these eschatological symbols for the church. They provide an example of what the church as an agent of new creation could look like in the midst of the injustice, deprivation, and degradation of the world in which it is situated.

This notion of the church may be developed further on the basis of the Pauline motif of the church-as-community as the temple or dwelling place of the Spirit (1 Cor. 6:19, Eph. 2:21). Its potential contribution can be seen in the way in which the motif of the temple or sanctuary is used in the Old Testament to integrate issues of worship, ecological fertility, and social justice. A few examples will demonstrate this point.

The church as the sanctuary of the Spirit is the sign and foretaste of the eschatological dwelling of God with creation. It should thus become the place where the people of God experience the presence of God, which transforms them into a community in fellowship with God and in harmony with the rest of creation. This in turn ought to transform their social life and through them bring renewal to creation. Thus when the Khanya Programme and the African Initiated Churches place communal worship at the center of a praxis that fans out to serve the poor and bring healing to the earth, they are giving expression to church as the sanctuary or dwelling place of the Spirit.

A few further aspects emerging from these case studies may be noted: first, the importance of a worshiping community. The model provided by the Khanya Programme and the tree-planting eucharists of the African Initiated Churches in Zimbabwe are particularly suggestive with regard to the centrality of revitalized worship. In both cases responses to issues of eco-justice are integrated into a renewal of worship and thus into the heart of the life of the church. This renewed worship becomes the center and dynamo for the praxis of eco-justice. The exclusive focus on God and God's transcendence in worship functions as a critique of other absolutes and illuminates the contrast to the brokenness, suffering, and degradation in the context surrounding the worshiping community. It also inspires them to engage in small but meaningful actions toward a transformation of these realities.

The church celebrates God's presence in the midst of creation and together with the rest of nature. It therefore examines ways in which the whole of creation can be included in worship, in anticipation of the eschatological worship of "every creature in heaven and on earth and under the earth and in the sea and all that is in them" (Rev. 5:13). This will only take place as the Word is proclaimed in such a way that the people of God are brought into a new awareness of their identity as the community of the new creation.[17]

The worshiping community, however, is also quite specifically an African community. Important aspects of inculturation are evident in our case studies, which are rooted, in various ways, in the African context. Some draw on symbols and ideas from traditional African culture and religion. They are all shaped by the particularities of the sociohistorical context of Africa, particularly South Africa. They are responses to the socioecological realities of Africa. In some cases it is traditional African ideas of a community that includes creation—of worship as a channel of blessing to the earth, and of a religion affecting the whole of life that have pointed to biblical themes neglected in Western theology.

It would be wrong to idealize Africa or the traditional African worldview. They are ambiguous and at times problematic, but they do provide a challenge to the church in the rest of the world to develop contextual responses to the eco-justice crisis, rooted in the biblical witness that challenges the dominant trends in society and the church.

Our case studies also speak of a church that is a community providing a new alternative, embodying something of the new creation as an alternative community whose life and praxis are a sign of the ultimate eschatological community of the new creation. It should thus be a community in which the fractures and divisions of human society are overcome and the relationship between humanity and the rest of creation is healed. This reality is only partially accomplished, because Christians live within a wide variety of intersecting communities that influence and shape their identity and thus the life and praxis of the church.

Finally, we may also speak of the church in these contexts as a penultimate community. It emphasizes both the reality of the transformation that has taken place and the incompleteness of the transformation. The church is a pilgrim community moving toward the new creation, but it is still characterized by much of the brokenness of the old creation. It lives in hope of new creation.

9

Issues of Community Empowerment

Peggy M. Shepard

INTRODUCTION

Access to power explains the politics of pollution and the environmental degradation that has turned our communities into the nation's dumping ground for life-threatening toxins and pollutants. There is a functional and significant link between racism, poverty, powerlessness, and the assault on certain communities. In West Harlem, our communities, which are poorer, less informed, less organized, and less politically influential, are more likely targets for abuse from polluters—whether they be corporations or governments. They are most likely to be targets of environmental racism that is the result of policies that site potentially hazardous facilities in low-income areas and communities of color specifically because they are less able to mobilize the resources necessary to wage an effective fight.

Research on issues of race and the environment indicates that people of color face a disproportionate impact from environmental problems. The racial composition of a community is the single variable best able to explain the existence or nonexistence of potentially hazardous facilities in that area. That is what we call environmental racism. Other than race, critical elements in the siting of potentially hazardous facilities appear to be lack of control over land use and the development process, and lack of access to the judicial system. The white middle-class-dominated movement of the '60s and '70s built an impressive political base for environmental reform and regulatory relief, but it did not address the disproportionate burden, that is, health burden, carried by the communities of color and of low income. At that time, few realized the implications of the NIMBY (Not In My Backyard) phenomenon. The hazardous-waste facilities, garbage dumps, and polluting industries were likely to end up in somebody's backyard and generally, they ended up in poor, powerless, black and Latino communities, rather than in affluent white suburbs. This pattern has proven to be the rule even though the benefits derived from industrial-waste production are directly related to affluence. Though case studies of Southern and Southwestern activists fighting for environmental justice are generally the rule, this statement by Robert Bullard is instructive on the dynamics in an urban environment as well: environmental racism has created "human sacrifice zones, exacerbated existing social inequities between blacks and whites, increased health risks to nearby residents, reduced property values, limited economic mobility and stigmatized entire communities as dumping grounds."[1]

THE WEST HARLEM COMMUNITY

Just the way a mugger looks for an easy mark, the environmental assault on communities of color and communities of poverty by government and corporations is systematic, deadly, and relentless. Access to power is a critical factor in the politics of pollution that has turned Harlem and other communities into a vast dumping ground. The dynamics of environmental racism take a number of forms, including decisions affecting land use, siting of facilities, enforcement of regulations, employment in mainstream environmental organizations, and the appointment of persons to serve on advisory and policy-making boards and commissions.

That Harlem residents describe their neighborhood as a dumping ground must have a significant psychological and emotional impact on youth, families, and community life. Our neighborhoods get the toilet bowl, the sludge, toxic emissions, the trash, the ash, and the buses, too.

Our neighborhoods get more of the trash because someone thinks the residents are trash too. Too often nowadays Harlem residents and other community activists use those phrases to describe their neighborhoods. Small wonder. Six out of seven Manhattan bus depots are located in northern Manhattan between 103rd and 181st Streets. Thousands of buses rumble through our neighborhoods belching a blanket of particulates. They weave and bob like boxers jostling for their personal space alongside the creaky delivery trucks roaring down Broadway beneath the rumbling elevated subway rushing toward Riverdale as it skips stops in neighborhoods on the "B" list. Squeaky garbage trucks ramble down narrow double-parked brownstone streets as they wind their way toward the Westside Highway and the swampy Viaduct road that services the Marine Transfer Station and the North River Sewage Treatment Plant. A dull whistle heralds the passing diesel-fueled Amtrak train as it races toward Albany.

"The urban ecosystem in this slice of New York is typical of the environmental witches' brew found throughout the United States. Does exposure to multiple toxic substances magnify the risk of disease and death? Should regulators set new emission standards to solve these problems," asks journalist Peter Hong. He reports that the Environmental Protection Agency (EPA) has launched studies to determine whether minorities, who often live in more polluted communities, face greater risks than assumed. An EPA spokesman admits that they need to develop a strategic plan for attacking concentrations of risk.[2]

The North River sewage treatment plant located in West Harlem is a state-of-the-art symbol of environmental injustice. Though the facility was originally slated some twenty years ago to be constructed along the Hudson River at 70th Street, a political not a scientific decision was made to relocate it upriver to 137th Street, after the well-informed and politically connected Upper West Side community mobilized to move the project there, with a little help from real estate developers. The $1.3 billion North River plant, which provided virtually no jobs or construction contracts to Harlem or northern Manhattan, began operation in May 1986.

Immediate community outrage at the sickening emissions and the disgusting odors from the plant led to mass meetings and four years of angry confrontation with the city administration under Mayor Ed Koch. That administration excelled in its ability to lie and stonewall. The community sought answers and resolution to demands that included calls for an independent engineering study of the plant, smokestack emission tests, permanent and continuous monitoring of these emissions, a new environmental-assessment study, a safety study on the thirty-acre River-bank State Park being constructed atop the plant, and the withholding of an operating permit until the community's demands were met. Clearly, some communities have insulated themselves from undesirable sitings while communities of color and poor communities have borne a dispro-portionate share of the city's pollution problem. Assess the impact of the North River plant, a nearby marine transfer station (where garbage is dumped onto barges), two bus depots within a five-block area (five of seven bus depots in Manhattan are located in or near Harlem), the diesel-fueled Amtrak train, the Westside Highway, the Trinity Crematorium (so out of compliance with air standards that the City itself shut it down), and the proposed biotechnology center that will raze the historically, culturally, and architecturally significant Audubon Ballroom and San Juan Theatre. Add the lack of managed open spaces, disgusting vacant lots created by the constant and improperly enforced renovation of buildings, lead and asbestos that often become airborne, and illegal dumping of toxic waste and medical waste in vacant lots that children explore.

Lead Poisoning

Lead poisoning is the number one threat to the health of children in the United States. There are 57 million housing units estimated by the U.S. Department of Housing and Urban Development to contain lead paint; of these units, nearly four million are occupied by toddlers and young children.[3]

More than 50 percent of New York City's lead-poisoning cases are in Bedford-Stuyvesant, Bushwick, Fort Greene, and Brownsville.[4] In Man-hattan, Washington Heights and East Harlem have the most cases. In the Bronx, it is Morissania, Mott Haven, and Tremont. In Queens, it is Jamaica.

In New York, the chief cause of lead poisoning is poorly maintained housing built before the ban on interior lead paint in 1960. Children do not have to eat lead paint chips to become poisoned. They can inhale, in-gest, and absorb lead from paint dust in living areas, and from dirt in playgrounds and vast areas of housing demolition sites where safety reg-ulations are not followed, and from automobile emissions. In 1984, it was estimated that 17 percent of all American children had elevated levels of lead in their blood that required intervention. For now, lead poisoning remains the most common and socially devastating environmental disease of young children—just ahead of asthma and respiratory ailments for children in New York City.[5]

Lead poisoning is a national disgrace that prevents a child's mind and spirit from proper development. A highly toxic metal, lead can produce a range of adverse human health effects particularly in children and fetuses. Effects include disorders of the nervous and reproductive systems, delays in neurological and physical development, cognitive and behavioral changes, and hypertension. Many poor children who are lead poisoned cannot learn to read or write, perform simple arithmetic, or master tasks that require basic coordination. It is a given that education is the prime vehicle for upward social mobility and a necessity for employment, and perhaps the only access to a hopeful future for many low-income children. Perhaps there is a correlation between the more than 50 percent of New York City children who are at risk for lead poisoning and the more than 50 percent of African American youth in New York City who are placed in Special Education classes because of so-called "learning disabilities" and often labeled hyperactive, a typical effect of lead poisoning. One study reports that children with moderate lead levels are six times more likely to have significant reading disabilities. Damage from regular exposure to lead is usually irreversible, and some effects—such as damage to hearing or IQ—often go undetected.[6]

The New York Environmental Planning Lobby (renamed Environmental Advocates) worked to draft and pass a state Comprehensive Lead Poisoning Prevention Act, which mandated universal lead screening. There may be some important new amendments in 2001 that would provide for a dedicated tax to finance lead-abatement programs and provide for training and state certification of abatement workers.

It is certain that with the advent of such a program, a lucrative industry will emerge. This is a prime opportunity for community-based job training and business development for the thousands of unemployed in the poor communities most affected by lead. Neighborhood housing-development groups have a significant opportunity to provide leadership and input on a range of activities: helping to develop inspection and abatement regulations covering all residential housing as well as preschools and day-care centers; providing technical assistance to other grassroots groups and to tenants on this issue; and organizing community-based training programs for abatement workers.

LAND USE AND TRANSPORTATION

Near urban freeway networks, with high concentrations of toxic auto emissions, urban residents are literally dying from the health hazards posed by smog, which also contributes to ozone depletion and global warming.[7] There is a direct connection between current energy policy and the real impact it has on people in an urban environment, because of the connection between global reliance on nonrenewable fossil fuels, and the disproportionate burden of environmental degradation it has on communities of color. Few of us realize the price that inner cities have paid for this nation's love of cars. Hundreds of our neighborhoods have lost most economic functions and vitality and have experienced the deterioration of housing stock, the destruction of human resources, waste of petroleum energy, pollution of air and water, and the degradation of urban biological resources. It is a story of investment decisions made without regard for community needs, a story of highways wrecking businesses and undermining the social integrity of neighborhoods. As a result, communities of color bear a disproportionate share of toxic contamination and health burdens, from lead and carbon monoxide in automobile emissions, to contamination of soil and groundwater under abandoned gas stations and other toxic-waste sites, and to noise and accidents caused by truck traffic that is too close to residential areas.

As government struggles with incentives to reduce energy consumption, transportation and energy planners often overlook conservation issues, the needs of our neighborhoods, and the potential contribution that inner-city communities might make to building new sustainable urban neighborhoods. We must refocus the debate and ask, How can we involve inner cities that have energy-efficient infrastructures already in place? How can we involve them as active participants in shaping and defining new policies?

Just as we see the parallels between the waste of land and biological resources owing to fragmented land-use decision making, and the waste of lives resulting from the same processes, there are important conclusions to draw about the connections between transportation, energy, and urban social justice.

The spaces in which we live affect our spirit and action much more than we realize. Oppressive physical surroundings perpetuate and reinforce their residents' oppression. The process by which our habitat is planned and built keeps people isolated, disempowered, and depressed. Insensitive and callous land-use siting policies invariably cut off community access to the waterfront, which can provide options for recreational and aesthetic use. Aesthetics appear to be superfluous when planners develop space in communities of color and poverty: static concrete plazas and vest-pocket parks are the uptown staple, while flowers, benches, shrubs, and waterfalls flourish downtown.

The loss of an economic base has left many cities with extensive areas of unused land. Derelict vacant lots demoralize nearby residents, cast a pall over renewal efforts, undermine property values, and inhibit the influx of capital needed for revitalization. Although this land now represents an obstacle to development and a burden for city governments, it can be turned into a significant resource when it is reclaimed for urban agriculture and recreational use.

The approach to management of vacant land can focus on its development through greening while taking into account the fact that city soil is often polluted with heavy metals such as lead, cadmium, and arsenic. These land-reclamation and greening strategies should not be thought of as temporary measures designed to attract developers but as a permanent open-space resource developed to support the growth of sustainable and more self-reliant communities—communities that can grow vegetables, plants, and trees to sell as well as producing and marketing herbs and jellies. The current economic crisis makes it progressively more difficult for municipal agencies to manage and maintain public facilities, especially open spaces. This has led to a broad range of service contracts and management leases to neighborhood organizations. Many services affecting our quality of life, such as garbage collection, public-housing maintenance, building-code inspection, sidewalk and street maintenance, and pest control, could be rendered effectively and economically at the grassroots level.

There is an opportunity to build partnerships between municipal governments, nonprofit community-based organizations, and unions whose members, as residents of many of these neighborhoods, are directly affected by these deteriorating services. Working together, unions and communities can work out options that affect environment and development issues—options that maintain jobs and create new ones. Communities are a voice not for simply shutting down plants but for making them safe for the community outside and the workers inside and advocating for workers on health and safety issues.

AIR POLLUTION

On a beautiful day you can no longer see forever. And, of course, please don't breathe deeply. Exercise and deep breathing on a bad day may send you to the hospital. And on smog alert days, caused by car and bus emissions, the impact is seen in increased emergency room admissions for respiratory problems.

Recent studies of the health effects of diesel particulates have concluded that the tiny inhalable soot particles may cause 50,000 to 60,000 deaths in the United States each year, more than any other form of urban air pollution. These fine particles evade the body's respiratory defense mechanisms and expose New Yorkers, especially children and the elderly, to increased risk of lung cancer, pneumonia, asthma, and other respiratory ailments.[8]

The impact of diesel bus soot is compounded by the fact that it is discharged at street level, precisely where pedestrians are walking and breathing. Buses lumbering along car-clogged streets produce more exhaust per city block than they would at normal speeds and they expel it into narrow, pollution-trapping street canyons—into a Harlem community whose topography, bordered by the East and West Side highways, is partially a valley.[9]

Death and illness from asthma has been increasing at an alarming rate in Harlem, a predominantly African American, economically disadvantaged urban community.[10] For the past three years, asthma has been the most common diagnosis seen in the Harlem Hospital Center Emergency Department, accounting for more than 6,000 visits each year and more than 7 percent of all emergency visits.[11] Asthma mortality rates have risen in the United States since the 1970s from 1.9 per 100,000 between 1974 and 1977 to 3.5 per 100,000 between 1982 and 1985. Urban areas accounted for 80.2 percent of asthma deaths, with most of those deaths concentrated in four areas: New York City; Fresno County, California; Cook County, Illinois; and Maricopa County, Arizona. New York City drives up the asthma mortality rate with 10.1 deaths per 100,000. In 1986, New York City had 3 percent of the national population, 6 percent of asthma hospitalizations, and 7 percent of deaths resulting from asthma. As in other asthma mortality zones, New York's cases have been concentrated in inner-city neighborhoods dominated by African American and Latino populations, such as in Central Harlem and the South Bronx. In 1990, Central Harlem's population of 115,393 was 87 percent African American with a median income of just under $15,000 and an unemployment rate of 15.2 percent. Whether because of race, poverty, or other complex circumstances of community disadvantage, Central Harlem demonstrates very high levels of asthma death and illness. Central Harlem has a rate of hospitalization for asthma that is three times higher than that of New York City for the 0–34 year-old age group.[12]

A review of Harlem hospital discharge records found that asthma admissions increased by 2.5 percent over the 1985–1990 period. In 1990 the overall asthma hospitalization rate was 123 per 10,000, approximately three times the New York City rate in the 0–34 age group. Hospital admissions were highest for the under-4-years-of-age group.[13]

Certainly the lack of access to primary care and inadequate self-care behaviors are important risk factors for asthma illness. But, doctors believe that environmental factors may impose a more serious handicap on management of asthma in Central Harlem than in other New York communities. It has been shown that higher levels of sulfur dioxides and air pollution are associated with asthma death, and Central Harlem consistently has the highest level of sulfur dioxide and particulates of all areas in the state of New York (according to the New York City forty-station Aerometric Network, 1960–80).[14]

"People of color tend to live in communities with high levels of air pollutants, both sulfur dioxide and suspended particulates. New York City is one of the regions where there are strong relationships between income and air pollution levels," according to Michel Gelobter, professor at Rutgers University.[15] Higher levels of sulfur dioxide and air pollution have been associated with higher asthma mortality rates. Thus, variations in air pollution levels may explain sudden surges in the number of persons coming to the Harlem Hospital Emergency Room for asthma.

Unfortunately, recently released statistics show rising rates of asthma illness and death among people of color. By 1989 the asthma death rate had increased 52 percent over the 1980 rate, which was more than twice the rate for white persons.[16]

The largest increase in asthma mortality was experienced among African American women, whose rates increased 63 percent compared with an increase of 37 percent among men. Overall, people of color accounted for 82 percent of all New York City asthma hospitalizations for 1982–1986.[17]

Doctors and community activists ask why the increase in asthma illness rates during the '80s was so much greater in Central Harlem. Are there other major differences in Harlem's risk factors for asthma that are important to consider? Harlem Hospital is beginning research to answer some of these questions. One can hypothesize, however, that a correlation does exist between the increased incidence of asthma and air pollution levels. Therefore, the environmental and health communities must begin to take action on this issue.

The siting decisions that bring polluting facilities and vehicles into our communities are often a matter of public policy. We have not done what we should to protest the Transit Authority's buying a new fleet of diesel buses and committing itself to a program of trap oxidizers to screen out the diesel particulates. Initial capital expenditures for diesel buses (approximately $200,000 each) are lower than those for Compressed Natural Gas (CNG) buses (approximately $250,000 each).[18] But the high purchase price of the trap oxidizers (as much as $15,000 per unit) in addition to their more frequent maintenance requirements make the cost of trap-equipped diesel buses high in the long term. The Toronto Transit Commission reports that CNG buses are less expensive to operate than conventional diesel buses. They cite an annual savings of $7,000 per bus.[19]

We cannot have a progressive program for real change in public policy while the Metropolitan Transit Authority (MTA)—a quasi-public entity—"does its own thing." That is the primary concern regarding authorities—that there is little or no accountability to the public.

The environmental community must develop a strong articulated agenda that is fought for, initiated, and implemented. There is significant advocacy work to do with the city and state administrations over the next four years. West Harlem Environmental Action (WE ACT) sued the MTA to stop them from building the fifth bus depot (out of six in 1988) in Northern Manhattan and the second in a three-block area in West Harlem. The MTA also had plans for a joint venture with a local development corporation to build low-income and seniors' housing over the bus depot. WE ACT was able to halt the development project but not the depot. The MTA—an authority—has special exemptions from having to do the Environmental Impact Statement that our lawsuit demanded.[20]

But environmental activists in this city must demand much more. We must demand—from city, state, and nation—accountability for and compliance with federal clean air standards. Above all, we must demand accountability for the health and well-being of all New York residents.

RECOMMENDATIONS

A health risk assessment of the Harlem community is essential, as is the development of a West Harlem community environmental health clinic. This is the same community where more than 50 percent of children under the age of six may be at risk for lead poisoning, where more youth under the age of nine are hospitalized for respiratory illness than for any other reason, where tuberculosis and AIDS is epidemic, and where the life expectancy of African American men and women is less than that of men in Bangladesh. There is a Third World here in New York City, whether it is called Harlem, Greenpoint-Williamsburg, or South Bronx.

The challenge for environmentalists and technocrats is to support the growing sense of ownership of this broadly defined environmental-justice movement that is being manifested at the grassroots level.

To address the need for education, training, and technical expertise, WE ACT began by producing community conferences focusing on information and on organizing skills and strategies relevant to environmental health issues, including the need to bring activists of all walks together in a coalition to merge social justice and environmental concerns. To further partnerships with neighborhood-based institutions, we are working in collaboration with City College of New York to produce a series of forums with elected and government officials that will help build their accountability to community residents. And we have designed a seminar series on a range of environmental health issues targeted to community leaders and residents. In partnership with Dr. Barry Commoner and the Center for Biology of Natural Systems at Queens College, we have begun efforts to strengthen neighborhood recycling by organizing a task force of block and tenant leaders to focus on impediments to recycling, better training, and innovative educational materials.

Through an active speakers' bureau, we have worked to raise public and media awareness of West Harlem as a symbol of environmental racism; we have also educated attorneys and have secured their pro bono services to support critical community concerns by speaking at law schools, bar associations, religious organizations, and educational institutions, and on radio and television programs. To add some virtual reality of our own, we conduct Toxic Tours of environmental hot spots in New York City's communities of color for the press, institutional groups, foundations, and students.

The need for coalitions and networks is critical if environmental-justice activists are to speak with a strong, unified voice and take action on city, state, regional, and national issues and legislation. In 1990, WE ACT began working with other New York City activists to form a citywide network that came together in 1991 as the New York City Environmental Justice Alliance. Last year, the alliance sponsored a forum for local, city, and state candidates for public office. In partnership with other nonprofits and mainstream environmental groups to form a Tri-State Transportation Campaign, the alliance has hired an executive director to coordinate outreach and education on targeted transportation issues in communities of color.

As steering committee members of the first National People of Color Environmental Leadership Summit in Washington D.C. in 1991, we also understood the necessity of working regionally to develop a multicultural, multiethnic North East Region Environmental Justice Network, which organized a regional gathering at Union Theological Seminary, New York, in 1992.

Organizing a movement, articulating and effecting a public policy agenda, requires long- and short-term strategies, and local, state, and federal objectives to achieve any measure of success. To gain self-determination over planning and land-use decisions in our communities requires longer-term strategies and a sharp analysis of power relationships. We may not always know who has power, but we know that its exercise can yield funding, legal resources, participation in decision making, and a priority niche for your issue on the public policy agenda. The fair distribution and allocation of resources by the "system" is often what community struggles are about.

And finally, the use of litigation has been an important tool in garnering attention, securing additional documents and data, allowing plaintiffs to negotiate important concessions, and achieving authority to enforce existing consent orders and agreements—even when you don't win the lawsuit. In 1988, WE ACT initiated action to sue the Metropolitan Transportation Authority to halt construction of another bus depot and to require the execution of an Environmental Impact Statement. We did not stop the depot, but we achieved a secondary objective by effectively halting the construction of senior citizens' housing atop the depot, which the community viewed as a significant health risk to the elderly.[21]

A significant event occurred on December 30, 1993, when a settlement of WE ACT's lawsuit against the City of New York for operating the North River plant as a public and private nuisance was signed by Judge Alice Schlesinger in the New York Supreme Court.[22] The settlement calls for a $1.1 million West Harlem Fund to be established to address the community's environmental and health concerns. WE ACT—in consultation with other plaintiffs—controls the fund and intends to use it to further institutionalize a West Harlem planning and advocacy organization. Its focus will be to develop partnerships to fund a West Harlem environmental health clinic that will treat respiratory ailments such as asthma while furthering research on the relationship between West Harlem's polluted air and the spiraling incidence of asthma illness and death. In addition, WE ACT will administer environmental education and advocacy projects, encourage the development of green businesses, and expand the scope of the Earth Crew Recyclers, a summer youth corps of African American and Latino teenagers, into a year-round environmental education and service program.

And, most important, the settlement gives plaintiffs the legal leverage—intended to ensure that the city administration completes its $50 million fix-up at the North River plant—and considerable power to use the court to enforce the city-state consent order and other agreements aimed at fixing and maintaining the North River plant.

10

These Stones
Shall Be God's House:
Tools for Earth Liturgy

Troy Messenger

FLIPPING THROUGH HYMNBOOKS OF A PREVIOUS GENERATION, one can easily see the estrangement of the earth from our worship. Particularly in evangelical Christian denominations, the burdens of life on Earth contrast sharply with hopes for heaven. "Should earth against my soul engage," the Christian trusted, there awaited "a land that is fairer than day."[1] If "while we walk the pilgrim pathway clouds will overspread the sky," then we could look forward to that heavenly realm of eternal fair weather.[2] According to these hymns, in the New Jerusalem it is always springtime, flowers never die, it never rains, and the sun never sets, because time is frozen in a perpetual morning.

> . . . time shall be no more,
> and the morning breaks eternal, bright, and fair. . . .
> On that bright and cloudless morning . . .[3]
>
> On that blessed morning clouds will disappear.[4]
>
> O they tell me of a home far beyond the skies,
> O they tell me of a home far away;
> O they tell me of a home where no storm clouds rise,
> O they tell me of an unclouded day.[5]

Though contemporary congregations spend much less time singing about our other home "over there," these hymn texts reveal a tension between earth-centered theology and liturgical practice that is as problematic today as it was a century ago. When we worship in spirit and truth—but not in earth-centered bodies—we deny a fundamental relationship we have as earth creatures at home in this world. If our orientation in worship is not toward the world in which we live, our theology will reflect that. It is not surprising that an industrial-era faith community "bound for the promised land," where "no chilling winds nor pois'nous breath . . . sickness and sorrow, pain and death are felt and feared no more,"[6] could have had a laissez-faire attitude toward the factories that spilled poisonous fumes into the air they breathed every day.

Earth theologies can not be effective without transformed worship. Worship is an essential companion to environmental justice because theology happens first and foremost in worship. Worship is primary theology. What we believe is being created week after week as the assembled reenact the sacred stories of God's action in the world. These actions testify to a theology that is being molded into our very selves.

Liturgical theology is not just about believing. It is about becoming. In worship, God's people come together in relationships with God, each other, and the world around them. These relationships are constantly being made, sustained, renewed, and redefined. Worship is an action of world-making. It is primary theology because these relationships are not only conceived but actualized at a given moment in a particular place. While singing or praying together, we not only understand the mystery of the unity of God's people, but we make it a reality. Worship becomes practice for living. In it we develop skills of interaction and love that become models for all of life. If worship works, the brokenness of our relationship with the earth will be restored. We will not only preach a theology of wholeness, but our worship will make that wholeness visible and present in our midst. Worship then becomes not about the earth, but a cocreator with earth.

In earth-centered liturgy, the earth is a partner in this common work of model-building. Even the most basic rituals illustrate the power of the earth's resources in combination with ritual action. A student in a Union Seminary course on ritual was assigned to do a ten-minute ritual using an object.[7] He chose rocks—one of the most basic elements of the world. We adapted this ritual and performed it at the liturgy workshop of the

Ecumenical Earth Conference. We began by selecting rocks, holding them, and getting to know them. We felt their weight and ran our hands over their surface. These were smooth, light-colored stones about the size of a hand, gathered from the bottom of a streambed. I invited the participants to think of a significant date in their lives and to write that date on the rock. Then we placed our stones, one at a time, in a pillar on a cloth on the floor and described our dates. Some were calls to vocations; others, engagements; still others, memorials. In this brief moment of sharing we brought a small, significant piece of ourselves into our common experience. In closing, I read a passage from Genesis 28 where Jacob marks his encounter with God at Bethel with a pile of stones. The passage ends thus: "this stone, which I have set up for a pillar, shall be God's house."[8]

Earth liturgy believes that the most basic elements of the earth are God's house. If God's spirit is indeed a creative life force moving throughout all creation, we ought to invite the earth to be our partner in worship. Authentic earth theology will emerge from congregations that take earth liturgy seriously. And the practice of worshiping faithfully with the earth will model interactions that allow us to live faithfully in our earth community.

The Tools of Earth Liturgy

For this work we need effective tools. Whenever people gather to worship, they use certain objects and practices that help them "do" the ritual work they have come together to perform. All of the things we use to make our common worship—prayers, icons, bread, hymns, vestments, buildings—help us in the difficult and ongoing task of molding healthy relationships. These special tools take rituals out of ordinary experience and set them apart where they have special significance for our lives. Too often, this break with the quotidian has meant a similar negation of the earth. But coming into the presence of the Holy does not necessitate forsaking the world in which we live. An incarnational theology suggests that the world around us is an appropriate place to seek God. Our break with the everyday can then be an opportunity to stop and listen to the earth.

Liturgies must reclaim the resources of the earth as the tools of worship if we are to rebuild our relationship with God, each other, and the environment. I propose here six tools—objects, time, space, sound, language, and action. We could add more, but these six elements are essential building blocks for rituals. As we allow the earth to be present in these tools, we will go a long way toward creating stones where God can dwell.

Earth Objects

Our simple workshop ritual shows that ordinary rocks can, in the company of sacred action, be God's house. Only in the most extreme forms of enlightenment Protestantism do we find worship that excludes sacred objects from liturgy. A. Verheul defines worship as "a personal meeting, under the veil of holy signs, of God with God's church and with the total person of each one of its members . . ."[9] These holy signs are simple objects that reveal and convey the essence of God.

We are familiar with the transformation of bread and wine. Whatever our eucharistic theology, the power of Holy Communion certainly lies in the connection of sacred history, ritual action, and ordinary foods. The act of taking in our daily bread is hallowed, and all table fellowship becomes a reflection of the liturgical archetype. Likewise, the waters of baptism literally wash our body at the same time they are recalling burial and the waters of birth. We reenact the life cycle and honor it with one of the basic elements of the earth as a way of marking our entrance into the fullness of the worshiping community.

Baptism and eucharist are paradigmatic rites for the earth community. These rites transform everyday human activities of eating, drinking, and washing into spiritual activities by which God can move in our common life. They teach us that rituals work when they are part and parcel of who we are as humans living in God's creation. Earth objects celebrate the beauty of the natural world—things like fire, water, soil, stone, wood, plants, natural fiber. Too often, our worship is filled with objects that don't help our liturgies—carpet, bad lighting, polyester paraments, gold anodized communion sets, photocopied service aids, silk flowers, artificial Christmas trees, wafers bearing no resemblance to bread, and baptismal fonts in which it is impossible to get very wet. Earth liturgies invite the possibility of bringing the stuff of the earth into our worship space and using it to celebrate our beautiful system of living, growing, and dying beings.

Earth Time

Liturgical time is slippery. Ritual scholars describe worship as taking place in a time out of time. Many see this disjunction with ordinary time as an essential component in defining ritual. Mircea Eliade argues that rituals take place in a creative moment temporally equivalent to the beginning of all things. He describes this repeated reenactment of creation as an "eternal return."[10] Christian theologians describe eucharistic *anamnesis*—the "remembering" of Christ's death in bread and wine—as a synchronic melding of past event, present moment, and future consequence. But these times do not negate the rhythms of human living. In liturgy, we do not live in the endless spring morning of nineteenth-century hymnody. We do worship in a time where it is possible for humans to touch the creative impulses of the beginnings of time as well as the glorious consummation of the ending of time. In worship, therefore, we acknowledge beginnings and endings, and the rhythms of movement and cycles between the two.

Being human means living in many concentric and sometimes conflicting temporal cycles. Our bodies feel the biological rhythms in daily, monthly, and lifelong cycles. Often these cycles are out of sync with work time, leisure time, lunar time, solar time, and particularly computer time or MTV time. Earth liturgy offers the possibility of healing these rhythms, of helping us synchronize our rhythms with the rhythms of God's creation.

At their roots, many of our modern liturgies were better connected with earth times. Ancient agrarian societies used rituals to bless the ground for planting, pray for rain, and give thanks for the harvest. Communities felt the winter darkness and marked the summer sun. As these rituals evolved into Christmas, Easter, and Pentecost we often lost our connection to the ancient rhythms of the earth. In writing seasons of liturgical significance onto our yearly calendar, it is essential that we not forget earth times. This might mean eucharistic prefaces that locate us in the season, blessing those who plant and harvest, reviving Rogation Day, celebrating Earth Day, marking births and deaths, comings and goings. Earth times must not be scripted out of liturgy, but used as ritual markers to celebrate the rhythms of God's creation and our place in that created order.

Earth Space

Often it is difficult to feel the rhythms of the earth because our worship spaces are so immune from the world. Worshiping in earth space can mean many things. It certainly means occasionally leaving our walled enclosures and worshiping where we can feel the elements. Contemporary congregations could learn from nineteenth-century Methodists who left their churches each summer to gather in a clearing in the woods to find spiritual renewal at annual camp meetings. At harvesttime, Jewish congregations similarly leave their synagogues for rustic booths during the festival of Sukkoth. Many of us have forgotten the power of joining our prayers with the grass under our feet and the sky over our head.

Built spaces best serve liturgical needs when these buildings are at home with their environment and congregation. The newly redesigned synagogue in West Vancouver, B.C., is an excellent example. Combining native woods with stones from Israel, the building integrates a sense of double place for this congregation. Sensitive to its particular location, the educational wing forms a bridge over an adjacent stream and shades a resting pool for migrating salmon. The interior is flooded with natural light and adapts easily to changing needs throughout the year with flexible seating and a movable wall.

St. Benedict the African, an African American Catholic congregation in Chicago, created an equally appropriate but entirely different liturgical space. Modeled on the design of an African hut, the round sanctuary focuses the creative energy toward the center of the worship space. Around the edges of the room, plants are growing in soil connected with the ground outside the building. The foundation does not cut off the structure from its environment but allows the environment to seep inside. At the entrance, one passes a large stone baptistry with running water.

Both of these are examples of worship space that can breathe with the breath of the world around us. They are organic to their people and connect the people with both their surroundings and their cultural and spiritual roots. And like the world, these spaces change; they are flexible and move with the seasonal needs of the congregation.

Earth Sound

During the Ecumenical Earth Conference we heard the sound of recycling. The *Music for Homemade Instruments* ensemble played an entire concert of carefully composed music on instruments made from garbage. Soda straws, refrigerator drawers, brake drums, cardboard tubes, electrical conduit, chopsticks, and other castaways became Indonesian gamelans, English bells, and katydids of the night sky. If somewhat tongue-in-cheek, this music reminds us that the world vibrates with music. Most of us left the concert with a little more curiosity about the sound lurking in our garbage.

As we become increasingly accustomed to the sound of digitized or synthesized sounds extracted from their environment, transformed, and delivered over high-tech sound systems, our worship is in need of rediscovering earth sound. In many traditions, a desire to transmit the spoken, amplified word with utmost clarity has led to the deadening (both acoustic and spiritual) of our worship spaces. Carpet, padded seating, and acoustical ceiling tile ensure that whoever is at a microphone is heard. They also ensure that everyone else is silenced. Earth sound begins with a room where the acoustics invite the congregation to sing, speak, and listen in many directions.

Earth sound also celebrates the breadth of sound from the ripple of water to the pounding of a drum. A healthy environment is diverse and has many species living together. Likewise our musical sounds should celebrate many cultures and traditions. Sounds from a single culture are as deadly as a single species monopolizing an ecosystem. Worship vibrating with earth sound would invite sounds from many sources—natural and musical, professional and amateur, presiders and congregation—reflecting the total range of cultures in a diverse congregation.

Earth Language

Linguistic philosophy since J. L. Austin has understood that language does things. It not only means but creates realities. Embedded in ritual contexts, language has the power to liberate and transform. Speaking for a just earth is an imperative, because in worship we not only advocate but create what we advocate.
Earth language certainly calls to mind images of the world around us. We speak of water and fire, times and seasons, and the God who lives and breathes in the myriad species of the world. We preach of justice for the victims of pollution. We confess our sin of squandering resources.

In the same way that earth sound reflects healthy ecosystems with a diversity of sounds, so also our corporate language will have a place for many people. Most important, our language will be inclusive, so that no group is left out of the presence of God. But earth language will also allow each person to speak, and in his or her own language. The Taizé community is an excellent example of this practice. Hosting youth from around the world, the songs and prayers of Taizé are in many languages. The simple, repeated phrases and familiar prayers create a harmony of voices where a person from any place is equally able to participate.

Earth Action

The earth is not passive. It is constantly in action. All of its many parts are constantly in motion—acting and counteracting. From continental plates to quantum particles, the earth is in motion. This suggests that if our worship models a healthy relationship with our environment, we, too, cannot be passive. Earth action means that the gathered faithful must have opportunities to act and react in worship. Liturgies become a creative interplay in which participants have options and real responsibilities for bringing about personal and corporate transformation. This participation will involve the whole congregation and the whole person of each member of that congregation. Participation will begin with familiar words and songs but will also include actions for the whole body and all the senses.

EARTH LITURGIES

Liturgies that respect and celebrate the earth can be both grand and simple. As our tools for worship would indicate, often small things hallow the earth, its rhythms, and our place in our environment. But there is also the place for festival worship that uses every means possible to build a just earth community. Following are two sample liturgies that demonstrate something of the range of possibilities for earth liturgies. Both start with ancient traditions and creatively adapt these to be highly effective rituals of community transformation.

The Feast of St. Francis

The Cathedral Church of St. John the Divine in New York City has a commitment to environmental justice that is evident throughout its ministry. The thirteen-acre cathedral grounds are the largest privately held park area in the city. On the border of Harlem and Morningside Heights is an oasis of green where the neighborhood comes together as a K–8 school, shelter, soup kitchen serving hundreds each week, senior outreach ministry, a recycling center, and several environmental ministries. Most of its almost $10 million budget goes directly to social outreach.

The cathedral is also an excellent example of a church that integrates these concerns for the environment and social justice with liturgy. Since 1985 the cathedral has observed the Feast of St. Francis on the first Sunday in October with children playing next to squawking peacocks. The cathedral is committed to the survival of this neighborhood, with preschool and after-school programs, a youth outreach program, and a festival Earth Mass. Each year thousands of people and their pets arrive before 8:00 A.M. to crowd into St. John's for the 11:00 A.M. service. Sometime after 1:00 P.M., when the congregation has received the bread and wine, the giant bronze doors are pushed open. Timidly making their way through these doors is a procession of beasts—elephant, pig, sheep, chicken, falcon, and even reverently carried algae—which make their way down the long nave to the crossing where they are blessed by the bishop. Following the service, the worshipers move outdoors to the cathedral grounds where they may have their own pets blessed by priests strolling through the petting zoo, animal adoption center, marionettes, face painters, and costumed dancers.

The liturgy connects faith and the earth in many wonderful ways. The Earth Mass, composed by Paul Halley and performed by the Paul Winter Consort, is a musical thread running throughout the service. The breadth of its musical styles is stunning. Latin liturgical chants weave in and out of jazz harmonies, African drumming, and the recorded calls of whales and wolves. The music itself lets us hear and feel what a connected earth sounds like. All of these melodies and rhythms are going on at once, but they respect one another and add to each other. The dogs in the congregation often join in on the hymns, but that is as it should be. And even the man in a robe and garland pushing a wheelbarrow and shovel in case the elephant should decide to "make an offering" is a holy man with a sacred role in this liturgy.

The Feast of St. Francis is for many residents of the Upper West Side the liturgical equivalent of Christmas or Easter. It is the one service they go to each year, and because of that, they consider St. John's their home. The service blesses the beasts that sustain people through the challenges of urban life. It helps maintain a relationship with the environment, which is tenuous at best in New York City. Moreover, this feast day is one of the critical public events that *makes* the Upper West Side what it is. By modeling the community as an ecological system where many cultural streams can merge and flourish with each other, other species, and the environment, the liturgy helps create that community. By doing so in such a large way, the cathedral also attracts the regional and national press to the environmental justice issues that it advocates.

Greening the Cross

Earth liturgies need not, however, include a cast of thousands. If we are respectful of our resources, perhaps we should do more with less. Our liturgies can, in fact, call us to our spiritual obligation to preserve our resources. On September 10, 1996, Union Seminary's chapel adapted the ancient Orthodox Greening of the Cross tradition for the blessing and dedication of the new seminary compost bin.

The service was planned and led by members of Larry Rasmussen's spring 1996 Ecology and Ethics class. The class led three services in the spring celebrating the cycle of life. The final service was planned for the fall to coincide with the completion of the compost bin. Titled "Prayers for the Earth," the service began in James Chapel with the community seated loosely throughout the space on cushions, chairs, and steps. A twelve-foot, rough-hewn cross lay across the steps at the front of the space, and candles and greenery were placed among the congregation. After gathering music and an introduction, the congregation was led through the greening ritual. While singing simple chants and praying, individuals took the greenery and flowers around them and attached them to the cross. This symbol of death became a tree of life. It was then carried in procession to the quadrangle and placed near the new compost bin. After prayers of dedication, the congregation shared fruit and mixed the rinds and cores into dirt to form the initial offering to the compost.

The service was not complex or expensive. It was less than thirty minutes in length. But it did use a variety of media to connect us with the earth, each other, and God. The service made sense in earth time as we anticipated autumn and the cycle of death and renewal, which would happen in miniature in our compost. Our space was earth space: the stone and wood floors and grass under our feet. We held the things of the earth, touched the wood of the cross, smelled flowers, ate fruit, and ran our hands through dirt. We sang Native American chants of the elements, played drums, and listened to the sounds of birds. We spoke of a world in which our spirits are at home in their earthly bodies. Each person had a variety of opportunities to act and interact with one another, our environment, and God. When it was over we had not only modeled something, but we had actually done something. We had opened our compost bin and made a community-wide commitment to take this small step together for the sake of the earth.

TOWARD EARTH-CENTERED LITURGY

These two examples illustrate the principles for earth-centered liturgy in two very different contexts. Placing them in juxtaposition highlights the flexibility of these principles. The tools of earth liturgy offer some very practical means of inviting the earth back into our worship. These tools suggest that at the most basic level, the earth should be present—in our rhythms, under our feet, in the things we hold, in what we hear, and in what we do. But the earth must be more than present. It must be a full participant.

The earth can teach us many things. Once the earth is joined with us in worship, we should learn from its marvelous capacity for renewal, how it flourishes in diversity, how ecosystems depend on every element participating fully. Earth liturgy takes the earth as its model and then models the human family in right relation to the earth. Practicing responsible living with the earth in worship is the first step in making it so.

We began by hearing the hymns that disparaged this earth-bound life and aspired to a land above and beyond this world. Let us close by hearing the words of promise that the Creator God who made us out of raw dirt is indeed at home with us, here and now; that in our worship we are connected by the hand that weaves us together with the very elements of the earth.

> Who knows the patterns of our lives before our days are spun?
> Who knows the reason why, and how, before it's all begun?
> The One whose hand weaves all with love and mystery and care;
> the One whose thread and warp and weft are flesh and earth and air![11]

Conclusion

THE CHURCH
ECOLOGICALLY REFORMED

Dieter Hessel

IN A CROWDED WORLD with conspicuous overconsumption alongside human deprivation, ominous species extinctions, land and water degradation, deforestation, overfishing, and other definite resource limits, a growing number of theologians, seminaries, church agencies, congregations, intentional communities, and individual members are responding in significant ways.[1] Such responses involve serious eco-theological study coupled with action to overcome severe social disparities and to care for creation by preserving and restoring special places, implementing locally sustainable food production, fostering responsible energy production and use, organizing communities to achieve environmental justice, and advocating policies and practices to reduce climate change.

Chapters in this volume show that, despite the impact of consumer-oriented "free market" economics on churches as well as societies, laity and clergy here and there are keeping the faith through spiritual attunement to natural as well as social ecology. They minister to places as well as people, serving both ecological integrity *and* social equity, holding together global/local concerns for the well-being of nature and humans. They try to embody an "eco-justice" orientation that grapples with environmental devastation and socioeconomic injustice, affirming the indivisibility of environmental and human rights, and demanding action for the common good.

Christians on six continents are joining this eco-justice journey. Yet compared with widespread church involvement in programs of social service and peace education/action, the churches have not institutionalized much care for creation or eco-justice ministry. Many Christians still do not see mission in terms of suffering with, healing, and liberating creation. They continue to affirm and practice "stewardship" in social terms, apart from ecological responsibility. Congregations typically conduct religion business as usual with little time for the shared human vocation of earth-keeping (Gen. 2:15), except perhaps for doing some recycling, exhorting members to reduce unnecessary consumption, and retrofitting church buildings for energy efficiency. In short, the bulk of clergy and laity who lead local, denominational, and ecumenical communities of faith tend to leave the well-being of creation to others called "environmentalists"; they have yet to "get it" with regard to an "ecological reformation of Christianity," that focuses on the new context of imperiled earth community and responds by reorienting liturgy, theology, ethics, and mission.[2]

As the world becomes hotter, stormier, less biodiverse, more unequal, more crowded, and more violent, the church must embody commitment to eco-justice. Not to do so will only induce lamentations, beginning a long requiem for nature. As Bill McKibben, author of *The End of Nature* (Random House, 1989) warned in a turn-of-the-millennium article addressed to Christians, "Spring now comes a week earlier across the northern hemisphere than it did 30 years ago. . . . This is an unbelievably large change for such a basic physical phenomenon. And all this with about one degree of global average temperature rise," that is likely to be followed by another four degrees of temperature rise in this century. "We are engaged in the swift and systematic decreation of the planet we were born onto; . . . we have ever more rapidly destroyed its inventory of life. . . . In our time the morally transcendent question is whether we will stop this decreation before it goes further; whether we will take the difficult steps to preserve God's creation in as intact and integral a form as is still possible."[3]

In these paradoxical times, when human domination of the earth intensifies along with human environmental awareness and action, it is especially pertinent for Christians to reconsider what on earth the church is for, including the where, what, and how of its ministry. Since "the central challenge today, both for the understanding of the church and for ethics, is to promote the rebuilding of sustainable human communities," the ecumenical community of faith must shift to an emphasis on post-anthropocentric (no longer so human-centered) worship, education, and witness.[4]

Documents such as *Baptism, Eucharist and Ministry* (1982) and *Confessing One Faith* (1991) that expressed a formal ecumenical "Faith and Order" consensus within anthropocentric and ecclesiocentric confines, are woefully inadequate for ecumenical Earth. There is urgent need for fresh theological-ethical reflection on the life and mission of the church as iconic participant in the new creation—the body of Christ working in human and natural communities to fulfill God's will. At stake is not just the church's practice (what it does) but also its nature (the church's being) as a believing community that "serves the fulfillment of God's purposes in creation as a whole" by grappling energetically and comprehensively with the crisis of ecology and equity.[5]

Reorientation to eco-justice is gaining enough spiritual and secular prominence to indicate that an ecological reformation of church and culture has begun. Such a reformation of religion and ethics takes seriously the reality of natural biophysical limits, the depths of the eco-justice crisis, and the intricate and interdependent relationships of humankind with the rest of nature. The ecological reformation also positively intersects, rather than competes with, struggles for economic, racial, and gender justice. Following is a brief description of the basic contours of this transformation involving world religions generally, and Christianity in particular.[6]

Steps toward an Ecologically Reformed Church

First, Christians need to acknowledge and abandon several bad theological habits that malformed the church's understanding of and relationship to nature. The church is just beginning to overcome four dysfunctional theological habits or alienating themes recently identified by Ian Barbour.[7]

(1) Christian thought separated God from nature. God was understood to be revealed primarily in historical events rather than in natural life, and God's transcendence was emphasized much more than God's immanence or living presence in creation. Reformed theology in Presbyterian circles intensified this bad habit in the way it interpreted the sovereignty of God, the authority of Scripture, and the human deputyship to dominate nature.

(2) Christian theology, following the lead of modern secular philosophy, separated humanity from nature. Humanity alone was said to be made "in the image of God," set apart from all otherkind, and given dominion. This translated into devastating utilitarianism, as exemplified currently in unfettered genetic engineering, which perpetuates human arrogance toward nature.

(3) There was also an increasing separation of redemption from creation. Nature became a mere backdrop for the drama of human salvation. Theology, preaching, liturgy, and ritual focused on the doctrine of personal redemption rather than the fulfillment of creation. Worship and pastoral activity today too often continue in this vein.

(4) The churches accepted and reinforced common assumptions about the domination of men over women (patriarchy), and the rights of human beings over nature. "Men and technology were identified with the first term in each of the following polarities of reason/emotion, mind/body, objectivity/subjectivity, and control/nurture. Women and nature were associated with the second term in each case." Eco-justice feminists have responded effectively with the critique that the oppression of women and the oppression of nature are rooted in a common set of hierarchical, dualistic, patriarchal assumptions.

Overcoming these bad theological habits involves decontaminating inherited Christian doctrine and liturgy and reconstructing faith affirmations and worship patterns to express more holistic organic models of God's relation to nature, and to undergird the human vocation of earthkeeping on a finite, fragile planet.

Reformation involves a shift of philosophical assumptions. So, a second step toward becoming a church and culture that cares for earth community is to connect with current cosmology and physics as well as the ecological and biological sciences that reorient us to reality. In the Protestant Reformation five hundred years ago, a new philosophy called Nominalism shifted attention from the great hierarchical chain of being to discrete individual things, resulting in new expressions of human liberty along with overly individualistic understandings of God, humanity, church, and society. Today, a philosophy of ecological realism, informed by current astronomy, biophysical sciences, ecofeminism, and nature writing, fosters respect for interrelatedness, spiritual kinship with otherkind, commitment to ecological sustainability, and advocacy for environmental justice.

In our time, faith and ethics are being reoriented by the new story of the cosmos and of planet Earth bodying forth the power, wisdom, and love of God. This dynamic evolutionary-process story focuses on relations and community, not on individuals and objects. Ironically, this is very much in keeping with the old biblical story of right relations reflecting the covenant God has made with the earth and humans. Current cosmology portrays the universe as emerging from a Big Bang or Great Flaring Forth 10 billion to 15 billion years ago when a tiny bit of matter exploded, becoming over billions of years the galaxies and stars and, roughly 4 billion years ago, bringing forth life itself on our planet, resulting in the richly diverse, infinitely interesting forms we know—from beetles to behemoths, from mushrooms to mice to wheat and giant cedars, from fish and birds, fungi and frogs to chimpanzees and human beings. We are all related; we all came from the same natural beginning. Earth's natural history, geologically recorded and ecologically alive, exposes a dynamic relational system that is reflective of the universe.

All of creation (or nature), the web of life on which we rely, is an interdependent community encompassing other creatures—plants and animals, spirits and ancestors—that have value as a part of one Sacred Whole, loved by God and deserving of profound human respect and care. As Jay McDaniel reminds us, "God is both a personal presence who 'knows our names' and to whom we can pray, but also an animating spirit within the whole of creation—a living God in relation to a creative universe."[8] God has given us humans responsibility for creation's health on and around planet Earth. The ecological and cultural quality of the planet's near future depends on our species developing an appropriate human-earth relationship.

A third aspect of the ecological reformation is to reexamine Scripture in the context of the deepening eco-justice crisis. Congregations and theologians are beginning to read and interpret the Bible with more alertness to nature (what goes on outdoors), while attending to God's special regard for the oppressed (the view from below), and appreciating culturally diverse understandings of faithfulness (insights from churches abroad and other religions). When rereading Scripture today, the view from "outdoors" needs to be linked with the view from "below" and the view from "abroad"; this trifocal perspective is essential for churches and ecumenical organizations that would serve both socioeconomic and ecological justice and seek the fulfillment of creation.

The Protestant Reformers half a millennium ago read Scripture anew to find basic criteria for their critique of malformed church tradition and to undergird a constructive revival of the right relatedness of faith. The twenty-first century eco-reformation involves recultivating the soil of biblical narratives to nurture earth-friendly praxis. Biblical scholars such as Brigitte Kahl characterize this as "a non-ecocidal, non-imperial reading." The Bible offers hidden treasure to ecologically alert readers who appreciate contemporary science and bring to bear insights gained from archaeological research and sociological and literary methods of interpretation. Rereading biblical passages from the perspective of earth community cuts through an overlay of modern anthropocentric misinterpretation, exposing how much Scripture has to offer as a critique of nature manipulation and destructive development. The Bible turns out to be a resource for celebrating daily life and guiding our ultimate redemption with (*not* apart from) the rest of nature.

Sabbath sensibility and covenant law featured in the Pentateuch foster deep respect for the well-being of creation while caring for "the widow, the fatherless, the sojourner." Exodus 23, Leviticus 19 and 25, and Deuteronomy 15 exemplify the covenant obligation to respond to the poor, to give animals rest, to let the land lie fallow, and to cancel debts periodically, if not redistribute land. Job 38–41 and a number of the Psalms underscore the values of relational integrity with everykind. Speaking to Job through the storm, God inspires Job's reverent awe for the revelatory power of wild creatures, natural places, and processes.

Proverbs 8:22-31 presents Woman Wisdom as the source of creation. The Gospel of John (1:1-5; 3:16) picks up this theme when affirming the power of the Logos—the ground and reason of being—to love the cosmos, and to restore its wholeness through incarnation. The epistles to the Ephesians (1:10; 2:19-22) and Colossians (1:15-20) celebrate the cosmic Christ who creates and reconciles all things. And the apocalyptic book of Revelation ends with a vision of the garden in the city, within which humanity is restored to health.

When the two creation accounts at the beginning of Genesis are reread with earth community in mind, Christians and Jews can begin to correct for P trumping J in tradition. Especially during the Modern period, secular cheerleaders for nature manipulation and destructive development, beginning with Francis Bacon, pursued dominion logic as humanity's mandate, following the lead of P—the Priestly liturgy that is

Genesis 1. ecotheology today takes an earth-friendlier path by focusing more attention on the second creation saga of J—the Yahwist account of primal humans in the Garden beginning in Genesis 2. As Theodore Hiebert has shown, the second creation saga views humans with humility as earth creatures—people of the land; Adama, from the soil—who share the same Creator's breath as do other animals, and who recognize that we are all mothered by earth.[9] The J account, which also appreciates God's theophanous presence in nature, culminates in the rainbow covenant God makes with "all flesh that is on the earth" (Gen. 9:12-13). Brigitte Kahl's chapter in this volume pursues in rich detail the theological implications of the stories in Genesis 2–4, introducing fresh insights to jar us out of the rut of routine interpretation.

A fourth step in ecological reform of Christianity is to theologize as if earth community matters. The objective is to recycle/reconstruct traditional affirmations about God, Christ, Spirit, world, church, soul/body, sin and evil, redemption and the eschatological vision of New Jerusalem or New Earth, and to re-present Christian theology and ethics in ecologically alert terms. Following are three examples.

(1) To engage the reality of one earth with a common destiny, the church-world relation needs to be reexamined. God-world-church, not God-church-world is our appropriate theologic. The well-being of the world (cosmos) is the objective of the Word becoming flesh. Ecclesiocentric theology, therefore, is beside the point. Christian communions cannot continue to assume that only the church has Truth to share with the world, or that the church is custodian of Earth's guiding Spirit. Such an assertion is patently false, when we remember that the Spirit blows where it will and we recall where environmental responsibility arose as well as who actually provided early leadership. Let us admit that the churches, across the conservative-liberal spectrum, have not led the pilgrimage toward sustainable community; instead Christian communions, while claiming to be exceptional, have mostly been quite conventional in their captivity to the culture of inappropriate development, production, and consumption in the late Modern period.

(2) We also should reconsider/restate what is meant by Spirit in light of the environmental crisis—something that Mark Wallace, of Swarthmore College does well in *Fragments of the Spirit,* a book that is biophilically informed by "earth friendly spiritualities." Wallace sees the Spirit as more than the power of reciprocity between the first and second persons of the

Trinity, or the interior power that redeems human beings. Following Rosemary Radford Ruether, *Gaia and God,* he urges us to reconceive the Spirit as a natural entity, a wild life-form.[10] "Long-standing de-emphasis on the Spirit's ecological identity is remarkable given the abundance of imagery about the Spirit drawn from the natural world within the Bible." The Spirit is both of God—the *vinculum caritatis* within the life of God, relating Father and Son—and the animator of earth community, with a cosmic role as the power of life-giving breath within creation. It is the Spirit of life, known to us as both personal agent (Thou) and inanimate force (It). Spirit and earth mutually indwell each other. This insight challenges the traditional doctrine of God, since "God as Spirit is vulnerable to loss and destruction insofar as the earth is abused and despoiled. While this association is beginning to be felt by many people today, most theologians are hesitant to postulate that ecologically toxic relationships with other life-forms place the presence of the Spirit in the world in fundamental jeopardy."[11] The point is that "God's fate and the world's future are fundamentally bound up with one another; God is so internally related to the universe that the specter of ecocide raises the risk of deicide; to wreak environmental havoc on the earth is to run the risk that we will do irreparable, even fatal harm to the Mystery we call God."[12]

Wallace invokes John Muir's nature writings as a resource for discerning the ecological work of the Spirit. "The theological demand of our time is to reimagine God as Spirit in a manner consistent with Muir's pneumatology of the wilderness . . . in which flashes of divine presence are refracted through the multifaceted complexity of all natural things. . . . Spirit is thinly clothed with a variety of life-forms. . . ." For Muir, nature is a living temple where the Spirit is at play in the flora and fauna of the wild.[13] Wallace concludes that a "reunderstanding of the Spirit in our time as a wild life-form who transgresses boundaries between humans and otherkind, while threatening to our traditional assumptions and identities, embodies the biblical promise of a new nature-intoxicated spirituality that knocks humankind off its hierarchical pedestal and replants it within the great earth mother, vitalized by the Spirit, who gives life to all beings."[14] This theological orientation overcomes the false distinction between love of God and love of nature.

(3) An ecologically reformed church inhabits the Earth lovingly as home, or *oikos,* "house of the earth." Developing this theme in *God's Spirit: Transforming a World in Crisis,* Geiko Müller-Fahrenholz proposes

that "the paradigm of *dominating* the earth which has guided most of human activity over the millennia needs to be replaced by the paradigm of *inhabiting* the earth, which aims at establishing compatible and sustaining forms of interaction between humans and nature. . . . In this connection the Greek word *oikodome* [building up a house] takes on considerable significance."[15] The focus shifts to "household politics" that undergird healthy, interacting ecosystems and cultures—planning, nurturing, ordering, correcting, even rebuilding communities, including households of faith, to be consistent with the ecological paradigm and the vision of ecumenical Earth.

The apostle Paul called his mission a service to the *oikodome* of Christ (2 Cor. 13:10). He urged members to behave toward each other in the spirit of *oikodome* (Rom. 14:19), so as to edify or upbuild the body of Christ (Eph. 2:21). "What the letter to the Ephesians calls 'the unity of the Spirit in the bond of peace' (4:3) could well be understood as an ecodomical covenant," argues Müller-Fahrenholz. He invites the church to enter with hope and confidence into a praxis of earth community or ecodomical unity. Regrettably, "The early church did not develop this ecodomical perspective; instead, it settled for another concept also derived from the word *oikos:* that is, *paroikia,* a word that means literally 'living away from home.' It is understandable that some of these small and persecuted Christian groups began to see themselves as communities of 'aliens and exiles' in a hostile world, whose true homeland was in the heavens (compare 1 Peter 2:11). Eventually each local Christian church came to be called *paroikia,* a home away from home, as it were, a place of refuge. . . . Obviously this helped to foster a dualism which despised the earth and glorified the world beyond."[16] Müller-Fahrenholz urges the ecumenical church to connect the two oikos themes: "The constructive and immanent thrust of ecodomical communities must incorporate the critical element of nonconformity."

Congregations and church-related organizations, which are reoriented to Earth as home, will develop real relations of solidarity with particular places, people, and life-forms jeopardized by inappropriate development or environmental injustice. In *Super, Natural Christians* (1997), theologian Sallie McFague enjoins us to interact with entities in (wilderness and humanly managed) nature "in the same basic way that we are supposed to relate to God and human beings, . . . as ends, not means, as subjects valuable in themselves, for themselves."[17] Loving creation this way is a natural follow-up to appreciating the spirit as a wild life-form. The struggle for eco-justice, of course, is not just in wild places to be preserved, but throughout the community of life including settled urban places, as this volume shows in Peggy Shepard's chapter on community empowerment for environmental action in West Harlem, and in the chapter on eco-justice ministry by the South African team.

A fifth step in ecological reformation for the sake of ecumenical Earth is to reshape liturgical life to highlight God's loving and just relation to habitat Earth, not only human beings. Christian worship, which has always expressed appreciative celebration of natural phenomena (doxology), needs to become more oriented to seeking the well-being of everykind in God's commonwealth, to ecological concern for the world reconciled in Christ, and to the eco-justice ethics and praxis that flow from the gospel. Troy Messenger's chapter in this volume introduces tools of earthier liturgy. And Kusumita Pedersen prods Christians to become morally inclusive of otherkind—that is, to welcome other species and the insights of other religions. For ecotheology and ecclesiology to have congruence, liturgy and education must open up to include voices of natural and religious diversity, and should learn from the ecumenical church about varied Christian practices of earth-keeping, as Larry Rasmussen also urges in his introduction to this volume.

A straightforward way to sharpen the question of liturgical reform in light of eco-theological and ethical emphases is to consider: what is and ought to be meant by deceptively simple references to "us" or "we" and "the oppressed" in church prayers, hymns, and preaching. "If God is for us, who can be against us?" asks Paul in Romans 8. But who does "us" encompass?—when we Christians refer to "us" created in God's image and given spirit, "us" who were chosen and brought to promised lands that we have messed up, "us" for whom Christ died, delivering "us" from death to life. *A Brief Statement of Faith,* the contemporary creed adopted in 1991 by the Presbyterian Church (U.S.A.), confesses, "In sovereign love God created the world good and makes everyone equally in God's image.... But we violate the image of God in others and ourselves, accept lies as truth, exploit neighbor and nature, and threaten death to the planet entrusted to our care.... Yet God acts with justice and mercy to redeem creation." That contemporary theological affirmation—an important though belated shift away from anthropocentrism in Reformed theology—is a benchmark on the pilgrimage of ecologically reformed and liturgically renewed churches toward the beloved community within habitat Earth.[18]

Earth community encompasses not only human cultures, but the whole creation of all of "us" together. Now which "us" is God acting with justice and mercy to redeem? Just to ponder the question shakes up familiar categories and suggests new combinations that portray "us" both generally and particularly. The ecological reformation will spread as public worship, spiritual development, lay education, and social action refocus on earth community—"us" understood comprehensively. In other words, God's priority concern or "preferential option for the oppressed" includes otherkind, as well as humankind. And responsiveness to all that is outdoors is a definite sign of the church's commitment to creation's well-being.

Sixth, an authentic reformation produces fresh ethical reflection and redefines faithfulness—that is, the human vocation—in common life, including politics and economics. The Protestant Reformation at the beginning of the Modern Era focused on justification/sanctification and the people's worldly calling within a post-feudal, though colonial, social order. Now, under conditions of problematic economic globalization (discussed in this volume's chapter by Ibrahim Abu-Rabi), the ecumenical focus should be on integral relatedness, earthy virtues, institutional change and public policies for social justice and the good of all. In this new context, Christian ethical teaching must specify environmental as well as social obligations, pinpointing the shared human vocation in every place and pursuit to express respect and care for Earth as God's creation and life's home, while seeking justice for biodiverse otherkind as well as culturally plural humankind.

Humanity belongs to one *oikumene* (household)—community of ecumenical Earth—that must concentrate on the well-being of life (as discussed in the chapter by Martin Robra, et al.) by acting for global/local justice, peace, and integrity of creation. In this volume's spiritually grounded moral perspective of eco-justice, earth community is one household (*oikos*), which benefits from an economy (*oikonomia*) that takes ecological and social stewardship (*oikonomos*) seriously. Toward this end, common global/local ethical standards need to be taught and observed. One available, promising expression of common ethics is the Earth Charter, which articulates an inspirational vision, basic values, and guiding principles for a sustainable way of living. The final version of the charter, issued by the Earth Charter Commission as a people's treaty in March 2000 after worldwide consultation with civil society groups, provides a coherent ethical map worthy of careful consideration and support by the world's religions and the United Nations.

As chapter 6 suggests, the Earth Charter intersects positively with ethical concerns of ecumenical Christianity. The charter contains spiritual affirmations about the community of life and the human role therein that are congruent with biblical-theological themes. For example, the first two sentences of the Earth Charter preamble's second paragraph announce, "Humanity is part of a vast evolving universe. Earth, our home, is alive with a unique community of life." Similarly, monotheistic faith today affirms that the whole cosmos—and this planet—bodies forth the power, wisdom, and love of God (now understood in more holistic, organic terms). In other words, the natural world is a tangible sign of the enlivening and restoring presence of God's Spirit. All of earth community is valuable to God, who relates directly to and cares about everykind. Consequently, humans are called to be earth-keepers with social and bio-responsibility for life's well-being who, in the words of the charter's general principles: "(1) respect Earth and life in all its diversity; (2) care for the community of life with understanding, compassion, and love; (3) build democratic societies that are just, participatory, sustainable, and peaceful; and (4) secure Earth's bounty and beauty for present and future generations."

The charter goes on to specify an integrated set of twelve organizing principles (or ethical guidelines)—applicable everywhere and at all levels of moral agency—to embody ecological sustainability, a just and sustainable socioeconomic order, and democracy and peace. Among the objectives expressed in these ethical principles are: Preserve biodiversity—"Protect and restore the integrity of Earth's ecological systems, with special concern for biological diversity and the natural processes that sustain life." Exercise caution and practice self-restraint—"Prevent harm as the best method of environmental protection, and when knowledge is limited, apply a precautionary approach." Protect animals—"Treat all living beings with respect and consideration . . . and protect them from suffering." But this environmental ethic is not a thing in itself. It is paired with commitment to secure human rights and socioeconomic justice in principles that enjoin us to: "Adopt patterns of production, consumption, and reproduction that safeguard Earth's regenerative capacities, human rights, and community well-being. . . . Affirm gender equality and equity as prerequisites to sustainable development and ensure universal access to education, health care, and economic opportunity. . . . Uphold the right of all, without discrimination, to a natural and social environment supportive of human dignity, bodily health, and spiritual well-being, with special attention to the rights of indigenous peoples and minorities." Such Earth Charter principles well express the necessary integration of ecological and social values in ethics and praxis for habitat Earth.

Seventh, to achieve the promise of ecological reformation, culture, religion, and politics must embody liberative commitment to racial and gender justice. James Cone's chapter in part 1, followed up by Peggy Shepard's narrative of community empowerment for eco-justice in part 3, eloquently highlight the struggle against environmental racism. So here I focus on the gender justice agenda—incorporating some insights of ecological feminism as a particular feature of the new reformation. From *New Woman, New Earth* (1975), and continuing in *Gaia and God: An Ecofeminist Theology of Earth Healing* (1992), and in "Ecofeminism: The Challenge to Theology" (2000), Rosemary Radford Ruether, a pioneering Christian explorer of the interconnections between domination of women and domination of nature, calls upon the church to discard the pattern of colonial thinking and gender hierarchy built into its doctrine of creation. She emphasizes that the ecofeminist vision and strategies aim "to liberate or heal these interconnected dominations," both at the ideological or cultural-symbolic level and at the socioeconomic level. [19]

Girls, communities, and biodiverse life worldwide are threatened by patriarchal domination and environmental destruction. Women, operating mostly in local, micro contexts close to the earth are, like nature, still being oppressed and disregarded—often barely visible to those who set macro political and economic policies. Consequently, women on every continent are making eco-justice responses that challenge exclusion or oppression of females and human disregard for nature. In the words of another pioneering ecofeminist, Elizabeth Dodson Gray, "Slowly, as if awakening from a long sleep, women are shaking the film of male concepts from our eyes and looking into life as if seeing it 'for the first bright time'. . . . As we awaken to our precarious ecological situation, women around the world become eco-justice activists. From Love Canal to the Chipco movement, women are mobilizing." [20]

At the beginning of the twenty-first century, ecofeminism has become a unifying symbol that goes to the heart of popular movements among women in Asia and Latin America as well as the Northern Hemisphere. During the Ecumenical Earth Conference that led to this volume, Beverly Harrison reported, "In Latin America, ecofeminism has replaced liberation theology as the label that most Christian women use. The reason is that male liberationists have been so continuously insensitive to the fundamental claims of justice, that many women across Latin America have turned to speak together of our embodied planet and its claim upon us as the very heart and soul of common life and work. . . . Women have come together sharing an integrated analysis of what we need. The basic rubric has become 'end the violence against Mother Earth and all her children.'" Women are acting assertively for the well-being of the people and places where they live, moving to manage limited resources of the web of life in an equitable, sustainable way, while demanding gender justice in economic life and social institutions, including the church.

Now, where were/are the churches in this struggle? In 1988, to sustain and expand upon the energy generated by the United Nations Decade for Women, the World Council of Churches (WCC) launched an "Ecumenical Decade of Churches in Solidarity with Women." Objectives of the decade were to empower women to challenge oppressive patterns of violence and structures of economic injustice at every level; to enable the churches to free themselves of racism, sexism, and classism; to give visibility to women's perspectives, actions, and participation in churches and communities; and to encourage the churches to take actions in solidarity with women. Major conferences and gatherings of women occurred in various regions around the world. In the United States, these ecumenical events were called "Re-Imagining Conferences" (which were met with virulent, conservative theological backlash led by males in the churches). At the same time, the WCC began a program of team visits to all its member communions to foster solidarity with women. This process revealed that gender inequality, domination, and violence often remain a common pattern within church as well as culture. So, in a December 1998 letter addressed to the Eighth Assembly of the World Council of Churches meeting in Harare, the women and men of the Decade Festival of the Churches in Solidarity with Women declared,

We hold firmly to the vision of a human community where the participation of each and every one is valued, where no one is excluded on the basis of race, sex, age, religion or cultural practice, where diversity is celebrated as God's gift to the world.

We hold firmly to the elimination of all forms of violence (sexual, religious, psychological, structural, physical, spiritual, military), and the culture of violence, especially as they affect the life and dignity of women. . . . The presence of violence in the church is an offense against God, humanity and the earth. . . . Violence against women is a sin.

We hold firmly to a vision of a world of economic justice where poverty is neither tolerated nor justified, where peoples of the south and east flourish with the people of the north and west, where a balance of power and wealth is restored, and where women and children no longer endure enforced and debilitating labour." This requires "cancellation of the internal and external debts of the world's poorest nations, . . . laws that protect women's rights to property and other rights, . . . equal pay for equal work, sustainable and livable wages, and honorable labour practices." In short, empowerment and equality of women is essential to earth community.

The eighth step in ecological reformation is to model sustainability with justice in individual and institutional activities. Individuals and institutions—households, governments, businesses, churches, and schools—teach sustainability with justice (or indifference to it) by example—as a way of life. The necessary transformation encompasses the lifestyles we lead as consumers, how we learn, work, and play, the way we operate organizationally and participate in the larger community. The focus is on best practices throughout society. Every organization and region needs to institutionalize "green" practices that lighten ecological impact, transform its educational processes to grapple with the environmental challenge, and refocus its public engagement to help build earth community. The church, of course, is present in a wide range of social institutions. The church ecologically reformed is much more than a set of congregations and ecclesial bodies. The church is the laity actively engaged with others of like mind in every social sector for justice, peace, and integrity of creation.

Theological Education to Meet the Environmental Challenge (TEMEC), an ecumenical program I have codirected for nearly a decade, concentrates on three aspects of sustainability: to give eco-justice themes and issues interdisciplinary attention at the curriculum's core, to embody just and sustainable community in campus operations, and to address global and regional issues of sustainability through public engagement.[21] The point is to help teachers, students, and administrators as well as schools of theology and universities to make eco-justice a central focus of scholarly work and learning, and of action at the individual, institutional, and social policy level. (While schools are featured in the following cases, many organizations, including congregations, can move in this direction with a similar threefold emphasis.)

Seattle University (Jesuit) offers a holistic, integrative bachelor's degree in ecological studies, which prepares students to understand not only the scientific nature of ecological issues, but the cultural and spiritual dimensions as well. Faculty and administrators explore these linkages. Students take courses in natural and social sciences, history, philosophy, theology, literature, and the arts. They engage in supervised fieldwork that brings together people from many different fields and careers seeking to understand the effects on communities as well as on the environment. Seattle University also models environmental conservation by making the campus itself a designated outdoor wildlife sanctuary that practices integrated pest management. The school also gives careful attention to recycling and to toxic-waste collection and disposal. The school's leaders recognize the profound ways Christian theology and spirituality give rise to reverence for all of creation. For a 1997 Earth Day liturgy at Seattle University that modeled the sacramentality of creation, music, banners, dance, and poetry were created by local Northwest artists who affirmed that ecology is a religious concern and a matter of soul. A vigil for extinct and endangered species was followed by a liturgy centered on the four elements, in connection with a national conference that explored Liturgy for Sustainable Communities.

Hendrix College in Conway, Arkansas, led by a special faculty committee on Sustainability and Global Education (SAGE) that is alert to its "crystallized pedagogy," has taken initiatives in four areas: reorienting the organizational culture of the college and planning special conferences,

revising curriculum to create an environmental studies major and pertinent general education requirements, assessing campus energy use and
the college food service while strengthening the recycling program, and
doing social outreach through workshops for public school teachers as
well as forming a Center for Sustainability and Spirituality in partnership
with Heifer Project International and Meadowcreek. The goal of SAGE is
to focus scholarship and teaching on pressing world issues such as biological and cultural diversity, the future of wild lands and natural resources,
as well as economic and cultural practices that respond to human needs
in more sustainable ways.

Claremont School of Theology in Southern California established an
Eco-Justice Task Force to coordinate planning for better formation of
ministers, teachers, and leaders with commitment to ecological regeneration and social-economic justice. The faculty who serve on this task
force have focused on teaching styles and course content relating to justice and sustainability, particularly in the Southwestern region. Theological learning is enhanced as students participate in the practice of a small
learning community that gathers weekly, incorporating worship, education, field trips, service, and recreation around a generative theme related
to eco-justice.

With the help of an outside consultant and the involvement of maintenance or food service directors, Claremont School of Theology has also
improved its recycling system and conducted audits of campus: buildings
for accessibility, energy efficiency, and water use; landscaping for water
efficiency, drought-resistant planting, and areas for vegetable gardening;
and food services to explore the sources and kinds of meals offered. In-
novations also include development of a meditation garden featuring
plants mentioned in the Bible, within a larger process of reclaiming and
enhancing campus green space.

The Lutheran School of Theology in Chicago and Meadville/Lombard
Theological School formed a lead cluster involving four other Chicago
seminaries, more than thirty faculty, active student groups, and several regional organizations. With support from TEMEC and the Program on
Ecology, Justice and Faith, leaders of this cluster launched the Chicago
Theological Initiative in Eco-Justice Ministry to coordinate course offerings and field education opportunities within the Association of Chicago

Theological Schools. This Chicago Theological initiative is structured to enable seminary students, within their M.A. or M.Div. studies, to pursue a concentration on ecotheology and ethics (leading to certification), while also gaining hands-on experience with "green zone" practices and civic engagement for eco-justice. Through this emphasis within seminary education, and through an internet site, Web of Creation (www.webof-creation.org), this initiative aims to explore the relationships between ecology, justice, and faith, to foster a theological vision of creation care that affirms the intrinsic worth of all members of the community of life, to give visibility to a credible cosmology and a coherent ethical framework for our common future, to strengthen religious leadership in environmental thought and action, and to develop requisite skills of ministry among clergy and laity.

NEW EMPHASES FOR THE CHURCH IN EARTH COMMUNITY

The above discussion has definite implications for church self-understanding and ministry, here stated in summary form.

God's project, involving humans, is Earth community, not only Christian community. God is acting with justice and mercy to redeem creation, not only human animals. So, a mark of ecclesial authenticity in response to the crisis of Earth and Humans would be to deliberately breach the walls between church and world, or Christianity and other religions, show in solidarity for just and sustainable community. This way of being church challenges Christian exceptionalism and exclusive definitions of salvation. As Larry Rasmussen recently put it, Christianity, other religious faiths, and life philosophies all must "become genuine earthfaiths and potent sources of earth patriotism and earth ethics."[22]

The Spirit that illumines earth's plight opens the way to a transformation of traditions. Theologians can participate by taking seriously the plight of people and nature together and reflecting on real praxis of just and sustainable community. This is the most direct way to overcome the modern Christian habit of divorcing social and ecological stewardship. The focus then shifts to local/regional/global responsibility for earth community inclusive of oppressed everykind.

Affirmations of belief and ethical teachings must be revised in light of a dialogue between the "Two Books"—of Nature and of Scripture—both of which are necessary, but neither of which is sufficient. In them together we encounter a more fulsome understanding of the Spirit, expressed interactively in the Universe-Earth story and the Biblical Covenant story.[23] When that revelatory interaction gets more emphasis in ecclesial life, constructive dialogue is more likely to occur with environmentalists who have been disappointed or put off by the church. This should also help the church to re-vision patterns of faithfulness in terms that are more fitting to an environmentally stressed world.

The churches' theological affirmations and liturgies should link appreciation of nature to explicit concern and care for nature. With this shift, preaching of the word, administration of the sacraments, and hymns and prayers of the people can become much more pertinent to the eco-justice crisis. Toward this end, theologians of the church need to give explicit attention to the environmental aspects of biblical narratives, ethical teachings, confessions of faith, the sacraments of baptism and holy communion, and hymns and prayers. With this new sensibility, Christian worship resources need to be reassessed and revised. (Denominational hymnals do convey nature appreciation, as well as concern for human reconciliation and well-being in the city, the nation, and internationally. But they include little emphasis on Christian responsibility to care for natural places and other species, and show a striking lack of focus on environmental ministry.)

The ecumenical movement has begun to articulate a basic social ethic for earth community, featuring the biblically rooted vision and values of eco-justice, a parallel expression of which is developed in the Earth Charter. As already indicated, an eco-justice ethic poses no either/or choices between caring for people and caring for the earth. The four basic, interactive norms of ecumenical eco-justice ethics can be summarized as follows:

- solidarity with other people and creatures—companions, victims, and allies—in earth community, reflecting deep respect for creation;
- ecological sustainability, that is, environmentally fitting habits of living and working that enable life to flourish and that utilize ecologically and socially appropriate technology;

- sufficiency as a standard of organized sharing—distributive justice—which requires basic floors and definite ceilings for equitable or "fair" consumption; and
- socially just participation in decisions about how to obtain sustenance and to manage community life for the good in common and the good of the commons.

Solidarity comprehends the full dimensions of earth community and of interhuman obligation. Sustainability gives high visibility to ecological integrity and wise behavior throughout the resource-use cycle. The third and fourth norms express requirements of distributive and participatory justice in a world that has reached or is exceeding resource production, pollution, and population limits. Observance of each ethical norm reinforces and qualifies the others. All four are core values that become corrective criteria to guide personal and institutional practice, social analysis, and policy advocacy. These four norms of eco-justice ethics, which are end-oriented and means-clarifying, give shape to activity that is both ecologically fitting and socially just.[24] Each church body and congregation needs to cultivate such a posture as basic Christian social teaching, to wrestle with its public policy implications, and to embody the value commitments of this ethic in particular locales, working with like-minded organizations.

The churches continue to experience an internal tug-of-war over what kind of message and mission to emphasize. The outcome of that struggle has direct implications for environmental education and policy advocacy. Only as the church remembers that the biblical story begins with accounts of creation and ends with the promise of New Jerusalem on earth, in the city, and to the degree that the church shows genuine appreciation for everykind and is clear about its responsibility for earth citizenship, can it participate meaningfully in the freighted eco-justice struggles occurring in countries and communities around the globe.

Ecumenical churches are developing a clear and compelling picture of what constitutes effective eco-justice-oriented ministry by individuals and congregations.[25] The appended outline of such ministry may be useful for a self-checkup of how well a congregation, community group, or educational institution actually equips participants to carry out basic earth community responsibilities. The special obligation of religious leaders, clergy and lay, in these times is to cultivate a renewed celebration of spirit within creation, a sense of awe, respect, humane pace, and appreciation of the wisdom of long-standing communities, and an ethic of justice, generosity, and caring for vulnerable people, creatures, and ecosystems. Otherwise, many more people will suffer from environmental degradation and social injustice, while numerous special places and wondrous otherkind are obliterated. During the next few decades the church faces a clear choice: either give in to humanly induced decreation, or participate in the ecological reformation to restore creation while seeking human well-being on this planet.

AGENDA FOR EARTH COMMUNITY MINISTRY

In addition to recovering an authentically biblical and scientifically informed appreciation of creation, adequate Christian theology views salvation holistically, encouraging human participation in social history and the natural world as one unified reality with a destiny of *shalom*. With that posture, churches can undertake the following earth-community responsibilities.

- Become informed and explore with others the environmental peril, related patterns of social inequity, and a theology and ethic of eco-justice.
- Inculcate sacramental respect for all creatures and careful stewardship of every place through worship, education, and service.
- Wrestle with the vocational and moral dilemmas of shifting to less consumptive lifestyles, more appropriate technologies, and a different pattern of economic life to serve eco-justice values. Offer special pastoral care to the laity whose work should be phased out.
- Appreciate insights from other living faiths and learn what resources they bring to the spiritual quest and vocational dilemmas of these times.
- Face issues of political and personal responsibility that come with the environmental challenge, exploring implications for daily work, community life, and public engagement.
- Foster constructive local responses to global problems, looking for international, ecumenical connections (for example, in response to climate change, the quest for food security, the urgent task of overcoming poverty).

- Encourage appropriate technologies at home and abroad (become informed about some of these—for example, renewable energy systems—and how to implement them locally).
- Explore urban and rural dimensions of ecology, participating in community organizations that care for place and act for environmental justice.
- Advocate changes in social policy and practice that serve the goals of ecology and equity (working with civil society groups, environmental specialists, public officials, as well as business and professional people who value justice and sustainability).
- Build communities of sustainable sufficiency, joining with others to envision and move toward reverential, sustainable development, and foster corporate responsibility consistent with this goal.
- Express individual lifestyle integrity and foster institutional practices consistent with a spirituality of creation-justice-peace, avoiding trivial and legalistic responses.[26]

Appendix
The Earth Charter*

PREAMBLE

We stand at a critical moment in Earth's history, a time when humanity must choose its future. As the world becomes increasingly interdependent and fragile, the future at once holds great peril and great promise. To move forward we must recognize that in the midst of a magnificent diversity of cultures and life forms we are one human family and one Earth community with a common destiny. We must join together to bring forth a sustainable global society founded on respect for nature, universal human rights, economic justice, and a culture of peace. Towards this end, it is imperative that we, the peoples of Earth, declare our responsibility to one another, to the greater community of life, and to future generations.

Earth, Our Home

Humanity is part of a vast evolving universe. Earth, our home, is alive with a unique community of life. The forces of nature make existence a demanding and uncertain adventure, but Earth has provided the conditions essential to life's evolution. The resilience of the community of life and the well-being of humanity depend upon preserving a healthy biosphere with all its ecological systems, a rich variety of plants and animals, fertile soils, pure waters, and clean air. The global environment with its finite resources is a common concern of all peoples. The protection of Earth's vitality, diversity, and beauty is a sacred trust.

* This final version of the Earth Charter was approved and released by the Earth Charter Commission at a meeting in Paris in March 2000.

The Global Situation

The dominant patterns of production and consumption are causing environmental devastation, the depletion of resources, and a massive extinction of species. Communities are being undermined. The benefits of development are not shared equitably and the gap between rich and poor is widening. Injustice, poverty, ignorance, and violent conflict are widespread and the cause of great suffering. An unprecedented rise in human population has overburdened ecological and social systems. The foundations of global security are threatened. These trends are perilous—but not inevitable.

The Challenges Ahead

The choice is ours: form a global partnership to care for Earth and one another or risk the destruction of ourselves and the diversity of life. Fundamental changes are needed in our values, institutions, and ways of living. We must realize that when basic needs have been met, human development is primarily about being more, not having more. We have the knowledge and technology to provide for all and to reduce our impacts on the environment. The emergence of a global civil society is creating new opportunities to build a democratic and humane world. Our environmental, economic, political, social, and spiritual challenges are interconnected, and together we can forge inclusive solutions.

Universal Responsibility

To realize these aspirations, we must decide to live with a sense of universal responsibility, identifying ourselves with the whole Earth community as well as our local communities. We are at once citizens of different nations and of one world in which the local and global are linked. Everyone shares responsibility for the present and future well-being of the human family and the larger living world. The spirit of human solidarity and kinship with all life is strengthened when we live with reverence for the mystery of being, gratitude for the gift of life, and humility regarding the human place in nature.

We urgently need a shared vision of basic values to provide an ethical foundation for the emerging world community. Therefore, together in hope we affirm the following interdependent principles for a sustainable way of life as a common standard by which the conduct of all individuals, organizations, businesses, governments, and transnational institutions is to be guided and assessed.

PRINCIPLES

I. Respect and Care for the Community of Life

1. RESPECT EARTH AND LIFE IN ALL ITS DIVERSITY.
    a. Recognize that all beings are interdependent and every form of life has value regardless of its worth to human beings.
    b. Affirm faith in the inherent dignity of all human beings and in the intellectual, artistic, ethical, and spiritual potential of humanity.

2. CARE FOR THE COMMUNITY OF LIFE WITH UNDERSTANDING, COMPASSION, AND LOVE.
    a. Accept that with the right to own, manage, and use natural resources comes the duty to prevent environmental harm and to protect the rights of people.
    b. Affirm that with increased freedom, knowledge, and power comes increased responsibility to promote the common good.

3. BUILD DEMOCRATIC SOCIETIES THAT ARE JUST, PARTICIPATORY, SUSTAINABLE, AND PEACEFUL.
    a. Ensure that communities at all levels guarantee human rights and fundamental freedoms and provide everyone an opportunity to realize his or her full potential.
    b. Promote social and economic justice, enabling all to achieve a secure and meaningful livelihood that is ecologically responsible.

4. SECURE EARTH'S BOUNTY AND BEAUTY FOR PRESENT AND FUTURE GENERATIONS.
    a. Recognize that the freedom of action of each generation is qualified by the needs of future generations.

b. Transmit to future generations values, traditions, and institutions that support the long-term flourishing of Earth's
human and ecological communities.

In order to fulfill these four broad commitments, it is necessary to:

II. Ecological Integrity

5. PROTECT AND RESTORE THE INTEGRITY OF EARTH'S ECOLOGICAL SYSTEMS,
WITH SPECIAL CONCERN FOR BIOLOGICAL DIVERSITY AND THE NATURAL
PROCESSES THAT SUSTAIN LIFE.
   a. Adopt at all levels sustainable development plans and regulations that make environmental conservation and rehabilitation integral to all development initiatives.
   b. Establish and safeguard viable nature and biosphere reserves, including wild lands and marine areas, to protect
   Earth's life support systems, maintain biodiversity, and
   preserve our natural heritage.
   c. Promote the recovery of endangered species and ecosystems.
   d. Control and eradicate non-native or genetically modified
   organisms harmful to native species and the environment,
   and prevent introduction of such harmful organisms.
   e. Manage the use of renewable resources such as water, soil,
   forest products, and marine life in ways that do not exceed
   rates of regeneration and that protect the health of
   ecosystems.
   f. Manage the extraction and use of non-renewable resources
   such as minerals and fossil fuels in ways that minimize
   depletion and cause no serious environmental damage.

6. PREVENT HARM AS THE BEST METHOD OF ENVIRONMENTAL PROTECTION
AND, WHEN KNOWLEDGE IS LIMITED, APPLY A PRECAUTIONARY APPROACH.
   a. Take action to avoid the possibility of serious or irreversible
   environmental harm even when scientific knowledge is
   incomplete or inconclusive.

b. Place the burden of proof on those who argue that a proposed activity will not cause significant harm, and make the responsible parties liable for environmental harm.

c. Ensure that decision making addresses the cumulative, long-term, indirect, long distance, and global consequences of human activities.

d. Prevent pollution of any part of the environment and allow no build-up of radioactive, toxic, or other hazardous substances.

e. Avoid military activities damaging to the environment.

7. ADOPT PATTERNS OF PRODUCTION, CONSUMPTION, AND REPRODUCTION THAT SAFEGUARD EARTH'S REGENERATIVE CAPACITIES, HUMAN RIGHTS, AND COMMUNITY WELL-BEING.

a. Reduce, reuse, and recycle the materials used in production and consumption systems, and ensure that residual waste can be assimilated by ecological systems.

b. Act with restraint and efficiency when using energy, and rely increasingly on renewable energy sources such as solar and wind.

c. Promote the development, adoption, and equitable transfer of environmentally sound technologies.

d. Internalize the full environmental and social costs of goods and services in the selling price, and enable consumers to identify products that meet the highest social and environmental standards.

e. Ensure universal access to health care that fosters reproductive health and responsible reproduction.

f. Adopt lifestyles that emphasize the quality of life and material sufficiency in a finite world.

8. ADVANCE THE STUDY OF ECOLOGICAL SUSTAINABILITY AND PROMOTE THE OPEN EXCHANGE AND WIDE APPLICATION OF THE KNOWLEDGE ACQUIRED.

a. Support international scientific and technical cooperation on sustainability, with special attention to the needs of developing nations.

b. Recognize and preserve the traditional knowledge and spiritual wisdom in all cultures that contribute to environmental protection and human well-being.

c. Ensure that information of vital importance to human health and environmental protection, including genetic information, remains available in the public domain.

III. Social and Economic Justice

9. Eradicate poverty as an ethical, social, and environmental imperative.

   a. Guarantee the right to potable water, clean air, food security, uncontaminated soil, shelter, and safe sanitation, allocating the national and international resources required.

   b. Empower every human being with the education and resources to secure a sustainable livelihood, and provide social security and safety nets for those who are unable to support themselves.

   c. Recognize the ignored, protect the vulnerable, serve those who suffer, and enable them to develop their capacities and to pursue their aspirations.

10. Ensure that economic activities and institutions at all levels promote human development in an equitable and sustainable manner.

   a. Promote the equitable distribution of wealth within nations and among nations.

   b. Enhance the intellectual, financial, technical, and social resources of developing nations, and relieve them of onerous international debt.

   c. Ensure that all trade supports sustainable resource use, environmental protection, and progressive labor standards.

   d. Require multinational corporations and international financial organizations to act transparently in the public good, and hold them accountable for the consequences of their activities.

11. AFFIRM GENDER EQUALITY AND EQUITY AS PREREQUISITES TO SUSTAINABLE DEVELOPMENT AND ENSURE UNIVERSAL ACCESS TO EDUCATION, HEALTH CARE, AND ECONOMIC OPPORTUNITY.

    a. Secure the human rights of women and girls and end all violence against them.
    b. Promote the active participation of women in all aspects of economic, political, civil, social, and cultural life as full and equal partners, decision makers, leaders, and beneficiaries.
    c. Strengthen families and ensure the safety and loving nurture of all family members.

12. UPHOLD THE RIGHT OF ALL, WITHOUT DISCRIMINATION, TO A NATURAL AND SOCIAL ENVIRONMENT SUPPORTIVE OF HUMAN DIGNITY, BODILY HEALTH, AND SPIRITUAL WELL-BEING, WITH SPECIAL ATTENTION TO THE RIGHTS OF INDIGENOUS PEOPLES AND MINORITIES.

    a. Eliminate discrimination in all its forms, such as that based on race, color, sex, sexual orientation, religion, language, and national, ethnic or social origin.
    b. Affirm the right of indigenous peoples to their spirituality, knowledge, lands, and resources, and to their related practice of sustainable livelihoods.
    c. Honor and support the young people of our communities, enabling them to fulfill their essential role in creating sustainable societies.
    d. Protect and restore outstanding places of cultural and spiritual significance.

IV. Democracy, Nonviolence, and Peace

13. STRENGTHEN DEMOCRATIC INSTITUTIONS AT ALL LEVELS, AND PROVIDE TRANSPARENCY AND ACCOUNTABILITY IN GOVERNANCE, INCLUSIVE PARTICIPATION IN DECISION MAKING, AND ACCESS TO JUSTICE.

    a. Uphold the right of everyone to receive clear and timely information on environmental matters and all development plans and activities which are likely to affect them or in which they have an interest.

b. Support local, regional, and global civil society, and promote the meaningful participation of all interested individuals and organizations in decision making.

c. Protect the rights to freedom of opinion, expression, peaceful assembly, association, and dissent.

d. Institute effective and efficient access to administrative and independent judicial procedures, including remedies and redress for environmental harm and the threat of such harm.

e. Eliminate corruption in all public and private institutions.

f. Strengthen local communities, enabling them to care for their environments, and assign environmental responsibilities to the levels of government where they can be carried out most effectively.

14. INTEGRATE INTO FORMAL EDUCATION AND LIFE-LONG LEARNING THE KNOWLEDGE, VALUES, AND SKILLS NEEDED FOR A SUSTAINABLE WAY OF LIFE.

a. Provide all, especially children and youth, with educational opportunities that empower them to contribute actively to sustainable development.

b. Promote the contribution of the arts and humanities as well as the sciences in sustainability education.

c. Enhance the role of the mass media in raising awareness of ecological and social challenges.

d. Recognize the importance of moral and spiritual education for sustainable living.

15. TREAT ALL LIVING BEINGS WITH RESPECT AND CONSIDERATION.

a. Prevent cruelty to animals kept in human societies and protect them from suffering.

b. Protect wild animals from methods of hunting, trapping, and fishing that cause extreme, prolonged, or avoidable suffering.

c. Avoid or eliminate to the full extent possible the taking or destruction of non-targeted species.

16. PROMOTE A CULTURE OF TOLERANCE, NONVIOLENCE, AND PEACE.

   a. Encourage and support mutual understanding, solidarity, and cooperation among all peoples and within and among nations.

   b. Implement comprehensive strategies to prevent violent conflict and use collaborative problem solving to manage and resolve environmental conflicts and other disputes.

   c. Demilitarize national security systems to the level of a non-provocative defense posture, and convert military resources to peaceful purposes, including ecological restoration.

   d. Eliminate nuclear, biological, and toxic weapons and other weapons of mass destruction.

   e. Ensure that the use of orbital and outer space supports environmental protection and peace.

   f. Recognize that peace is the wholeness created by right relationships with oneself, other persons, other cultures, other life, Earth, and the larger whole of which all are a part.

THE WAY FORWARD

As never before in history, common destiny beckons us to seek a new beginning. Such renewal is the promise of these Earth Charter principles. To fulfill this promise, we must commit ourselves to adopt and promote the values and objectives of the charter.

This requires a change of mind and heart. It requires a new sense of global interdependence and universal responsibility. We must imaginatively develop and apply the vision of a sustainable way of life locally, nationally, regionally, and globally. Our cultural diversity is a precious heritage and different cultures will find their own distinctive ways to realize the vision. We must deepen and expand the global dialogue that generated the Earth Charter, for we have much to learn from the ongoing collaborative search for truth and wisdom.

Life often involves tensions between important values. This can mean difficult choices. However, we must find ways to harmonize diversity with unity, the exercise of freedom with the common good, short-term objectives with long-term goals. Every individual, family, organization, and community has a vital role to play. The arts, sciences, religions, educational institutions, media, businesses, nongovernmental organizations, and governments are all called to offer creative leadership. The partnership of government, civil society, and business is essential for effective governance.

In order to build a sustainable global community, the nations of the world must renew their commitment to the United Nations, fulfill their obligations under existing international agreements, and support the implementation of Earth Charter principles with an international legally binding instrument on environment and development.

Let ours be a time remembered for the awakening of a new reverence for life, the firm resolve to achieve sustainability, the quickening of the struggle for justice and peace, and the joyful celebration of life.

Notes

Preface

1. "Ecumenical Earth: New Dimensions of Church and Community in Creation" was the title of the conference. An account by journalist Leon Howell is available in *The Union News*, itself available from the Office of Communications, Union Theological Seminary, 3041 Broadway, New York, New York, 10027.

Introduction

1. See James H. Cone, "Whose Earth Is It Anyway?" chapter 1 in this volume.

2. See Kusumita Pedersen, "Inclusion and Exclusion: Reflections on Moral Community and Salvation," chapter 2 in this volume.

3. Held at and sponsored by Union and Auburn theological seminaries, New York City, in October 1998: "Ecumenical Earth: New Dimensions of Church and Community in Creation."

4 Quoted from the movie *A Time to Kill*.

5. John Howard Yoder, *Body Politics: Five Practices of the Christian Community before the Watching World* (Nashville: Discipleship Resources, 1997), 13.

6. The phrase is a direct reference to Donald W. Shriver Jr.'s excellent volume *An Ethic for Enemies: Forgiveness in Politics* (New York: Oxford University Press, 1995).

7. From panels in the Hall of Biodiversity, American Museum of Natural History, Central Park West at 79th Street, New York, NY 10024-5192.

8. Ibid.

9. Spectrum of Habitats video, Hall of Biodiversity, American Museum of Natural History, Central Park West at 79th Street, New York, NY 10024-5192.

10. The phrase is Douglas John Hall's, from *Professing the Faith: Christian Theology in a North American Context* (Minneapolis: Fortress Press, 1993), 317.

11. Dale T. Irvin, *Christian Histories, Christian Traditioning: Rendering Accounts* (Maryknoll, N.Y.: Orbis Books, 1998), 127. I draw substantially from Irvin for the formulation of all these assumptions.

12. The Greek word *oikos* (household) is the root for both, as it is for "economic."

13. Irvin, *Christian Histories, Christian Traditioning*, 129.

14. Dorothee Soelle, *Against the Wind: Memoir of a Radical Christian,* trans. by Barbara Rumscheidt and Martin Rumscheidt (Minneapolis: Fortress Press, 1999), 103.

15. Alfred W. Crosby Jr., *The Columbian Exchange: Biological and Cultural Consequences of 1492* (Westport, Conn.: Greenwood Press, 1974), 12.

16. See Brigitte Kahl, "Fratricide and Ecocide: Re-Reading Genesis 2–4," chapter 3 in this volume.

17. Martin Luther King Jr., *Where Do We Go from Here: Chaos or Community?* (Boston: Beacon Press, 1968), 167.

18. This discussion draws from Irvin, *Christian Histories, Christian Traditioning*, 108-9.

19. Quoted in Michael Krauss, *Alaska Native Languages: Past, Present and Future* (Alaska Native Language Center, University of Alaska, Fairbanks, 1972), 23. I have taken it from Michael Oleksa, *Orthodox Alaska: A Theology of Mission* (Crestwood, N.Y.: St. Vladimir's Seminary Press), 171.

20. Oleksa, in *Orthodox Alaska,* 178, is drawing from Richard John Dauenhauer, *Glacier Bay Concerto* (Anchorage: Alaska Pacific University Press, 1980), 39.

21. Cited by Oleksa in *Orthodox Alaska,* 179.

22. Ibid., 172.

23. Cited by Oleksa, *Orthodox Alaska,* 209, using Dauenhauer's "Conflicting Visions in Alaskan Education" (University of Alaska, Fairbanks, Alaska, 1980), 20.

24. F. Eboussi Boulaga, *Christianity without Fetishes: An African Critique and Recapture of Christianity* (Maryknoll, N.Y.: Orbis Books, 1984), 224. My thanks to Dale Irvin for pointing me to Boulaga. See Irvin's discussion, *Christian Histories, Christian Traditioning,* chapter 7.

25. Irvin, *Christian Histories, Christian Traditioning,* 138–41.

26. Ibid., 141.

27. See Hessel, "The Church Ecologically Reformed," the conclusion to this volume.

28. See the forthcoming book on sustainable development and sustainable community in World Council of Churches' work, authored by David Wellman and published by the WCC. See also the distinctions drawn and described in Larry L. Rasmussen, *Earth Community, Earth Ethics* (Maryknoll, N.Y.: Orbis Books, 1996).

29. These concluding pages draw in part from my chapter, "The Right Direction, but a Longer Journey," in *Ecclesiology and Ethics: Ecumenical Ethical Engagement, Moral Formation and the Nature of the Church,* ed. Thomas F. Best and Martin Robra (Geneva: WCC Publications, 1997), 105–11.

30. Cone, "Whose Earth Is It, Anyway?" chapter 1 in this volume, and Pedersen, "Inclusion and Exclusion: Reflections on Moral Community and Salvation," chapter 2 in this volume.

Chapter 1

1. Cited in Samuel Rayan, "The Earth Is the Lord's," in *Ecotheology: Voices from South and North,* ed. David G. Hallman (Geneva, Switzerland: WCC Publications, 1994), 142.

2. See papers and Bible studies ed. James W. van Hoeven, *Justice, Peace and the Integrity of Creation* (World Alliance of Reformed Churches Assembly, Seoul, Korea, August 1989); and Preman Niles, *Resisting the Threats to Life: Covenanting for Justice, Peace and the Integrity of Creation* (Geneva, Switzerland: WCC Publications, 1989).

3. Basil Davidson, *The African Slave Trade: Precolonial History 1450-1850* (Boston: Little, Brown, and Co., 1961), 80.

4. Eduardo Galeano, *Open Veins of Latin America: Five Centuries of the Pillage of a Continent* (London: Monthly Review Press, 1973), 50.

5. See Adam Hochschild, "Hearts of Darkness: Adventures in the Slave Trade," *San Francisco Examiner Magazine,* August 16, 1998, 13. This essay is an excerpt from his book, *King Leopold's Ghosts: A Story of Greed, Terror and Heroism in Colonial Africa* (New York: Houghton Mifflin, 1998). Louis Turner suggests that five million to eight million were killed in the Congo. See his *Multinational Companies and the Third World* (New York: Hill and Wang, 1973), 27.

6. See Charles Carroll, *The Negro a Beast, or, In the Image of God* (Miami: Mnemosyne Pub. Co., 1969).

7. See Reinhold Niebuhr, "Justice to the American Negro from State, Community and Church" in his *Pious and Secular America* (New York: Charles Scribner's Sons, 1958), 81.

8. Malcolm X, *By Any Means Necessary* (New York: Pathfinder Press, 1970), 56.

9. George Breitman, ed., *Malcolm X Speaks* (New York: Grove Press, 1965), 197–98.

10. Reinhold Niebuhr, "The Assurance of Grace" in *The Essential Reinhold Niebuhr: Selected Essays and Addresses,* ed. Robert M. Brown (New Haven, Conn.: Yale University Press, 1986), 65.

11. "A Christmas Sermon on Peace, 1967" *A Testament of Hope: The Essential Writings and Speeches of Martin Luther King, Jr.,* ed. James M. Washington (New York: HarperCollins, 1991), 254.

12. See Delores Williams, "A Womanist Perspective on Sin," in *A Troubling in My Soul: Womanist Perspectives on Evil and Suffering,* ed. Emilie M. Townes (Maryknoll, N.Y.: Orbis Books, 1993), 145–47; and Williams's "Sin, Nature, and Black Women's Bodies," in *Ecofeminism and the Sacred,* ed. Carol J. Adams (New York: Continuum, 1993), 24–29; Emilie M. Townes, *In a Blaze of Glory: Womanist Spirituality as Social Witness* (Nashville: Abingdon Press, 1995), 55; and Karen Baker-Fletcher, *Sisters of Dust, Sisters of Spirit: Womanist Wordings on God and Creation* (Minneapolis: Fortress Press, 1998), 93.

13. Robert Bullard, *Dumping in Dixie: Race, Class, and Environmental Quality* (Boulder, Colo.: Westview Press, 1990), 31.

14. Cited in Bunyan Bryant and Paul Mohai, eds., *Race and the Incidence of Environmental Hazards: A Time for Discourse* (Boulder, Colo.: Westview Press, 1992), 2. See also

"African American Denominational Leaders Pledge Their Support to the Struggle against Environmental Racism," *The A.M.E. Christian Recorder,* May 18, 1998, 8, 11.

15. Cited in Robert D. Bullard, ed., *Unequal Protection: Environmental Justice and Communities of Color* (San Francisco: Sierra Club Books, 1994), 20.

16. Benjamin Chavis is now known as Benjamin Chavis Muhammad and is currently serving as the National Minister in Louis Farrakhan's Nation of Islam.

17. Bunyan Bryant, ed., *Environmental Justice: Issues, Policies, and Solutions* (Washington, D.C.: Island Press, 1995), introduction, 5. Benjamin Chavis defined environmental racism as "racial discrimination in environmental policy-making. It is racial discrimination in the enforcement of regulations and laws. It is racial discrimination in the deliberate targeting of communities of color for toxic waste disposal and the siting of polluting industries. It is racial discrimination in the official sanctioning of the life-threatening presence of poisons and pollutants in communities of color. And, it is racial discrimination in the history of excluding people of color from the mainstream environmental groups, decision making boards, commissions, and regulatory bodies." (Robert Bullard, ed., *Confronting Environmental Racism: Voices from the Grassroots* [Boston: South End Press, 1993], foreword, 3.)

18. *National Black Church Environmental and Economic Justice Summit,* Washington, D.C., December 1–2, 1993, The National Council of Churches of Christ in the U.S.A., Prophetic Justice Unit. This is a booklet with all the speeches of the meeting, including the one by former Vice President Gore.

19. See Ronald A. Taylor, "Do Environmentalists Care about Poor People?" *U.S. News and World Report,* April 2, 1984, 51.

20. John Lewis's quotation is cited in Deeohn Hahn-Baker and David Hahn-Baker, "Environmentalists and Environmental Justice Policy," in Bryant, *Environmental Justice,* 68.

21. Alice Walker, *Living by the Word: Selected Writings 1973–1987* (San Diego: Harcourt Brace Jovanovich, 1988), 173.

22. See Taylor, "Do Environmentalists Care about Poor People?"

23. Ibid., 51.

24. Audre Lorde, *Sister Outsider: Essays and Speeches* (Trumansburg, N.Y.: Crossing Press, 1984), 110.

25. Catherine Keller, *From a Broken Web: Separation, Sexism, Self* (Boston: Beacon Press, 1986), 5.

26. See Elie Wiesel, "Nobel Peace Prize Acceptance Speech," December 10, 1986.

27. Cited in Leonardo Boff, *Cry of the Earth, Cry of the Poor,* trans. Phillip Berryman (Maryknoll, N.Y.: Orbis Books, 1997), 2.

Chapter 2

I would like to express my gratitude to Lucinda Mosher, Uwe Gielen, and the Venerable Karunegoda Piyatissa for their help in developing this article.

1. Loren Eiseley, *The Firmament of Time* (New York: Atheneum, 1960), 174.

2. Ibid., 175–78.

3. The Karaniya Metta Sutta is found in the Khuddhaka Nikaya of the Pali Tripitaka, in the Khuddaka-Patha, and in the Sutta-Nipata.

4. As cited in Harvey Aronson, *Love and Sympathy in Theravada Buddhism* (Delhi: Motilal Banarsidass, 1980), 49.

5. I am indebted for this information to the Venerable Karunegoda Piyatissa.

6. Bhadantacariya Buddhaghosa, *The Path of Purification (Visuddhimagga)*, translated from the Pali by Bhikkhu Ñyanamoli (Colombo: M. D. Gunasena & Co., Ltd., 1976), 334–35.

7. For a recent overview, see Paul Williams, *Mahayana Buddhism: Doctrinal Foundations* (New York: Routledge, 1989).

8. See Aronson, *Love and Sympathy;* Buddhaghosa, *Path of Purification.*

9. See Anantanand Rambachan, *Gitamrtam: The Essential Teachings of the Bhagavad Gita* (Delhi: Motilal Banarsidass Publishers, 1993), chapter 5. Citations from the Bhagavad Gita follow the translation by Winthrop Sargeant, *The Bhagavad Gita*, revised edition ed. Christopher Chapple (Albany: State University of New York Press, 1994).

10. Ibid., 39.

11. See Raimundo Panikkar et al., eds., *The Vedic Experience: Mantramanjari*, 3rd Indian edition (Delhi: Motilal Banarsidass Publishers, 1994), 304–6.

12. I have heard brief versions of this opening prayer at a number of gatherings. The complete opening, I am told, takes an hour and a half to recite in full.

13. Jordan D. Paper, "The Sacred Pipe: The Historical Context of Contemporary Pan-Indian Religion," *Journal of the American Academy of Religion* 56:4 (1988), 643-65; and William K. Powers, *Yuwipi: Vision and Experience in Oglala Ritual* (Lincoln: University of Nebraska Press, 1982).

14. Powers, *Yuwipi,* 14.

15. Address at the conference "Religion and Ecology: Discovering the Common Ground," October 20, 1998, United Nations, New York.

16. Susan Opotow, ed,, "Moral Exclusion and Injustice." Special issue of *Journal of Social Issues*, 46:1 (1990), 1.

17. Ibid., 13.

18. Robert Jay Lifton, *The Nazi Doctors: Medical Killing and the Psychology of Genocide* (New York: Basic Books, 1986), chapters 19–20.

19. Albert Bandura, "Selective Disengagement and Moral Control," in Opotow, "Moral Exclusion and Injustice," 27–45.

20. See Opotow, "Moral Exclusion and Injustice"; Bandura, "Selective Disengagement and Moral Control"; and Ervin Staub, "Moral Exclusion, Personal Goal Theory and Extreme Destructiveness" in Opotow, "Moral Exclusion and Injustice," 47–63.

21. Ralph Blumenthal with Judith Miller, "Japan Rebuffs Requests for Information about Its Germ-Warfare Atrocities," *New York Times*, March 4, 1999, A12.

22. Staub, "Moral Exclusion," 58.

23. Ibid.

24. Opotow, "Moral Exclusion," 4.

25. Staub, "Moral Exclusion."

26. Opotow, "Moral Exclusion," 179.

27. Ibid., 17.

28. The Princeton Religion Research Center reports that 53 percent of Americans believe in hell. It is interesting that many more—71 percent—believe in heaven, perhaps an indication that indeed people believe in hell "for others" as von Balthasar says. (George Gallup Jr. and Sarah Jones, *One Hundred Questions and Answers: Religion in America* [Princeton: Princeton Religion Research Center, 1989], 14.)

29. S. Mark Heim, *Salvations: Truth and Difference in Religion* (Maryknoll, N.Y.: Orbis Books, 1997), 34.

30. Wilfred Cantwell Smith, *Towards a World Theology: Faith and the Comparative History of Religions* (Philadelphia: Westminster Press, 1981), 171.

31. Ibid., 170.

32. Hans Urs von Balthasar, *Dare We Hope "That All Men Be Saved"? with a Short Discourse on Hell,* trans. David Kipp and Lothar Krauth (San Francisco: Ignatius Press, 1988), 163–65.

33. Ibid., 196.

34. Ibid., 188–90.

35. Ibid., 215.

36. Ibid., 184–86.

37. Ibid., 178.

38. Dermot A. Lane, *Keeping Hope Alive: Stirrings in Christian Theology* (Mahwah, N.J.: Paulist Press, 1996), 162–63.

39. Ibid., 167.

40. Catechism of the Roman Catholic Church, 1994, 164–65.

41. Clark H. Pinnock, *A Wideness in God's Mercy: The Finality of Jesus Christ in a World of Religions* (Grand Rapids, Mich.: Zondervan, 1992), 12.

42. Ibid., 19.

43. Ibid., 76.

44. Ibid., 157.

45. Church of England, *The Mystery of Salvation: The Story of God's Gift* (London: Church House Publishing, 1995), 198–99, cited in Lane, *Keeping Hope Alive,* 143.

46. Lane, *Keeping Hope Alive,* 143.

47. Thomas F. Best and Martin Robra, eds., *Ecclesiology and Ethics: Ecumenical Engagement, Moral Formation and the Nature of the Church* (Geneva: World Council of Churches, 1997), 5–6.

48. Ibid., 16.

49. David B. Burrell and Elena Malits, *Original Peace: Restoring God's Creation* (Mahwah, N.J.: Paulist, 1997), chapters 6 and 14.

50. Morton Deutsch, "Psychological Roots of Moral Exclusion," in Opotow, "Moral Exclusion and Injustice," 21–25.

51. Brian Swimme and Thomas Berry, *The Universe Story: From the Primordial Flaring Forth to the Ecozoic Era—A Celebration of the Unfolding of the Cosmos* (San Francisco: HarperSanFrancisco, 1992).

52. Sri Chinmoy, *The Wings of Joy* (New York: Simon & Schuster, 1994).

53. Unpublished talk, New York, August 1998. In a dialogue with his students,

Sri Chinmoy was asked how it is possible to identify oneself with insects or other "lower forms of life."

54. Stephanie Kaza, *The Attentive Heart: Conversations with Trees* (New York: Fawcett Columbine, 1993); Sallie McFague, *Super, Natural Christians: How We Should Love Nature* (Minneapolis: Fortress Press, 1997); Brian J. Walsh, Marianne B. Karsh, and Nik Ansell, "Trees, Forestry and the Responsiveness of Creation," *Cross Currents* 44 (1994), 149–62.

55. Loren Eiseley, *The Unexpected Universe* (New York: Harcourt Brace Jovanovich, 1969), chapter 4.

56. Ibid., 87–88.

Chapter 3

1. About the problems around Bible and nature see Theodore Hiebert, *The Yahwist's Landscape: Nature and Religion in Early Israel* (New York: Oxford University Press, 1996), 3–29.

2. I follow the translation of Everett Fox, *In the Beginning: A New English Rendition of the Book of Genesis* (New York: Schocken Books, 1983).

3. The mutual dependence of earth and humanity in Genesis 2 has been seen by a growing number of authors in recent years; compare Ellen van Wolde, "Facing the Earth: Primaeval History in a New Perspective," in *The World of Genesis: Persons, Places, Perspectives,* Philip R. Davies and David J. A. Clines, eds. (Sheffield: Sheffield Academic Press, 1998), 30.

4. The superior position the Yahwist narrative attributes to the arable soil (Adama) as being served (*'abad*) by human beings next to God has been observed by Hiebert, *The Yahwist's Landscape,* 66–67. He also pays attention to God's role of having the ultimate power to produce and sustain life on the one hand, and act as a divine farmer on the other hand, one who has his place on the Adama (2:7, 8; 4:14), plants the garden there (2:8), puts the humans to work on it (2:8, 15), and controls their work (3:8).

5. One of the rare noticeable exceptions is Ilana Pardes, "Beyond Genesis 3: The Politics of Maternal Naming," in *A Feminist Companion to Genesis,* Athayla Brenner, ed. (Sheffield: Sheffield Academic Press, 1993), 173–93. See also Brigitte Kahl, "And She Called His Name Seth (Gen. 4:25): The Birth of Critical Knowledge and the Unread End of Eve's Story," *Union Seminary Quarterly Review* 53 (1999) 19–28.

6. Hermann Gunkel, trans., *Genesis* (Macon, Ga.: Mercer University Press, 1997), 43.

7. Gerhard von Rad, trans., *Genesis: A Commentary* (London: SCM Press, 1972): ". . . blood was more pleasing to JHWH," 104; compare also Riane Eisler, *The Chalice and the Blade: Our History, Our Future* (New York: Harper & Row, 1988). According to Eisler, Cain represents a peaceful, gynocentric agrarian culture; Abel with his slaughtered sheep, on the other hand, an aggressive, virile, pastoral people, who was preferred by Yahweh, "the fierce and angry god of war and mountains" 44, 64.

8. Compare Norman K. Gottwald, *The Tribes of Yahweh: A Sociology of the Religion of Liberated Israel 1250–1050 B.C.E.* (New York: Orbis Books, 1979), 577–80.

9. von Rad, *Genesis,* 104; Karl Barth, *Church Dogmatics,* II/2 (Edinburgh: T & T Clark, 1957), 340–42.

10. Claus Westermann, trans., *Genesis 1–11: A Commentary* (Minneapolis: Fortress Press, 1984), 297.

11. Walter Brueggemann, *Genesis: A Bible Commentary for Teaching and Preaching* (Atlanta: John Knox Press, 1982), 56.

12. Compare Pardes, "Beyond Genesis 3," 178–80.

13. Either as a man created with God or as a man walking with God, like Enoch in 5:21.

14. This parallelism has been widely observed, but without consideration of its gender and earth implications. As a male parallel of the female fall account of Genesis 3, the story of Genesis 4 repeats its major narrative elements: divine decree-temptation-transgression-divine question-human defense-punishment/expulsion-divine protection. The key terms of sin and fall occur in Genesis 4 for the first time (4:7), and the death predicted in 2:17 only happens in 4:8.

15. That the term man/*ish* points toward a "condensation" of Cain and Adam has been also observed in the very insightful analysis of Pardes, "Beyond Genesis 3," 182–83, which, however, does not reflect the impact of 3:16 on the concept of man/*ish*.

16. I owe this pivotal insight to K. Deurloo, *Kain en Abel* (Amsterdam: Ten Have, 1967); compare also Ellen van Wolde, "The Story of Cain and Abel: A Narrative Study," *Journal for the Study of the Old Testament* 152 (1991), 25–41.

17. Gordon J. Wenham, *Genesis 1–15* (Waco: Word Books, 1987), 103 sees it as no coincidence that only the second son respects that the firstborn by right belongs to God.

18. E. A. Speiser, trans., *Genesis* (Garden City, N.Y.: 1964), 30: "The manifest contrast however, is between the unstinted offering on the part of Abel and the minimal contribution of Cain."

19. The close and dramatic relationship between earth, water, human, and blood in Hebrew gets an additional emphasis by the striking similarities between the four terms used in Genesis 2–4, all of which contain two, three, or four of the same letters aleph, daleth, mem, he; compare van Wolde, "Facing the Earth," 29, and "The Story of Cain and Abel," 37.

20. It is interesting that in the Babylonian Creation Epics the mixture between earth and blood is seen quite differently. In the Atrakhasis Epic, for example, the ringleader of the divine strike is executed as punishment for the rebellion, and his blood together with earth is used to create the human race. One could see this as a concept that integrates an imperial order and the violence it is based upon right into the very substance of humanity.

21. This point has been strongly underlined by van Wolde, "Facing the Earth," 46, who in her analysis of Genesis 1–11 points out that the earth/Adama doesn't only have a face (2:6; 4:14; 6:1, 7; 7:4, 23; 8:8, 13) and a mouth (4:11), but is treated by God as an independent subject, whose perspectives he may share, even if it is

opposite to that of the human beings like in the story of the flood and the disper-
sion. "God is presented as the divine being acting on behalf of the earth and the
entire creation, not only as the defender of the human subject," 47.

22. The correspondence between 4:1 and 4:25 with regard to Eve's "more modest" or even mourning attitude when naming her third son is also seen by Um-
berto Cassuto, *A Commentary on the Book of Genesis,* trans. Israel Abrahams (Jerusalem:
Magnes Press, Hebrew University, 1961), 246; and Pardes, "Beyond Genesis 3,"
186–87, without, however, recognizing the dimension of resistance that emerges
when 4:25 is linked back to the immediately preceding verses, 4:23-24.

23. This would mean that the younger brother motif has to be explained in
terms of Genesis 2–4, that is, as inscribing a strongly critical pro-earth, pro-
brother, and pro-women compound into the Genesis of Israel. This "genetic
principle" implies constant challenge to the established hierarchies of superior
and inferior, in and out, oneness and otherness. For a review of literature see
Everett Fox, "Stalking the Younger Brother: Some Models for Understanding a
Biblical Motif," *Journal for the Study of the Old Testament* 60 (1993), 45–68.

24. Compared with Gen. 4:17-22 some of the names of Cain's descendants are
slightly changed and appear in different order in Genesis 5, but all are there until
Lamekh. They are, however, put into a position after and secondary to Seth/Abel
and Enosh now, and some of them seem to be remarkably transformed. Lamekh,
for example, will announce a new relationship between Adama and Adam in 5:29.
Compare Brueggemann, *Genesis,* 69–70.

25. Compare Brigitte Kahl, "And She Called His Name Jeth (Gen 4:25): The
Birth of Critical Knowledge and the Unread End of Eve's Story," *Union Seminary
Quarterly Review* 53, 1–2 (1999), 19–28.

Chapter 4

1. See, for example, A. Ahmad, *Islam and the Environmental Crisis* (London: Taha
Publishers, 1997); F. Denny, "Islam and Ecology: A Bestowed Trust Inviting Balanced Stewardship," *Earth Ethics,* 10:1 (fall 1998), 10–11; F. Rahman, *Major Themes of
the Qur'an* (Minneapolis: Bibliotheca Islamica, 1989), especially chapter 4.

2. In the case of India, for example, see R. Mukerjee, *The Rise and Fall of the East
India Company* (Berlin: Veb Deutscher Verlag der Wissenschaften, 1958).

3. See Henry Kissinger, *Years of Upheaval* (Boston: Little, Brown and Company,
1982), and *White House Years* (Little, Brown and Company, 1979). On the domestic
effects of the Cold War in the United States, see James T. Patterson, *Grand Expectations: The United States, 1945–1974* (New York: Oxford University Press, 1996).

4. See J. Decornoyn, "Capital privé, développement du sud et solidarité mon-
diale: Les multinationales, omniprésentes et . . . impuissantes," *Le Monde Diploma-
tique* (Novembre 1988), 8–9; M. Horsman and A. Marshall, *After the Nation State*
(London: Harper Collins, 1994); K. Ohmae, *The Borderless World* (London: Harper
Collins, 1990) ; and Robert B. Reich, *The Work of Nations : Preparing Ourselves for 21st
Century Capitalism* (New York: Knopf, 1991). According to Samir Amin, "Although

the new [1990s] globalization has inhibited the ability of the nation-state to manage its domestic economy, it has not cancelled out the presence of the state." Samir Amin, *Fi muwajahati azmat 'asrina [Face to Face with the Crisis of Our Age]* (Cairo: Sina Li'l Nashr, 1997), 71.

5. B. Karlin, "Space: New Frontier for US Entrepreneurs," *International Herald Tribune*, September 14, 1988.

6. Decornoyn, "Capital piveé," 9.

7. Amin, *Fi muwajahati*, 20–21.

8. See Z. Laidi et al., *L'ordre mondial relache* (Paris: Presses de la Fondation Nationales des Sciences, 1994).

9. See S. Strange, *The Retreat of the State: The Diffusion of Power in the World Economy* (Cambridge: Cambridge University Press, 1998).

10. Amin, *Les défis de la mondialisation* (Paris: L'Harmattan/Forum du tiers-monde, 1996).

11. Amin, *Fi muwajahiti*, 133.

12. Immanuel Wallerstein, *After Liberalism* (New York: The New Press, 1995), 15.

13. See Daniel T. Griswold, "Blessings and Burdens of Globalization," *The World and I* (April 1998), 30–35.

14. See Robert Boyer and Daniel Drache, eds., *States against Markets: The Limits of Globalization* (London: Routledge, 1996).

15. See Peter Martin, "La mondialisation est-elle inévitable? Une obligation morale," *Le Monde Diplomatique* (June 1997), 14. The author claims the following: "Les débats sur la mondialisation se polarisent généralement sur ses enjeux économiques. Je voudrais, pour ma part, mettre en avant les arguments profondément moraux qui plaident en sa faveur, et que l'on peut résumer en une phrase: l'intégration accélérée de sociétés autrefois marginalisées est la meilleure chose qui soit arrivée du vivant de la génération d'après-guerre. La mondialisation constitue une authentique collaboration par-delà les frontières, des sociétés et des cultures, contrairement aux collaborations factices des dialogues Nord-Sud et des élites bureaucratiques. Non seulement elle a sapé les fondations de l'empire du mal soviétique, mais elle est en train d'en faire autant en Chine. Même sans ces effets politiques directs, ses vertus auraient été extraordinaires: elle a provoqué une énorme amélioration du bonheur humain dans les sociétés ayant su saisir les chances qu'elle offre. Cette transformation produira les effets exactement inverses de ceux invoqués par les gens qui, à gauche, en font le procès. Sous son impulsion, le pouvoir se déplacera irrésistiblement des pays développés vers le reste du monde. C'est le désir d'empêcher à tout prix ce transfert qui sous-tend la vision du monde des critiques de la mondialisation. Leurs arguments, de mon point de vue, reposent sur un désir viscéral de préserver le statu quo et de pérenniser l'hégémonie de leur idéologie profondément conservatrice. . . . Les critiques les plus raffinés admettent que des millions d'emplois ont été créés. Mais, disent-ils, il ne s'agit pas de véritables emplois, mais d'une exploitation éhontée de la main-d'oeuvre. Allez dire cela aux travailleurs bien formés de Hongkong, de Singapour, de Malaisie, de Thaïlande, aux ouvriers de l'électronique d'Acer, aux ouvriers de l'automobile de Daewoo. Allez dire cela

aux travailleurs de la Chine méridionale qui ont échappé à la vie misérable et éreintante des campagnes et qui avancent—effectivement dans les pires conditions de travail—vers une authentique prospérité et une authentique autonomie de vie."

16. Ignacio Ramonet, "Régimes globalitaires," *Le Monde Diplomatique* (January 1997), 1. According to Ramonet, "On appelait 'régimes totalitaires' ces régimes à parti unique qui n'admettaient aucune opposition organisée, qui subordonnaient les droits de la personne à la raison d'Etat, et dans lesquels le pouvoir politique dirigeait souverainement la totalité des activités de la société dominée. A ces systèmes succède, en cette fin de siècle, un autre type de totalitarisme, celui des 'régimes globalitaires'. Reposant sur les dogmes de la globalisation et de la pensée unique, ils n'admettent aucune autre politique économique, subordonnent les droits sociaux du citoyen à la raison compétitive, et abandonnent aux marchés financiers la direction totale des activités de la société dominée."

17. See Paul Hirst and Graham Thompson, *Globalization in Question: The International Economy and the Possibilities of Government* (Cambridge: Polity Press, 1996).

18. Charlene Spretnak, *The Resurgence of the Real: Body, Nature and Place in a Hypermodern World* (New York: Addison-Wesley Publishing Company, 1997), 34.

19. See C. de Brie, "Le couple Etat-nation en instance de divorce," *Le Monde Diplomatique* (May 1989).

20. See Nancy Birdsall, "Life Is Unfair: Inequality in the World," *Foreign Policy* (summer 1998), 95–113.

21. Benedict Anderson, *Imagined Communities: Reflections on the Origin and Spread of Nationalism* (London: Routledge, 1991), 140.

22. Pierre Bourdieu, "L'essence du neoliberalisme," *Le Monde Diplomatique* (March 1998), 3.

23. See Charles William Maynes, "The Perils of an Imperial America," *Foreign Policy* (Summer 1998), 36–49.

24. Even some European, most notably French, intellectuals are discussing ways to respond to what they see as the American cultural menace on Europe, and are seeking ways to protect cultural diversity and reviving their cultural independence vis-à-vis the United States of America. See Paul-Marie de la Gorce, *Le Dernier Empire* (Paris: Grasset, 1996), and Ignacio Ramonet, "L'empire americain," *Le Monde Diplomatique* (February 1997), 1. Henry Kissinger reflects the American view on this matter: "A united Europe is likely to insist on a specifically European view of world affairs—which is another way of saying that it will challenge American hegemony in Atlantic policy. This may well be a price worth paying for European unity, but American policy has suffered from an unwillingness to recognize that there is a price to be paid." Henry Kissinger, *White House Years* (Boston: Little, Brown and Company, 1979), 82. Another architect of contemporary American policy argues that the strategic task of the United States is to prevent the emergence of a dominant and antagonistic Eurasian power and to create a stable continental equilibrium with the United States as the political arbiter. See Zbigniew Brzezinski, *The Grand Chessboard: American Primacy and Its Geostrategic Imperatives* (New York: Basic Books, 1997), especially chapter 2.

25. "Le post-colonialisme est un phenomene tres recent qui date du debut des années 1990, comme suite à la chute des regimes communistes, la Guerre du Golfe et l'effritement du peu d'unite que le Tiers Monde etait parvenu a construire. . . . Le post-colonialisme est, avant tout, le preduit du 'nouvel ordre mondial.'" Mahdi Elmandjra, *La decolonization culturelle: Defi majeur du 21eme siecle* (Marrakech, Morocco: Editions Walili, 1996, and Paris: Futuribles, 1996), 208.

26. See for example Muhammad 'Abid al-Jabiri, *Introduction a la critique de la raison arabe* (Casablanca: Editions le Fennec, 1995) and *al-Mashru' al-nahdawi al-'arabi [The Project of Arab Renaissance]* (Beirut: Markaz Dirasat al-Wihdah al-'Arabiyah, 1996).

27. de la Gorce, *Le Dernier Empire,* 16.

28. Claude Julien, *L'empire americaine* (Paris: Grasset, 1968), 25. The same ideas are presented by Jean-Jacques Servan-Schreiber in *Le defi americain* (Paris: Denoel, 1967).

29. Edmund Wilson, *The American Earthquake: A Chronicle of the Roaring Twenties, the Great Depression and the Dawn of the New Deal* (New York: Da Capo Press, 1996), 569.

30. Muhammad 'Abid al-Jabiri, "al-'Awlamah, nizam wa aydiyolojiyah," in *al-'Arab wa tahadiyat al-'awlamah* (Rabat : al-Majlis al-Qawmi li'l Thaqafah al-'Arabiyah, 1997), 15. A number of Islamist and Arab nationalist thinkers share the above views. For example, the Egyptian Islamist Muhammad Ibrahim Mabruk contends in a very controversial book that the United States encourages pragmatism in the Muslim world as a means of colonizing this world in a new way. See Muhammad Ibrahim Mabruk, *Amerika wa'l islam al-nafi'i* (Cairo: Dar al-Tawzi'i wa'l Nashr al-Islamiyah, 1989), especially 191–211. See also 'Adil Hussein, *al-Iqtisad al-misri: mina al-istiqlal ila al-taba'iyah* (Cairo: Dar al-Mustaqbal al-'Arabi, 1986), and Ramzi Zaki, *Mushkilat misr al-iqtisadiyah* (Cairo: Dar al-Fata al-'Arabi, 1982).

31. Richard Falk, "Vers une domination mondiale de nouveau type," *Le Monde Diplomatique* (May 1996), 16. Professor Falk goes on to describe in detail the new meaning of freedom that is being invented by the supporters of cyberspace technology: "M. John Perry Barlow, éminent futurologue, cofondateur de la Fondation de la frontière électronique de Davos (fait significatif, ce village suisse accueille chaque année les responsables du capitalisme mondial), a publié une "Déclaration d'indépendance du Cyberspace". Elle s'ouvre par ces mots: "Gouvernements du monde industrialisé, géants fatigués faits de chair et d'acier, j'arrive du Cyberspace, la nouvelle habitation de l'esprit. . . . Vous n'êtes pas les bienvenus parmi nous. Vous n'êtes pas souverains là où nous rassemblons." Et de défier ouvertement tout contrôle territorial: "Vos concepts juridiques de propriété, d'expression, d'identité, de mouvement et de contexte ne s'appliquent pas à nous. Ils sont basés sur la matière. Il n'y a pas de matière ici." M. Barlow s'engage à "créer une civilisation de l'esprit dans le Cyberspace." Elle sera, selon lui, 'plus humaine et plus juste que le monde auparavant créé par vos gouvernements'. Dans cette optique, l'Etat n'est à l'évidence en rien source de pouvoir, d'identité, d'autorité légale."

32. See Joseph Nye and William Owens, "America's Information Edge," *Foreign Affairs* (March–April 1996).

33. S. Sassen, *Losing Control? Sovereignty in an Age of Globalization* (New York: Columbia University Press, 1996).

34. Nye and Owens, "America's Information Edge," 29–30.

35. See William Greider, *One World, Ready or Not: The Manic Logic of Global Capitalism* (New York: Simon and Schuster, 1997); and A. Gresh, "Les aleas de l'internationalisme," *Le Monde Diplomatique* (May 1998), 12.

36. See Richard Barnet and John Cavanagh, *Global Dreams: Imperial Corporations and the New World Order* (New York: Simon and Schuster, 1994); and M. L. Bouguerra, *Le recherche contre le Tiers-Monde* (Paris: Presse Universitaire de France, 1993).

37. For a detailed discussion of this subject, please consult Claude Liauzu, *Race et civilisation: L'Autre dans la culture occidentale* (Paris: Syros, 1992).

38. Elmandjra, *La decolonization culturelle*, 175.

39. Ibid., 188.

40. Ibid.

41. See Ibrahim M. Abu-Rabi, "Beyond the Post-Modern Mind," *American Journal of the Islamic Social Sciences* 7 (September 1990), 235–56.

42. See Jean-Marie Domenach, *Enquete dur les idees contemporaine* (Paris: Points, 1987); and Charlene Spretnak, *Resurgence of the Real*, 2.

43. Richard Falk, *Explorations at the Edge of Time: The Prospects for World Order* (Philadelphia: Temple University Press, 1992), 48.

44. See Leonardo Boff, *Ecology and Liberation: A New Paradigm*, trans. John Cumming (Maryknoll, N.Y.: Orbis Books, 1995); and David R. Griffin and Huston Smith, *Primordial Truth and Postmodern Theology* (Albany: State University of New York Press, 1989). One must note that Christian thinkers and theologians were quicker than their Muslim counterparts in providing ethical answers to the challenges of globalization. Please consult Hans Küng, *A Global Ethic for Global Politics and Economics* (New York: Oxford University Press, 1998), especially chapter 2.

45. Rahman, *Major Themes*, 79.

Chapter 5

1. It is necessary to make a distinction between globalization as a historic process that developed over centuries in different phases and the recent political and economic project of the intentional globalization of capital, production, and trade.

2. Eighth General Assembly of the World Council of Churches, Harare, Zimbabwe, December 13–14, 1998.

3. The World Council of Churches (WCC) produced a number of publications on globalization: Bas de Gaay Fortman and Berma Klein Goldewijk, *God and the Goods: Global Economy in a Civilizational Perspective* (Geneva: WCC, 1998); Julio de Santa Ana, ed., *Sustainability and Globalization* (Geneva: WCC, 1998); Richard Dickinson, *Economic Globalization: Deepening the Challenge for Christians* (Geneva: WCC-Unit III, 1998); and Chris Arthur, *The Globalization of Communications: Some Religious Implications* (Geneva: WCC, 1998).

4. See Steven C. Rockefeller, "Global Interdependence, the Earth Charter, and Christian Faith," chapter 6 in this book.

5. The WCC study process on ecclesiology and ethics explored how churches function as moral communities and introduced a new understanding of the role of the WCC as space maker for processes of community building, linking the local and the global. See Thomas Best and Martin Robra, eds., *Ecclesiology and Ethics* (Geneva: WCC, 1997); and Lewis Mudge, *The Church as Moral Community* (New York: Continuum, 1998).

6. See Larry Rasmussen, *Earth Community, Earth Ethics* (Maryknoll, N.Y.: Orbis Books, 1996), 90–97.

7. Eighth General Assembly of the World Council of Churches, Harare, Zimbabwe, December 13–14, 1998.

8. *Resisting Domination—Affirming Life. The Challenge of Globalization,* Appendix II to the Report of the Policy Reference Committee II (Geneva: WCC Document No. RC-II 1), §§ 20 and 21.

9. For the implications of globalization for contextual theologies, also see Robert Schreiter, *New Catholicity* (Maryknoll, N.Y.: Orbis Books, 1997).

10. Rasmussen, *Earth Community, Earth Ethics,* 138–54.

11. Conference in Brasov, Romania, 1995.

12. *Dalits* are socially and culturally despised and oppressed people who belong to the lowest caste categories of the Indian society.

13. The case study process had the following components: (1) historical study on the "Response of the Indian Churches to the Issues of the Poor and Poverty," (2) research studies on three major causes of poverty in India, namely, caste, gender, and economic reforms, (3) experiential study with the poor sharing their views of themselves and their predicament, and (4) reflective study: workshops, conferences, and consultations.

14. This design was based on the suggestions of the Brasov meeting and developed by a local preparatory committee at Nairobi, together with Unit III of the WCC.

15. Margot Kaessmann, "Glimpses of the New Ecumenical Movement," in WCC-Unit III, Sam Kobia, ed., *ECHOES* 12 (1997), 38–39.

16. Ibid.

17. Compare *Continuing the Journey,* "Report of the Theology of Life Consultation at the Union Theological Seminary, April 1998," in WCC-Unit III, Sam Kobia, ed, *Working on Theology of Life: A Dossier* (Geneva: WCC, 1998), 124.

18. See Kathryn Tanner, *Theories of Culture: A New Agenda for Theology* (Minneapolis: Fortress Press, 1997).

19. WCC Unit III JPC, "The Legacy of JPC: From Canberra to Harare.: Reflections of the Unit III Commission" (Geneva: 1998), 11–12.

20. See Lewis S. Mudge, "Toward a Hermeneutic of the Household," *The Ecumenical Review* 51:3 (July 1999), 253.

Chapter 6

1. "Fides et Ratio," John Paul II, an encyclical letter to the bishops of the Catholic Church on the relationship between faith and reason (Rome: September 14, 1998), 104.

2. Information on the history of the Earth Charter project and on current Earth Charter activities in different countries can be found on the Earth Charter Web site at www.earthcharter.org.

3. *Our Common Future,* Report of World Commission on Environment and Development (WCED) (New York: Oxford University Press, 1987), 332–33.

4. Unlike a hard law treaty, a soft law document such as the Universal Declaration of Human Rights is regarded as a statement of intentions and aspirations and it is not considered to be legally binding. Soft law documents like the Universal Declaration of Human Rights, however, frequently evolve over time into hard law. In addition, any declaration of fundamental ethical principles that gains wide acceptance can function as a soft law document that influences the development of international law even if it has not been formally endorsed by the United Nations.

5. *Caring for the Earth* (Gland, Switzerland: IUCN, UNEP, WWF, 1991), 10, and *Strategies for National Sustainable Development: A Handbook for Their Planning and Implementation* (London, U.K.: Earthscan Publications, in association with IUCN and IIED, 1994), xiii, 13.

6. *Human Development Report 1998* (New York: Oxford University Press, 1998), 14–16.

7. The concept of the intrinsic value of all species is employed in international law in instruments like the Biodiversity Convention. In the Earth Charter Benchmark Draft 2, this concept was used in the first supporting principle that appears under principle 1. The relevant supporting principle calls for recognition of "the interdependence and intrinsic value of all beings." Some philosophers, however, object to the use of the concept of intrinsic value. For example, many Buddhist philosophers are critical of language of this nature because it can be interpreted to mean that all beings possess a self in the form of some independent unchanging entity. This idea they deny, preferring to emphasize the interdependence of all beings and the idea that the being of a person or thing is made up of its relations with the other beings that make up its environment. In addition, a number of contemporary Western philosophers have raised critical questions about how and in what sense individual beings can be said to possess intrinsic value. Given the controversy, a decision was made by the drafting committee to delete reference in the Earth Charter to intrinsic value and instead to include an affirmation that all beings are interdependent and worthy of respect regardless of their value to humanity. This language conveys the essential idea, and it is language that the critics of the term *intrinsic value* are prepared to support.

8. See, for example, Albert Schweitzer, *The Philosophy of Civilization*, trans. C. T. Campion (New York: Prometheus Books, 1987), chapters 22–27.

9. Alexander Kiss and Dinah Shelton, *International Environmental Law* (New York: Transnational Publishers, Inc., 1991), 6.

10. *The Beijing Declaration and Platform for Action,* Fourth World Conference on Women, Beijing, China, September, 4–15, 1995 (New York: Department of Public Information, United Nations, 1996), part 2, chapter 4, section C, "Women and Health," 94, 58.

11. *Human Development Report 1998,* 2.

12. In Geneva on April 27, 1999 the United Nations Commission on Human Rights adopted the resolution on "Promotion of the Right to Democracy" by a roll-call vote of 51-0 with China and Cuba abstaining. See the *Journal of Democracy* (July 1999), 180–81. See also Amartya Sen, "Democracy as a Universal Value," ibid., 3–17.

Chapter 7

1. World Commission on Sustainable Development, *One Earth Community* (Oxford: Oxford University Press, 1987).

2. Donella H. Meadows et al., *The Limits to Growth: A Report for the Club of Rome's Project on the Predicament of Mankind* (New York: Universe Books, 1974).

3. Wesley Granberg-Michaelson, "Creation in Ecumenical Thought," in *Ecotheology: Voices from South and North,* ed. David G. Hallman (Geneva: World Council of Churches Publications, 1994).

4. World Council of Churches, *Now Is the Time: A Report from the Seoul World Convocation on Justice, Peace and Integrity of Creation* (Geneva: World Council of Churches Publications, 1990).

5. World Council of Churches, *Searching for a New Heaven and a New Earth: An Ecumenical Response to UNCED* (Geneva: World Council of Churches Publications, 1992).

6. David G. Hallman, ed., *Ecotheology: Voices from South and North* (Maryknoll, N.Y.: Orbis Books, 1994).

7. Visser 't Hooft Endowment Fund for Leadership Development, *Sustainable Growth: A Contradiction in Terms?* (Geneva: Visser 't Hooft Publications, 1993).

8. David G. Hallman, *Creation and Justice in the World of Politics: The Ecumenical Community and the United Nations Challenge Each Other,* a paper examining ecumenical involvement in the recent UN world conferences in Rio, Vienna, Cairo, Copenhagen, and Beijing, prepared for a consultation of the World Alliance of Reformed Churches, April 1996 (available from the author).

9. The World Council of Churches (WCC) has published several resources including *Accelerated Climate Change: Signs of Peril, Test of Faith* (1994), "The Church and Climate Change" in the *Ecumenical Review,* 49:2 (April 1997), and the two current documents *Climate Change and the Quest for Sustainable Societies* (1998), and *Mobility: Prospects for Sustainable Mobility* (1998). Copies of the latter three can be ordered through the WCC in Geneva.

10. Hallman, *Ecotheology.*

Chapter 8

1. Justice, sociologically seen, may also be understood as the outcome of the way in which we regulate our lives together in society, through constitutions, agreements, contracts, regulations, and laws. Jürgen Habermas's view comes closest to this definition; compare Jürgen Habermas, *The Theory of Communicative Action,* vol. 1, *Reason and the Rationalization of Society,* trans. Thomas McCarthy (Boston: Beacon Press, 1984).

2. For more information on South African environmentalism and church-based responses, see *A Rainbow over the Land: A South African Guide on the Church and Environmental Justice* (Cape Town: Western Cape Provincial Council of Churches, 2000).

3. *Ikhaya* is an Nguni word whose nuances and depth of meaning are not dissimilar to that of the Greek *oikos.* For a great many black South Africans who experienced, directly or indirectly, the effects of the massive forced migratory labor system that was part of South Africa's history for so many decades (going back to the early part of the century), the issue of a "home place" is profoundly deep. It is also profoundly ecological.

4. As in the internationally publicized case against Thor Chemicals in Kwa-Zulu Natal for mercury poisoning, a case that not only brought to light the hazards to which the factory workers were exposed, but provided evidence of mercury solution run-offs into the dam that serves some hundreds of thousands of black South Africans in a poor, shack settlement area, Inanda.

5. The best analysis of these effects of poverty and their impact on human beings in South Africa remains that of Francis Wilson and Mamphela Ramphele, *Uprooting Poverty: The South African Challenge: Report for the Second Carnegie Inquiry into Poverty and Development in Southern Africa* (Cape Town: David Philip, 1989). They focus in particular on fire, water, and earth as key touchstones for measuring poverty.

6. The Gini Coefficient, which measures levels of inequality in a society, shows this contradiction starkly. South Africa, with Brazil, consistently has the highest Gini Coefficient in the world, that is, the greatest inequality among income earners, among economies where data allows adequate measurement.

7. We do not mean that this criterion exhausts the meaning of "eco-justice." Yet it remains crucial, not only in the context of poor or developing countries such as South Africa, but also globally.

8. The Constitution of the Republic of South Africa, 1996 as adopted on May 8, 1996 and amended on October 11, 1996 by the Constitutional Assembly, chapter 2, clause 24.

9. See J. Cock, "Towards the Greening of the Church in South Africa: Some Problems and Possibilities." GEM Discussion document (Johannesburg: Group for Environmental Monitoring, 1991), 1–21. See also J. Cock, "Towards the Greening of the Church in South Africa: Some problems and possibilities," *Missionalia* 20:3 (1992), 174–85.

10. Lynn White, "The Historical Roots of Our Ecological Crisis," *Science* 155, 1203–07.

11. Important recent academic conferences include: a 1987 symposium of the Institute for Theological Research (UNISA) called "Are We Killing God's Earth?" the 1991 annual meeting of the Missiological Society of South Africa on "Mission and Ecology," the 1991 annual meeting of the Theological Society of South Africa on JPIC; workshops in January 1997 on "Church and Environment" at the University of Cape Town; and the 1997 meeting of the Theological Society of South Africa on creation theology.

12. For references to most of these, see Ernst Conradie, *Christian Theology and Ecology: An Indexed Bibliography* (Bellville: University of the Western Cape, 1998).

13. See J. Cock, "Towards the Greening of the Church in South Africa: Some Problems and Possibilities," *Missionalia* 20:3 (1992), 174–85; and "The Gold Fields Faith and Earthkeeping Project: A Theological and Ethical Discussion," in *Questions about Life and Morality: Christian Ethics in South Africa Today*, Louise Kretzschmar and Len Hulley, eds. (Pretoria: J.L. van Schaik, 1998).

14. Khanya Programme Newsletter 5:1, 4, Winter 1997. More information is available at www.sa-eastcape.co.za/khanya/.

15. See also Ernst Conradie, *Hope for the Earth: Vistas on a New Century* (Bellville: University of the Western Cape, 2000), chapter 20.

16. Paul S. Minear, *Images of the Church in the New Testament* (Philadelphia: Westminster Press, 1960), proposed that the image of the firstfruits draws together a number of convictions; the following are suggestive for our discussion: (1) God's lordship over all being, (2) the dedication to God of agricultural produce, (3) the appearance and presentation of the first fruit as a pledge of the coming harvest, and (4) the power of the first to sanctify and to cleanse what is to follow.

17. Ibid., 112.

Chapter 9

1. Robert Bullard, *Dumping in Dixie: Race, Class and Environmental Quality* (Boulder, Colo.: Westview Press, 1990).

2. Peter Hong, "Do Two Pollutants Make You Sicker than One?" *Business Week* (September 28, 1992), 77–78.

3. Louis W. Sullivan, "Strategic Plan for the Elimination of Childhood Lead Poisoning" (Department of Health and Human Services, 1991) A2–A3.

4. Eric A. Goldstein and Mark A. Izeman, *The New York Environment Book* (Washington, D.C.: Island Press, 1990), 132.

5. Sullivan, "Strategic Plan," A2.

6. Ibid.

7. Henry Holmes, "Energy Policy and the Urban Predicament," presentation to the Urban Habitat Program of the Earth Island Institute (San Francisco, 1992), 2. These communities have an important stake in the debate about sustainable development and energy policy, yet advocacy systems for energy and transportation issues in communities of color are virtually nonexistent.

8. Renee Skelton and Richard A. Kassel, *End of the Line for Dirty Diesels: Why New York City Needs Natural Gas Buses* (New York: Natural Resources Defense Council, 1993), introduction, 1.

9. Ibid., chapter 1, 1.

10. Asthma episodes are triggered by stimuli that lead to airway obstruction, causing wheezing and shortness of breath. Airborne allergens also appear to play a role in the development of asthma in some persons.

11. Charles Felton, Sally E. Findlay, Lynne Richardson et. al., unpublished data observations, Harlem Hospital, 1993.

12. Jean Ford, "Identifying Risk Factors for Hospitalization and Death in Central Harlem," presentation to the American Thoracic Society International Meeting, May 1993.

13. Ibid., unpublished data

14. Ibid.

15. Michel Gelobter, "Toward a Model of Environmental Discrimination," in *Race and the Incidence of Environmental Hazards: A Time for Discourse,* ed. Bunyan Bryant and Paul Mohai (Boulder, Colo.: Westview Press, 1992), 64–81.

16. Ford, Presentation to the American Thoracic Society International Meeting.

17. Ibid.

18. Ibid., chapter 4, 14.

19. Ibid., chapter 3, 11.

20. *Delores Beauford et al. v MTA,* Index #5028/88, New York Supreme Court. The court held that the Manhattanville depot was exempt from doing an environmental impact statement required by Public Authorities Law, Section 1266(c)(11) because the depot was a replacement project (1998).

21. Ibid., 2. The court held that should any use (major residential development above or adjacent to the depot) be contemplated in the future, the Public Authorities Law exemption would not be applicable, and the possible environmental impact statement requirement, not only for such residential use but also for the bus depot itself, would need to be revisited.

22. Ibid.; *West Harlem Environmental Action v New York City Department of Environmental Protection,* No. 16743/92, New York Supreme Court (1992).

Chapter 10

1. Sanford E. Bennett, "Sweet By and By."

2. E. E. Hewitt, "When We All Get to Heaven."

3. James M. Black, "When the Roll is Called up Yonder."

4. Lewis E. Jones, "We Shall See the King Someday."

5. J. K. Alwood, "The Unclouded Day."

6. Samuel Stennett, "On Jordan's Stormy Banks."

7. Timothy Mayotte created this ritual in the fall of 1997 for Janet Walton's and Troy Messenger's "Ritual Performance and Ritual Criticism."

8. Gen. 28:18-22a.

9. Ambrosius Verheul, *Introduction to the Liturgy: Towards a Theology of Worship,* trans. Margaret Clarke (London: Burns & Oates, 1968), 19.

10. Mircea Eliade, *Myth of the Eternal Return,* trans. Willard R. Trask (New York: Pantheon, 1954), 51–53.

11. James Gertmenian, "The Weaver's Shuttle Swiftly Flies," *New Century Hymnal* (Cleveland: Pilgrim Press, 1990).

Chapter 11

1. For an overview, see my essay "Where Were/Are the Churches in the Environmental Movement?" in Dieter T. Hessel, ed., *Theology for Earth Community: A Field Guide* (Maryknoll, N.Y.: Orbis Books, 1996), chapter 16.

2. See James A. Nash, "Toward the Ecological Reformation of Christianity," *Interpretation* 50:1 (January 1996), 7–8; and his earlier book, *Loving Nature: Ecological Integrity and Christian Responsibility* (Nashville: Abingdon Press, 1991), especially chapters 4–5.

3. Bill McKibben, "Climate Change and the Unraveling of Creation," *The Christian Century* (December 8, 1999), 1196–97.

4. Konrad Raiser, "Ecumenical Discussion of Ethics and Ecclesiology," *The Ecumenical Review,* 10.

5. S. Mark Heim, "What Is the Church?" *The Christian Century* (Oct. 23, 1996), 1001.

6. This conclusion discusses the *church's* ecological reformation. But that should not exclude attention to the implications for, and insights from, other world religions in ecumenical Earth, regarding which current information is available from the Forum on Religion and Ecology (FORE), Department of Religion, Bucknell University, Lewisburg, PA 17837. FORE fosters cross-disciplinary dialogue on worldviews and environmental ethics that builds on a series of conferences resulting in major volumes on Religions of the World and Ecology, published by the Harvard University Center for the Study of World Religions.

7. Ian G. Barbour, "Religion in an Environmental Age," in *Earth at Risk: An Environmental Dialogue between Religion and Science,* ed. Donald B. Conroy and Rodney L. Petersen (Amherst, N.Y.: Humanity Books, 2000).

8. Quoting Jay McDaniel in an ecumenical forum on "Religion, Ethics, and the Earth Charter," *Earth Ethics,* vol. 11, no. 1 (spring, 2001).

9. See Theodore Hiebert, *The Yahwist's Landscape: Nature and Religion in Early Israel* (New York: Oxford University Press, 1996).

10. Rosemary Radford Ruether, *Gaia and God: An Ecofeminist Theology of Earth Healing* (San Francisco: HarperSanFrancisco, 1992).

11. Mark I. Wallace, *Fragments of the Spirit: Nature, Violence, and the Renewal of Creation* (New York: Continuum, 1996), 138.

12. Ibid., 141.

13. Ibid, 154–58.

14. Ibid., 167–68.

15. Geiko Müller-Fahrenholz, *God's Spirit: Transforming a World in Crisis* (New York: Continuum, 1995), 108–9.

16. Ibid., 109–10.

17. See Sallie McFague, *Super, Natural Christians: How We Should Love Nature* (Minneapolis: Fortress Press, 1997), chapters 1 and 2.

18. The anthropocentric tendency of Reformed Confessions was well documented by George Kehm, "The New Story," in Dieter Hessel, ed., *After Nature's Revolt: Eco-Justice and Theology* (Minneapolis: Fortress Press, 1992), especially 199–201.

19. See Rosemary Radford Ruether, "Ecofeminism: The Challenge to Theology," in *Christianity and Ecology: Seeking the Well-Being of Earth and Humans*, ed. Dieter Hessel and Rosemary Radford Ruether (Cambridge: Harvard University Center for the Study of World Religions, 2000), 97.

20. *The Egg: An Eco-Justice Quarterly*, 13:1 (Winter, 1992–1993).

21. As director of the Program on Ecology, Justice and Faith, I developed the TEMEC initiative in partnership with Richard Clugston, executive director of the Center for Respect of Life and Environment (CRLE) in Washington, D.C. Individually and together we secured significant foundation grants to implement this ecumenical program from 1992 forward. Aspects of the TEMEC program we codirected are described in articles that appeared in CRLE's journal, *Earth Ethics*, 1995–1998. We have related closely to a set of theological schools and universities that became "Lead Institutions for Eco-Justice" committed to the threefold emphasis of this program. Case examples that follow are from four of these lead institutions. A fifth lead institution, Union Theological Seminary, New York, was the site of the conference on ecumenical Earth that led to this volume.

22. Larry Rasmussen, "Conversion to Earthfaith," *The Cresset* (May 1996), 9.

23. Along this line see Dieter Hessel, "Spirited Earth Ethics: Cosmological and Covenantal Roots," *Church and Society* (July–August, 1996).

24. Dieter Hessel, "Ecumenical Ethics for Earth Community," *Theology and Public Policy*, vol. 8, 1 and 2 (1996), 22–24, presents these four norms in more detail.

25. For example, see Dieter Hessel, *Social Ministry*, rev. ed. (Louisville: Westminster John Knox, 1992) chapter 10; and the list of *Environmental Justice Resources* and *Environmental Justice Covenant Congregation Program* of the National Council of the Churches of Christ in the U.S.A., available from P.O. Box 968, Elkhart, IN 46515, Ph: 800-762-0968. Also see the resources available from regional organizations such as Earth Ministry, 1305 NE 47th Street, Seattle, WA 98105.

26. For practical lifestyle-change suggestions, see Michael Schut, ed., *Simpler Living, Compassionate Life: A Christian Perspective* (Denver: Morehouse Group, 1999).

Index

CPSIA information can be obtained
at www.ICGtesting.com
Printed in the USA
FSHW020459210520
70443FS